RECLAIMING
GOODNESS

RECLAIMING GOODNESS

*Education and the
Spiritual Quest*

HANAN A. ALEXANDER

University of Notre Dame Press

Notre Dame, Indiana

Designed by Wendy McMillen
Set in 10/13 Meridien by Em Studio Inc.
Printed in the U.S.A. by Sheridan Books, Inc.

Library of Congress Cataloging-in-Publication Data

Alexander, Hanan A.
    Reclaiming goodness : education and the spiritual quest /
Hanan A. Alexander
        p.   cm.
    Includes index.
    ISBN 0-268-04003-6 (cloth : alk. paper)
    1. Spiritual Life.   2. Moral education   I. Title.
BL624.A43   2001
291.4—dc21   00-010905

∞ *This book is printed on acid-free paper.*

This book is dedicated to the memory of

Eli Samuel Resnikoff

fellow seeker and beloved friend.

Contents

Preface

This book is about the spiritual awakening of recent decades and its relation to education and democracy. "Spirituality" is a slippery term. Its meaning is often vague; and it connotes different things to different people. Some use the term to denote devotion to a supernatural deity or to describe pious adherence to religious doctrines or practices.[1] Others understand it as depicting a sense of belonging or inner feeling that is generally discovered outside of organized religion.[2] I prefer a more encompassing approach that captures similarities between religious and nonreligious uses of the term. According to one especially compelling example, spirituality implies a quest to live meaningfully through honest self-assessment that eschews insignificant desires and aggravations—what one author calls "the small stuff"[3]—in order to embrace a higher purpose.[4] Yet, even this definition is not very precise because the purposes of a spiritual life can be found in many different places.

For some, the purpose of such a life is located within ourselves and is discovered by getting in touch with our passions or desires or "inner child." Others look for spiritual direction in collective vision or group consciousness. Living meaningfully in this view involves fellowship within a community of shared memory and commitment. A third approach seeks spiritual fulfillment outside the self and the community in experience of, or unity with, a divine being achieved through rituals and symbols. The ambiguity generated by these conceptions of spiritual purpose is complicated by the fact that each entails some attitudes that are uplifting and moving and others that are incoherent and morally problematic.

This book offers an analysis of these approaches to the spiritual life that differentiates their inspirational from their dangerous tendencies. It develops an alternative model of spirituality wherein we discover our best selves in learning communities devoted to a higher good. In addition to addressing the quest for life's meaning, this alternative also addresses concerns about identity, community, morality, purpose, and transcendence. I call a comprehensive response to these "big" issues a vision of the "good life." Spirituality, in this view, is about acquiring and living by such a vision. People are searching for spirituality today, I argue, because comprehensive visions of the good are conspicuously absent from modern culture.

"Good" is used here as an ethical concept in the classical sense in which the "good life" indicates a concern with how life ought to be lived.[5] In this view, the spiritual quest entails a hunger for ethical vision; but this does not mean that those who lack a spiritual dimension in their lives are unethical. Rather, without a vision of the good it is unclear what it means to be ethical—to live in accord with a higher ideal.[6] Today's spiritual seekers experience their moral intuitions as fragmented and ungrounded. They are unsure about their stances and seek guidance in the higher ideals of a community that can provide them with identity, meaning, and purpose. The exploration of ideals worthy of devotion, both natural and supernatural—this-worldly and otherworldly—is called theology. The spiritual quest, therefore, is not only an ethical but also a theological pursuit.

Contrary to a common misconception that dichotomizes thinking and feeling, passionate devotion to higher ideals is entirely consistent with an intelligent consideration of these ideals. To embrace them, we need not only commit ourselves emotionally, we must also think critically about the significant life-choices these ideals entail; we must make these choices freely, and learn from our mistakes. Critical thinking, free will, and learning from error are crucial values for a democracy. There is, therefore, a profound connection between spirituality and democracy—and between spirituality and liberal education which prepares leaders and citizens to function effectively in a democratic society.

This sort of education is not merely a means to an end, such as getting a better job, acquiring knowledge, gaining a political or religious identity, or insuring group or ideological survival. Acquiring a liberal education involves cultivating a spiritual vision of the good. Absent such a vision, we lack the criteria for assessing and selecting values. In this case, there would be no way to determine which job is better, or what knowledge is worth acquiring, or with which ideal to identify, or what groups or ideologies should survive. Education is process and product rolled into one; it is a value to be achieved, and educational institutions ought to express those convictions we cherish most. There is, therefore, a reciprocal relationship between spirituality—living according to a vision of the good—and education. Not only does spirituality, which is acquired through education, need critical thinking as a cornerstone, education also needs to be grounded in a spiritual vision so that it, too, can be meaningful.

A Return to Ethics and Theology

I am proposing, in other words, a return to ethics and theology in educational thought, albeit with an expanded mandate that includes exploration of natural as well as supernatural ideals.[7] Since the end of the last century, education in the United States and other parts of the Western world has undergone a process of secularization. This led to a decline of interest in issues pertaining to values and spirituality in educational research, philosophy, policy, and practice, and to extraordinary confusion over the methods and content of moral and religious instruction. Education consequently came to be viewed as primarily concerned with transmitting the knowledge and skills needed to prepare for economic productivity.

There is, however, a renewed interest in normative pedagogy today that marks an important turn away from viewing education as an agent of epistemology and economic instrumentalism, and toward understanding it as an emissary of goodness. According to this alternative, the first task of education is not to produce good lawyers, doctors, and MBAs, but rather to cultivate good people. This can be understood as a spiritual awakening in educational thought. A similar renewal of interest in "the good" is underway in ethical and religious thought.[8] Much modern moral philosophy has focused on *justifying* individual rights, often in the context of a theory of justice.[9] It has aimed not to construct coherent accounts of how to live but rather to dissect and defend moral concepts, prescriptions, and behaviors.[10] Similarly, much modern religious thought has been concerned with justifying correct belief, or protecting religious faith from skepticism, rather than with offering religious community and faith as a primary source of meaning in life. Of late, however, both moral and religious thought have become concerned not so much with analyzing behavior and belief as with returning to synthetic, holistic conceptions of the good life, with conceiving a comprehensive and coherent picture of how we ought to live.

The ensuing discussion is thus part of a realignment in educational, ethical, and religious thought from value-free analysis of individuals and their rights toward passionate engagement with communities envisaging the good. Rather than dichotomizing "feelings" and "reasons," as has been so common in modern thought, this trend synthesizes religiosity—passionate devotion to higher ideals—with intelligence.[11] Ideals are not only fostered within religious institutions but also by cultural endeavors, such as art, literature, music, or politics. These too can be pursued with "religiosity" in the sense in which I am using the term.[12]

The synthesis that is emerging might be called a "Copernican revolution," after the sixteenth-century Polish astronomer Nicolaus Copernicus. His theory that the Earth revolves daily on its own axis and annually around the Sun revolutionized the science and theology of his day. Immanuel Kant invoked his name and spirit when he revolutionized the philosophy of knowledge two centuries later.[13] I hope to contribute to a similar paradigm shift in educational thought.[14]

Why Study Spirituality and Education

The view developed here is not in keeping with popular attitudes that oppose spirituality to critical thinking. The failure of modern thought to offer compelling visions of the good life has sent people searching. In the absence of more compelling alternatives, some have found answers in narcissistic spiritualities that emphasize values emanating from the self or in a revival of Marxist ideology that focuses on the ills of cultural in addition to economic oppression. Others have found solace in the darker corners of human history. The religious right has become increasingly attractive to many because it offers a clear account of the difference between right and wrong.

The result has not only been the increased influence of the kind of fundamentalism that leads to terrorism in the Middle East and around the globe. It has also meant a growing influence in the Islamic world, in post-Soviet Eastern Europe, and in many Western countries of religious fanaticisms that seek to replace democracies with their own theocratic or dogmatic regimes. It has been said that the greatest threat to democracy today is neither fascism nor communism but self-centered subjectivism and neo-Marxist relativism on the left, and religious fundamentalism on the right.

Both sides have misused education. Subjective individualists often understand education as a process of deconstructing values imposed on us by tradition and community. Neo-Marxists understand education as a tool for reconstructing society in the image of their own ideologies. Fundamentalists see education as a way of insuring religious commitment, ethnic identity, and communal continuity. All of these views share an instrumental attitude toward education as a means to ends that students are not to question.

This attitude restricts the potential reflective dimension of education, and limits the freedom of learners to make intelligent value
choices. The result should more properly be called indoctrination
rather than education.

There is a desperate need for us to recognize the profound connection between spirituality and the critical reasoning that is crucial to democracy. In this context, education involves initiation
into, and renewal of, communities devoted to nondogmatic ideals
located beyond both the self and the collective. This book illumi-
nates that link. Many people are searching for this kind of spiritual perspective. They are moderate in their political views and
troubled by the self-centered narcissism of modern individualism,
yet they disdain both the neo-Marxist relativism and the religious
extremism that threatens liberal societies around the world. They
are seeking a picture of the good life that provides spiritual sustenance without blunting their capacity to reason and evaluate.

Some of these spiritual seekers have had disappointing experiences with formal religion or education. Despite their penchant for
moderation, they treat the mainline, middle-of-the-road organizations in which they were often raised with suspicion. They mis-
trust modern institutions and enjoy experimenting with the novel
or the extreme. This presents a special challenge for religious and
educational leaders attempting to respond to their concerns. A recent special issue of the *New York Times Magazine* referred to this
process as "God decentralized":

> A new breed of worshiper is looking beyond the religious in-
> stitution for a do-it-yourself solution. . . . The religious institu-
> tions that used to deliver orthodox practice to the unquestion-
> ing masses are under challenge—not just by smaller institutions
> but by individuals who want to reshape religion for themselves.
> God is being decentralized. . . . More and more, Americans ap-
> pear to be turning to religion (in *some* form, however unortho-
> dox) even though they are unsure if they believe in God. . . .
> Doubt and zeal, invention and tradition: The American religious
> landscape continues to expand.[15]

For too long this silent moderate majority has allowed the assumption to prevail that extremism is more "authentic" than temperance, and that passion and centrism don't mix. And for too long these centrists have deceived themselves into believing that spiritual community, sacred memory, tradition, theology, and ritual have limited appeal and even less to say to contemporary society. The time has come to reengage the middle course between "mystical fusion with the world" through self or group consciousness and "sectarian withdrawal from it."[16]

Audience and Methods

While education is a significant thrust of this book, it is primarily about the spiritual crisis of our time. It is written for spiritual seekers in all walks of life who sense that, for values to make sense, we need to examine and embrace them with our minds as well as our hearts. This includes scholars interested in philosophy, theology, religion, and education, as well as teachers, parents, and religious leaders.

Because these issues have wide applicability, I have employed concepts and examples not only from my own background as a philosopher and a rabbi, but also from a variety of literary and faith traditions, and from the experience of daily life. Although the weightiness of the topic warrants careful reasoning, arguments are presented with a minimum of jargon. When, on rare occasions, I have found it necessary to use technical terms, these are explained in the text. Similarly, examples drawn from my own tradition are widely accessible, often with parallels in other cultures.

I begin by arguing in the first two chapters that modern thought has failed to advance a compelling ethical vision. This has spawned a spiritual crisis, a questioning of our most basic beliefs and assumptions. But how can we respond to the moral failings of the Enlightenment without sacrificing the freedoms and traditions of criticism that constitute its political successes? This calls for comprehensive conceptions of the good that entail three democratic values: critical thinking, freedom, and fallibility.

One or more of these values are denied in several influential conceptions of spirituality because the extreme—and often incoherent—versions that tend to be popular assume a tension between rationalism and romanticism. Responding to the spiritual crisis of modernism, the four central chapters contend that we must abandon this tension in favor of ethical visions based on intelligent feelings and a loving rationality. This can be accomplished through an intelligent approach to spirituality. It requires that we define ourselves in the context of learning communities that foster the virtues of integrity, humility, and literacy. These virtues lead to a form of fulfillment rooted in moral agency.

The book concludes with an exploration of what an intelligent spiritual education is all about. Instrumental conceptions of education that tend toward indoctrination are rejected in favor of teleologically oriented spiritual pedagogy that nurtures meaning and purpose. This sort of pedagogy is found in *organic communities* in which the values and concepts taught to children and students are naturally reinforced by adult role models. It lies at the heart of "liberal education," to the extent that such an education embraces the core values of liberal society. Can these ideas work? If education is intrinsically valuable, the relevant question is not whether an approach to pedagogy "works," but whether it properly represents a communal vision of the good. Spiritual renaissance is possible when education and community are united in their devotion to what we cherish most.

Following Aristotle, Maimonides held that the good life is to be found in the midway between extremes. He called this the golden mean.[17] By pursuing extremes rather than a middle road, the recent awakening has sacrificed the core of what spirituality is all about—leading a good life; and in becoming distanced from its spiritual roots, education has given up its primary mission—the cultivation of goodness in people. The aim of this book is to reclaim the intelligent heart of spirituality and the ethical soul of education.

Acknowledgments

Sometimes books write themselves. The author sets out to say one thing, but only finds the voice to say something else. I did not set out to write a book about spirituality and education but rather to critique a movement concerned with the continuity of my own religious community. Yet, as I delved more deeply into the problems that beset this movement, it became clear that these are not unique to a particular faith, tradition, or ethnic group but are rooted in historical dynamics and conceptual misunderstandings that lie at the heart of education in contemporary culture. I am grateful to Jeffrey Gainey of the University of Notre Dame Press for encouraging me to discover the universal themes in my own particular experience.

This book is the culmination of a long journey. When I entered the Graduate School of Education at Stanford, Elliot Eisner was completing *The Educational Imagination,* in which he articulated his conceptions of qualitative and artistic evaluation, and Nel Noddings was writing *Caring,* in which she gave voice to a new feminist ethic. Their unapologetic embrace of education as a normative activity impressed me. Although ambivalent about normative concerns, I was also drawn to the precision and rigor of analytic philosophy represented by the intellect and wit of Denis Phillips. It seemed to me then, as now, that conceptual tools as powerful as those employed by philosophical analysis should be used to understand our most cherished commitments. I owe a deep debt to each of these extraordinary teachers whose imagination, care, and intelligence have been my models and whose passion, commitment, and encouragement vibrates in every line of this book.

I have enjoyed a long and fulfilling association with the University of Judaism. Its indelible mark is reflected in these pages. I have long treasured the friendship and counsel of its rector, Rabbi Elliot Dorff, and its librarian emeritus, Dr. Louis Shub. I was privileged to serve as academic dean and vice president under two remarkable presidents, Rabbi David Lieber, who has been my mentor and teacher, and Rabbi Robert Wexler, who has been a colleague and friend. I was also honored to work closely with two distinguished community leaders who chaired the university's board of directors, Jack Ostrow, of blessed memory, and Francis S. Maas. I am profoundly thankful to all of these men for the intellectual life that informs these pages and the institution that made it possible. I am also grateful to the university for a research fellowship and additional research funding, to my students in the Fingerhut School of Education who commented on these ideas in class discussions and private conversations, and to colleagues on the faculty and staff whose hard work enabled me to take time to complete this project.

This work could never have been completed without the time afforded by a study leave spent as a visiting professor at the University of Haifa during the 1996–97 academic year at the invitation of Gabi Salomon, then dean of the faculty of education. There I met wonderful new colleagues, including Miriyam Ben Peretz, Ilan Gur Zeev, and Shifra Shoenmann, with whom I enjoyed important conversations that contributed to this work. I am grateful to them all.

During that year, I was invited to give talks on this project at the Hebrew University and the Schechter Institute for Judaic Studies in Jerusalem, the Tel Aviv University, the Leo Baeck College in London, London University's Institute of Education, and the Free University of Amsterdam. I was also asked to conduct a seminar on my research at the Jerusalem Fellows. I am grateful to Steven Cohen, David Zisenwein, Brenda Bacon, Michael Shire, Howard Dietcher, and Siebren Miedema for these invitations, and to my students at the Jerusalem Fellows for helpful comments and suggestions.

Like most authors, I strive to help readers understand what I have to say without too much unnecessary effort. Analytic philosophers pride themselves on clarity, but we too often confuse it with technical precision. I am grateful to Fanny Levy and Suzanne Rice for teaching me to write more clearly and accessibly, without sacrificing analytic rigor, to David Dortort for his keen insight and gentle prodding, and to numerous readers for comments and criticism, including Thomas McCambridge, Barry Rosenblatt, Sherman Rosenfeld, Saul Wachs, Donald Arnstine, Daniel Pekarsky, Alven Neiman, Paul Farber, and an anonymous reviewer. I also benefited from conversations with members of the California Association for Philosophy of Education, the Philosophy of Education Society, the Philosophy of Education Society of Great Britain, the American Educational Research Association, the Jewish Education Research Network, the Association of Professors and Researchers in Religious Education, and the International Seminar on Religious Education and Values where I first tested some of these ideas among professional colleagues.

Credit for any insight this volume may offer should be shared with those I have mentioned, but responsibility for errors or misunderstandings remain mine alone. Finally, to my children, Aliza, Yonina, and Yehuda, who sacrificed time with their Abba so that he could be locked up in his study, and to my soul mate, Shelley, who reads every word I write and supports me in all that I do, I owe more than words can express.

CHAPTER ONE

Spiritual Awakening

There was a time when I knew the goal but not the road; now it is the opposite. Perhaps not even that. There is more than one path open to us. Which one leads toward God, which one leads toward man? I am just a wanderer. Still I go on searching. Perhaps all I seek is to remain a wanderer. . . . I am searching for a special course; one that lies between words and silence.

Elie Wiesel[1]

The story is told of a pious old man who would go to a special place in the forest at a designated time each year to light a fire and to pray for forgiveness from God for himself, his family, and his people. It was to this same place that his father would go each year. The words that the old man recited and the rituals that he performed were the very same words and rituals that his father had recited and performed. The old man had learned to pray in this way from his father, just as his father had learned from his father before him.

The day came when the old man died, and it fell to his son to take his place. But something happened in the transmission of this age-old practice, and the son did not remember the words he was to recite. So when the appointed time drew near, the son went to the place that his father had shown him. There he lit the fire just as his father had taught him and recited the following prayer: "Dear God, I know the place, and I know how to light the fire, but I do not know the words to my father's prayer. But I am here and I have my father's feelings of remorse in my heart. Let that be enough to atone for my sins and those of my family and my people." And it was enough.

When it came time for the old man's grandson to take his father's place, he was unable to learn the words of the prayer, since his father had forgotten them, and he was unable to find the place because he no longer lived in the area. But he remembered that his father had lit a fire. So when the appointed time approached, he went into the forest to a place of his own choosing, lit a fire, and recited the following prayer: "Dear God, I have forgotten the place, and I never knew the words. But I know how to light the fire and I am here with remorse for my sins and those of my family and my people. Let that be enough." And it was enough.

As the years went by, it became increasingly difficult to pass on the family traditions from one generation to the next. It did not take long before most of them were forgotten altogether. One day a young man, who knew very little of his family heritage, felt guilty for the way in which he and his family had treated their neighbors. Although he had apologized, and the neighbor had accepted his apology, he was not satisfied that he had done enough to make amends. His sister had told him that once their ancestors had a special ritual that they would perform to help make things right. She knew that her ancestors lit a fire somewhere in the forest, but she did not know what they said.

And so the young woman and the young man recited the following prayer: "Dear God, whoever and whatever you are, we do not know you very well, and frankly we don't even know if we believe in you, but we do know that our ancestors once believed in you. We have forgotten the day and we never knew the place. We're told that once there were rituals, a fire, and a forest; and we have heard rumors of some words that were recited. We never learned any of these. But we do know that we have done wrong and that we want to make it right. So we ask, if you are indeed the source of forgiveness, that our feelings of remorse and our deeds of reconciliation be enough." And they were enough.[2]

The Spiritual Quest

But were they really enough? We hope they were enough for God! But what about for this young man and woman who know little of their family's heritage or history, whose community and education offer them few ideals, who have no mechanism to expiate guilt, and who must differentiate right from wrong on their own, indeed, who must sort out whether there even is a right and a wrong?

There are, of course, many people who feel little need to connect with their religious or cultural heritage, or history, or community in order to decide on the values by which they will live. Some may have had family experiences that were stifling rather than ennobling, or felt oppressed rather than inspired by the religion of their ancestors or the values of their culture. But there are also many others who are searching today for a spiritual dimension in their lives that connects them to their past, or their culture, or their community, or their God. They are looking for identity and a sense of self, for community and belonging, for awe and wonder, and meaning in life. They quest after ethical vision and desire transcendent purpose.

Theological Questions

There is an unprecedented interest in spirituality today, specifically in spirituality grounded in tradition. Bookstores are filled with volumes of spiritual inspiration. Political leaders and public intellectuals discuss the "politics of meaning." Religious figures call for heightened fervor in their houses of worship. Study groups abound that explore sacred texts and mystical practices. And schools are being called to nurture student character and foster caring communities.[3]

This spiritual interest involves a number of "big" questions that are interrelated: (1) The Identity Question. What does it mean to be true to myself, to be the sort of person I should be, the best that I can be, to embrace my true identity? (2) The Community Question. In which communities will I flourish, will my family thrive. In which can I learn ethical ideals, or discover memory and history, or experience the security and fulfillment of belonging? (3) The Moral Question. If I am to be a moral person, a good person, how should I relate to others, both among those who belong to the communities that I have joined and among those who do not belong? (4) The Question of Meaning and Purpose. What is the meaning of life, its ethical vision or higher purpose? (5) The Question of Transcendence. What is worthy of ultimate commitment, loyalty, worship, or devotion?

Where does one turn to answer questions such as these? There are a number of places that offer partial answers. Some have understood questions about identity, community, and meaning as psychological or sociological, so they have looked to these fields of inquiry. However, the spiritual search is not only about understanding the way things are, but also about how they ought to be. Empirical social sciences such as psychology and sociology lack the vocabulary to address questions about values. Others have focused on the moral angle and have sought answers in philosophical ethics. This is a step in the right direction since all of these questions involve a normative dimension. Nevertheless, moral philosophy, like the social sciences, has its limits. It tends to ignore matters of ultimate meaning and transcendent purpose in favor of that which can be observed and defended logically. Undoubtedly, this is why the people who are searching today look beyond the confines of empirical and rational discourse.

Those who look for answers beyond the realm of logic often turn to poetry and the arts. They claim that answers to ultimate questions are ineffable, mysterious, and unexplainable. Poetry and the arts bridge the expressible and the inexpressible; they display for deliberation feelings and experiences that lie beyond the limits of ordinary language. Surely, answers to many of these questions are expressed in symbols, rituals, pageantry, performance, and metaphor. These forms of representation may express content about how life ought to be lived, but unless we are to accept that content without question, at least some of it must also be accessible by means of ordinary language so that we can assess how and whether it should be practiced.

For some people, spirituality involves a search for values that requires using critical judgment to differentiate between the positive and the negative. Since critical thinking is at the heart of education, some have looked to educational thought and practice for answers. There is certainly an educational dimension to each of these queries involving the skills as well as the value of critical thinking. However, without the moral content of some tradition, or literature, or community, educational processes alone cannot supply satisfying answers to life's "big" questions. Of course, all of these questions are addressed in one form or another by the spectrum of religious communities and many of the most compelling answers are found in faith traditions; but organized religion does not hold a monopoly over spirituality, so I don't view the issue as exclusively "religious." People also discover ideals to live by within national, racial, ethnic, intellectual, cultural, artistic, linguistic, gender, and sexual orientations.

I prefer, therefore, to view these as theological questions. I use the term "theology" not as the study of a transcendent deity alone, but rather as the pursuit of any higher good worthy of devotion. Some call this "natural" as opposed to "revealed" theology, because it is not based in historical faith commitments but in experiences people share by virtue of their common humanity, or culture, or historical epoch. Paul Tillich called it "theology of culture."[4] It is a quest that integrates the exploration of psychological, sociological, philosophical, poetic, educational, and religious issues by asking what our most sacred commitments should be. The search for spirituality, then, is fueled by a theological hunger, a yearning for identity, community, morality, meaning, and transcendence that can be satisfied only by a vision of a higher good. To find such a vision we must explore theology: the study of higher ideals, which requires the use of critical thinking skills acquired through education.

Learning to devote oneself to a higher good means adopting a comprehensive picture of how life ought to be lived organized around our most cherished beliefs, practices, and images. In Western religions these key values are expressed in terms of faith in God—a supernatural deity who is the creator of the universe and the author of its moral code.[5] There are also nonreligious conceptions of the good. Rather than drawing on the divine, for example, many nontheistic feminists idealize the image of a caring mother as their higher good.[6] I call the holistic portrait of life based on these sorts of fundamental commitments "a vision of a good life." The search for spirituality can be understood as a quest for such a vision, for an all-encompassing set of values to guide our lives that is most often found in a religious tradition, or a cultural heritage, or a caring community.[7]

An Unwholesome Disinterest in Our Souls

The genesis of today's search for the spiritual life is often attributed to a rebellion against the overly rational character of modern life. Many people feel today that the institutions upon which they have depended for moral guidance—families and communities, churches and synagogues, schools and colleges—have failed to offer a satisfactory response to life's ultimate questions. These institutions are excessively dry and intellectual, speaking too much to the head and not enough to the heart. They have been so interested in accommodating themselves to modern culture, in transmitting its rationalist values and advancing its program of scientific analysis and technological progress, that they have lost interest in our souls, in values that foster inner peace, interconnectedness, and faith in higher ideals. The life they generate is self-centered, fragmented, and focused more on means, instruments, and techniques than on worthwhile ends. This has left many of us yearning for a more fulfilling way of life.

A prominent rabbi was asked by congregants to speak with their son because he had become involved with a cult. The young man was raised in the liberal synagogue of which the rabbi was spiritual leader. He had been educated in its religious school and celebrated coming of age in its sanctuary. He had also attended a fine private high school and been accepted to the most prestigious Ivy League colleges. In short, he had received the best preparation for life that a liberal faith community had to offer. The parents were distraught that their son should be attracted to such a mindless, manipulative, and fanatic way of life as a cult. They wanted the rabbi to find out where, as parents and as a community, they had gone wrong. When the rabbi met the young man, he said to him, "All they want is your soul. All they are really interested in is your soul." To which the young man responded, "At least someone is interested in my soul." This sense of failure, of unwholesome disinterest in our souls, has brought on a crisis, a questioning of the basic assumptions that have governed our lives.

In response, some people have sought the spiritual in subjective feelings, or group solidarity, or religious dogma. Often, the beliefs and practices associated with these solutions are transmitted through emotional exhortations, mechanical training, and rote memorization of doctrines or texts. Followers are not expected to question the "why and wherefore" of these beliefs and practices. In extreme cases, such as cults, assent to these sorts of commitments is sometimes accomplished by means of manipulation, brainwashing, or mind control. These approaches to the inculcation of belief and practice are instances of indoctrination. Questioning and critical reasoning are not part of the equation.

Spirituality, however, is a value term. It involves a vision of the good. For those engaged in this search, to say that a person or institution embodies spirituality is a mark of praise; and to say that they lack this trait is to voice a complaint. The answer to our spiritual quest cannot be wholly irrational, therefore, since the concept requires that we be able to distinguish between positive and negative values. Whether the source of value derives from personal intuition, or the collective will, or the word of God, understanding the difference between worthy and worthless involves the exercise of critical judgment. Compelling persons to adopt commitments through manipulation or brainwashing hampers their capacity to make such judgments. The very purpose of controlling a person's mind through denial of love, or infliction of pain or the use of drugs is to subjugate her will. To be capable of distinguishing a good from a bad life, we must be able to choose our values freely.

For this kind of choice to be genuinely free, it must be possible for a person to miss the mark. Moral decisions are not necessary conclusions that couldn't be otherwise. They are not derived mechanically from indubitable premises. Even when we base them on good reasoning, moral judgments are contingent; they could always be otherwise because they involve the ambiguities, vagaries, and unpredictability of real life. This is why rules, reasons, and methods of analysis cannot make moral decisions; only people can do so.

Although modernity may have overemphasized the role of reason at the expense of emotion in guiding our lives, we do not solve the problem by throwing the intelligent baby out with its rational bath water. Any answer to our spiritual quest requires an intelligent dimension that embraces critical thinking, free will, and fallibility. I argue that these very dichotomies between reason and feeling, thinking and acting, that are so characteristic of modern thinking lie at the core of our current spiritual paralysis. Our very capacity to offer and absorb criticism is predicated on the emotional security born of having been properly cared for. Critical rationality begins with love!

The intelligent dimension of spirituality ties it closely to education. Unlike mechanical training and rote learning, teaching in the fullest sense involves the transmission, not merely of beliefs and practices, but also of methods for assessing and evaluating them. It follows that education is not first and foremost about acquiring knowledge, or gaining identity, or insuring group continuity, as is often supposed, but rather about empowering a person to choose a vision of the good life. There is, in other words, a symbiotic relationship between spirituality properly conceived and education. Intelligent spirituality can only be transmitted by means of education; and all education worthy of the name is an agent of a spiritual vision. Moreover, if we think of democracy as the sort of society that values intelligence—critical judgment, freedom, and fallibility—then intelligent spirituality and education are partners in a commitment to the core values of that society. So, to the extent that liberal education involves the preparation of leaders and citizens for liberal, democratic societies, it is also a form of spiritual education. This, in brief, is the thesis of this book.

A Theology of Education

If the ensuing account of spirituality can be called a "theology of culture," then the spiritual pedagogy that flows from it can be seen as a "theology of education."[8] The task of this sort of natural theology is not to develop an account of spirituality and education grounded in a systematic interpretation of a particular faith, but to clarify the conditions under which it is logically possible to offer any account at all. To be sure, these conditions do presuppose substantive assumptions, but not the sort typically found in revealed theology such as ideas concerning the nature of divine communication. Instead, these conditions address the assumptions required for ethical discourse to make sense and the relation of these assumptions to open society, education, and the spiritual quest.

Such an analysis would be empty, however, without some grounding in particular traditions, since neither education nor spirituality can be actualized outside the context of distinct ethical visions. The ensuing discussion is, therefore, full of illustrations. These are drawn from a variety of secular, Christian, and Jewish sources. Many are taken from the Hebrew Bible, since it is revered by Christians, Jews, and Moslems, and played a significant role in the development of secular humanism. Hence, an interpretation of biblical theology—shaped by rabbinic teachings—is in some sense implicit in this volume. Its point is to illuminate spiritual life and pedagogy in general, not biblical or Jewish thought in particular. However, it may be easier to grasp what I have to say about spirituality and education if I summarize at the outset some key points about my reading of this one influential faith tradition.[9]

Understanding spirituality and education as related to ethics leads to an interpretation of biblical religion as empowering rather than coercive.[10] God, on this account, is not an authoritarian, omniscient dictator but a loving parent and consummate teacher who seeks to pass on fundamental truths about the human condition to children and students. Like every good parent, He can become disappointed and even angry with His children; and like every good teacher, She not only conveys concepts to Her students through explanations and experiences, but learns from interacting with them as well.[11] Holiness resides not in an all-perfect being, as some philosophers would have it, but in a fallible presence who—as our role model—takes responsibility for and learns from mistakes. The biblical god is not characterized by a need to exert power over others, but is impassioned by a desire to empower others to chart their own courses.

Whatever actually happened at Sinai, the Hebrew Bible produced a revolution in human self-perception according to which we are not ignorant and controlled by omnipotent gods, but are intelligent and capable of controlling ourselves. Biblical authority lies not in any particular view of *how* God spoke at Sinai, but in an account of *what* was said that enables us to become responsible moral agents capable of making sense of our lives. People are like God in that they can distinguish between right and wrong as they are given to understand it and free to act on that understanding. Moreover, parents and teachers imitate God when they seek to identify and confirm those divine sparks in children or students that enable them to become intelligent agents of their own actions. Parenting and teaching are thus sacred activities.

Biblical and democratic thought share important themes concerning the sanctity and moral potential of each human being. The task of education, in this interpretation, is to actualize that potential through initiation into a spiritual community. Realizing moral potential requires that we exercise control over ourselves, not over others; so the impetus to follow divine teaching cannot stem from coercion. It must flow from understanding the role of that teaching in liberating us from self-defeating attitudes and actions. To force behaviors and beliefs on people, therefore, is to undermine the very point of the biblical message. Free people must be taught, not merely trained—educated, not indoctrinated.[12] Religious faith cannot be enforced, whether by the necessary conclusions of philosophical arguments or through the coercive actions of religious authorities. It is a practice, and must be nurtured within communities that share memory and meaning.

Consider how communal celebration of the Sabbath communicates these ideas. In Exodus 20:8–12 we are enjoined to "*remember* the Sabbath day and keep it holy" because God did so when creating the world (Genesis 2:1–4).[13] Memory is a mental act of which we are capable because, with God, we are intelligent. We can make distinctions between holy and ordinary days, and between right and wrong (Genesis 3:8). In Deuteronomy 5:12–16 we are told to "*observe* the Sabbath" as a reminder of Israel's slavery in Egypt. Observance is an act of will of which we are capable because we are not slaves, either to human task masters or to our own creative labors. Also with God, we are free to rest. The Sabbath lies at the heart of the Bible's ethical code—it is the fourth of the Ten Commandments—because it demonstrates that people, like God, are intelligent and free to make their own mistakes; and its commemoration enshrines these concepts in the very cycle of communal life.

Modern political theory is not antithetical to biblical religion but to the dogmatic misreading of that religion as obsessed with coercive authority and power. Today's spiritual crisis is a product of an overreaction against that obsession which resulted in a suppression of ethical deliberation about the nature of the good. Our current malaise is not a product of too *much* freedom born of the modern rejection of traditional religion as posited by the religious right; and the solution is not a wholesale rejection of modernity for a nostalgic religion of the past. Nor is our current difficulty a result of too *little* freedom stemming from the rigidity of modern rationality in religious institutions, as argued by the left; and the solution is neither a new-age spirituality centered on the self nor a revolution of the powerless.

Our problem lies in a *misconception* of the nature of freedom as vested in individuals independent of communities with visions of a higher good such as that revealed at Sinai. Divine commandments—both the inspiring and the disconcerting—are liberating. Without them—or practices very much like them—there is no way to make sense of what it means to be liberated. They are neither to be accepted blindly nor adopted at face value, but rather to be interpreted and reinterpreted, under the guidance of learned teachers, in order to accommodate our ever-expanding understanding of the human condition. Individuality—identity or selfhood—is a spiritual concept. It is constituted ethically and theologically, by affirming a vision of the good. In this instance, God—the teacher and symbol of ethical ideals—is discovered and embraced in communities that study, practice, and celebrate Torah.[14]

Part of the work of retrieval required by our current predicament is surely a rereading of both biblical texts and modern political philosophy in ways that recognize these affinities.[15] To reread these—and other—traditions in ways that embrace a more wholesome interest in our souls, we need a better understanding of the attitudes this spiritual awakening is challenging, where they came from, and why they are problematic.

Spiritual Crisis

Our modern way of life is a product of two seventeenth- and eighteenth-century revolutions, the Enlightenment and the Emancipation. The Enlightenment project challenged the scriptural faith of medieval life and replaced it with new forms of reasoning, inquiry, and knowledge. Physics replaced theology as the queen of the sciences, and epistemology—the study of knowledge—overtook ethics as the central concern of philosophy. This new thinking became the basis for a modern way of life based on scientific reasoning and technological advancement.

The Emancipation project is the social, economic, and political program that resulted from the Enlightenment. Individuals became citizens of nation-states that were to pursue the socioeconomic interests of their constituents. Many of those who have benefited from the successes of the Emancipation project have become aware that Enlightenment individualism does not provide a sufficiently satisfying conception of goodness. Here is where the search for spirituality begins. To see why, let us look a bit more closely at the rise and decline of the Enlightenment ideology and its impact on the new interest in spirituality.

The Medieval Synthesis

Prior to the advent of medieval religious philosophy in the ninth century, the spiritual life of Moslems, Christians, and Jews was based on faith in the divine origins of sacred scripture. To each of these communities, the Koran and the Christian and Hebrew Bibles taught the truth about how and why the world came into being and set forth the life that God expected of the faithful. These people made sense of the world through the eyes of scripture.

The rediscovery of Aristotle by the Moslems challenged the naiveté of these theologies by offering an additional source of truth and value—philosophical reason. Aristotle's philosophy undermined long-held assumptions about the nature of knowledge and the source of ethical ideals. Although many continued to adhere to the simple faith of their ancestors, others such as al-Farabi the Moslem, Maimonides the Jew, and Aquinas the Christian, came to believe in the veracity of both reason and revelation. They needed to explain the truth of revelation, given that some of its convictions could not be sustained rationally, such as the world being created in six days, the Red Sea splitting on Moses' command, and the sun standing still at the behest of Joshua. To preserve their way of making sense of the world, they needed to explain how the beliefs and practices of Islam, Christianity, and Judaism were possible given Aristotelian reasoning. Philosophy provided the tools for reconciling these two sources of truth.

By the middle of the fourteenth century, a well-developed synthetic religious philosophy had emerged, sometimes called "scholasticism," that reconciled the truths of scripture with Aristotelian rationality. According to this synthesis, revelation and reason are completely compatible. One need make no intellectual sacrifices in order to embrace faith in God and a life devoted to His word. By the middle of the fifteenth century, much of the religious and intellectual life of Europe, North Africa, and the Middle East was divided. There were rationalists (mostly intellectuals and scholastics) and nonrationalists (clerics or mystics or people of simple faith who had little exposure to or sympathy for philosophy). Both alternatives offered a clear conception of a higher good to which one was expected to devote one's life.

The Emergence of Enlightenment

The Enlightenment emerged in the seventeenth century as a critique of both the scholastic synthesis of the rationalists and the simple faith of the nonrationalists. It advanced a new sort of rationality that turned out to be less compatible with medieval faith than the Aristotelian variety. Aristotle's rational method was deductive. He began with fundamental assumptions such as the existence of God as a necessary prime mover. These were proved by means of arguments that made little or no reference to empirical reality. From these premises he deduced other important claims about the nature of the universe. For Aristotle, it was not material reality within space and time that was most crucial for discovering the truth but abstractions and essences that lie beyond our sensory experience. This metaphysical focus was remarkably compatible with biblical religion.[16]

The French philosopher René Descartes argued that the scholastic synthesis failed not only because it presumed the truth of scripture but also because it accepted the veracity of Aristotelian rationalism. He pioneered a new kind of reasoning known as "skepticism" that questioned any premise that was not "clear and apparent." In place of both simple faith and the scholastic synthesis of faith and reason, Descartes offered a philosophy without presuppositions that would rest solidly on a foundation purged of doubt by means of skepticism. Whereas Aristotle's rationality could be reconciled with religious and cultural custom such as that contained in Scripture, Descartes was skeptical of anything based on mere "example and custom." According to Ernest Gellner, in Descartes's view:

> [e]ntire societies are deeply committed, with fervor and often with arrogance and with infuriating complacency, to blatant absurdities. This being so, how can we trust our own strong collective convictions. We know them to be fools. Are we ourselves exempt from folly? . . . Liberation from error requires liberation from culture, from, "example and custom." . . Liberation is to be achieved by purification through doubt: that which is based only on custom and example is dubitable but . . . that which is rational is not. Culture and reason are antithetical. Culture is questionable. Reason is not. Doubt and reason must jointly purge our minds of that which is merely cultural, accidental and untrustworthy.[17]

Benedict Spinoza, a Dutch Jew, applied Descartes's theory to theological studies. He demonstrated that the Hebrew Bible could be understood as the political constitution of an ancient people with limited ethical consequences for his day.[18] Spinoza's analysis was quickly extended to Western religion in general. The Scottish empiricist David Hume showed that religious belief could make no defensible claims to empirical knowledge; it did not represent truth and could never be more than mere opinion.[19] In the wake of Hume's analysis, it became clear that the tension between faith based on scripture and the new critical rationality based on skepticism was much deeper than that between the naive faith of the medievals and Aristotelian rationality. The good life according to scripture was under attack.

In place of medieval conceptions of goodness, the leader of the eighteenth-century German Enlightenment, Immanuel Kant, argued that the basic principles of biblical morality could be sustained on the basis of critical reason alone, without reliance on scripture. Kant argued not for a synthesis of reason and revelation but for a new kind of faith which he called a "religion of reason."[20] It consisted primarily in a rational morality derived from the duty to treat other people as ends rather than means. He called this the "categorical imperative."[21] Kantian ethics provided not so much a vision of how to live a good life as it did a basis for justifying the rightness of specific behaviors. No longer was it assumed that people would share a common vision of how life should be lived. Instead, they agreed only to a common approach for the justification of their behaviors. Individuals could choose their own visions of the good, but based on a universal logic embedded in consciousness.[22]

The British political philosopher John Locke extended this ethical analysis to political theory by conceiving of a society that would allow people with different faiths, or with no faith at all, to participate in a common civic culture and political system without sharing a vision of the good.[23] Lockean society was neutral with respect to competing moral ideals. This led to a separation of religion and state that denied religious institutions the power to enforce their beliefs and practices. People could now choose freely to live without religion; and secularism was born. Religious denominations would have to compete for the loyalty of their constituencies in an open marketplace of ideas.

A Modern Synthesis

During the nineteenth and twentieth centuries, liberal Protestants, Catholics, and Jews replaced scholasticism with a new synthesis that turned out to be more problematic and fraught with tension than its predecessor. In contrast to the scholastic synthesis that posited the rationality of scientific knowledge, religion, and ethics, the new liberal synthesis admitted the rationality of scientific knowledge only; religion and ethics were excluded. This protected them from the critiques of Spinoza and Hume, but not without a price.

Secularism, which was made possible by the Lockean separation of church and state, promoted science and technology as the basis for common belief and public policy. Religion and ethics, on the other hand, were restricted to the emotional sphere. They were said not to conform to the theoretical logic of Descartes and the empiricists. Instead, they either followed their own sort of reasoning or expressed pure feeling that defied logical discourse altogether. Since religion and ethics could not be subjected to empirical critique, they were assumed to be private, personal, and subjective. As such, they could have little influence on the public domain. To adapt to modernism, advocates of a religious or moral life retreated to a position in which religion and ethics would have increasingly limited influence over society and the public.

This dichotomization of knowledge on the one hand, and religion and ethics on the other, meant that spiritual values and concerns were relegated to the place of worship or the home but were excluded from the public spheres of work or politics. In the United States, where this exclusion was mandated by the constitutional separation of church and state, religious education was removed from the public arena and restricted to the supplemental school of the church or synagogue or to the independent parochial school. Value instruction in state-sponsored schools lost its moral compass. If ethics are private and grounded in ineffable feelings, there is little in the way of moral instruction that school teachers can offer students. With the added challenge by the multiculturalists regarding the possibility of state schools transmitting any common values, the very idea that education should initiate students into a vision of the good life, secular or religious, has been called into question.[24]

People regarded the spiritual concerns expressed in religion and ethics as largely irrelevant to the world at large. Those domains where spirituality was allowed to exert influence, such as the church and synagogue, were also influenced by Enlightenment rationalism. Worship became more decorous and less emotional, more concerned with liturgical structure and less with creating community and meaning. People joined churches and synagogues more for their schools than for their worship services. Bible study became Bible stories, and ethical questions were reduced to the level of that which could be learned in kindergarten.[25]

Since public and private values were no longer mutually reinforcing, the religious programs of these schools were marginalized in the broader culture. With limited support from the culture at large and scarce resources in terms of both time and money, the education in religion and values that these institutions were able to offer was meager. Low salaries and part-time instructional schedules made it difficult to attract properly prepared staffs or to market adequate curriculum materials. Many people serving in these schools have been volunteers.

All of this was mitigated for Christians only by virtue of the fact that they represent the North American majority, so schools and society could be counted on to convey at least the external vestiges of their faith, such as the celebration of Christian holidays. For Jews, the problem was intensified because the pressure to assimilate into the secular or Christian majority was enormous, and the external environment was neutral at best or, more likely, hostile to the preservation of Jewish or religious identity. The liberal synthesis was showing signs of strain; it contained the seeds of its own demise.

The Unraveling of Modernism

Those who, despite their impoverished religious education, maintained a spiritual commitment to churches and synagogues were often ambivalent about their religious identities because the soci-

ety did little to validate them. Graduates of this system often identified more strongly with their secular professional and political
allegiances for which there was far greater status and public recognition. In response to their ambivalence toward religion, some
abandoned the liberal synthesis for a more secular lifestyle. Others pursued what they perceived to be a more "authentic" form
of their old-time religion.

Yet, even among those who have remained committed to the
liberal synthesis, there has been a retreat from modernism. The
term "education" in the expression "religious education," for example, is seen in some circles as too modern and secular. They
experience contemporary education as dry, heartless, and value-
less; as focused on getting a better job rather than on becoming a
better person. The term "education" is being replaced in many
churches and theological seminaries, therefore, by such expressions as "Christian nurture" or "pastoral theology." This reflects the
belief that modern education has little to say about the cultivation
of faith and the inculcation of values.

Many Jewish leaders have also begun to recognize that the
modern synthesis they embraced for so long speaks to the hearts
and minds of fewer and fewer of their contemporaries and their
children. Fearful for the future of the Jewish people in North
America, they hope that improvements in the Jewish educational
system can increase identification with a Jewish conception of the
good life. This concern has come to be known as the Jewish continuity crisis. It is a spiritual crisis that stems from the difficulties
within modern thought at articulating adequate visions of how
one ought to live.

The popularity of the term "spirituality" that is the subject of
this book can also be seen as a retreat from the modernism that
has infused our religious institutions. If moderns saw traditional
religion as antiquated, irrelevant, and meaningless, today's spiritualists experience religious liberalism as dry, unfeeling, and empty.
In its effort to reconcile tradition with modernity, the modern synthesis embraced too much modern rationalism and not enough

traditional feeling. "Spirituality," on the other hand, permits an embrace of some of the positive aspects of religion without the need to affiliate with "modern" churches or synagogues.[26]

The enlightenment synthesis has begun to unravel not only because of its emotional flatness but also because of flaws in the concepts on which it was founded. It turns out that Cartesian logic, Kantian ethics, and Lockean politics are themselves deeply problematic. Philosophers concerned with the interpretation of texts—with hermeneutics—have demonstrated the impossibility of Descartes's presuppositionless philosophy. Martin Heidegger argued, for example, that when we read a text, we do not approach it as a tabula rausa—a blank slate. On the contrary, in order to read and understand anything, we must first know the language in which it was written. Every language is full of concepts, ideas, and assumptions that are embedded in the meaning of words and in grammatical structure. Heidegger calls these assumptions the "pre-understanding" that a reader brings to a text.[27]

His student, Hans-Georg Gadamer, pointed out that history, culture, and language also influence this pre-understanding. Readers bring not only linguistic but also historical and cultural assumptions to understanding a text. All communication is like textual interpretation in this respect; we bring the assumptions of our language, history, culture, and personal background to discourse with others.[28] Karl-Otto Apel called this the "a-priori of communication."[29] Philosophy is no different from any other discourse. It must take place within a community that shares language, culture, history, and education. Consequently, the very idea that philosophy could be founded on presuppositionless first principles is simply untenable.

Postmodern philosophers who are critical of modernism have also shown how Kant's rational morality and Locke's neutral society are problematic. Kant's moral vision rests on the idea that people value rationality. But why value reason above anything else? Kantians respond with a so-called transcendental argument in which reason is self-justifying. According to this sort of argument, the very question "Why be rational?" presupposes the value of rationality because it calls for a reason. Since the rationalist accepts no justificatory grounds other than reason, there can be no acceptable defense of rationality that does not already assume what it purports to establish. Rationality cannot be justified without assuming that which calls for justification.

Moreover, Alasdair MacIntyre has shown that Locke's liberal society is not as neutral as it made itself out to be, but is rather an expression of the liberal and often secular values of one culture that are imposed on others as a price of admission. There is, accordingly, no neutral way to adjudicate between competing conceptions of the good, so there is no firm foundation on which to anchor our webs of belief.[30]

Rationalism and Romanticism

This late twentieth-century rebellion against rationalism is not new; it has been part of modernity since its inception. Indeed, at each stage in its development, a non- and sometimes anti-rational reaction occurred that is often called romanticism. Certainly, contemporary life in the West has been organized around the rational assumptions of the Enlightenment; it has also been plagued by conflicts with the nonrational.

In the seventeenth century, the Enlightenment generated the foundations of modern mathematics and science and the basis for a neutral liberal society. A romantic response emerged that criticized the lack of feeling and emotion in the new rationality and complained of its emphasis on the universal over the individual. Then, in the eighteenth century, the scientific revolution translated to technology, and a reaction against the pervasiveness of instrumental reason developed. At the same time, the lack of community in the newly industrialized world was bemoaned.

As the emergence of logical analysis became the model for studying behavior and the basis for social policy, twentieth-century Western societies rapidly secularized and urbanized. Concern was

voiced about the penchant of logicians for analyzing the formal relations between ideas while ignoring their content. It was also noted
that behavioral analysis paid too much attention to the mechan-
ics of mind and the structure of society, and not enough to personal feelings and communal yearnings. Antiformalism emerged,
along with organic thinking that used biological metaphors to describe human life in terms of integrated wholes rather than dis-
connected parts. Conservative politicians and antiliberal religious
leaders began to speak nostalgically about the more cohesive
community of yesterday, in which people were less logical and
analytical.

Most recently, we have witnessed dramatic changes in the physical sciences. Quantum physics relativized our assumptions about
the relations between time, space, and matter. The sands began
to shift under that which appeared to the early modern empiricists
and those who accepted their views as fixed and "objective." If
external reality—matter—is not fixed in space and time, then perhaps related assumptions about the nature of knowledge and
inquiry should also be questioned. This led postmodern critics to
doubt whether logic is a given of consciousness rather than a creation of culture; whether knowledge is "objective" rather than
constructed; and whether the natural and social sciences are governed by reason rather than by individual and cultural biases.

Most of these thinkers echo and even trace their intellectual
origins to earlier romantic revivals. They claim to shut down the
debate, proclaiming the end of modern rationalism and the victory
of their own forms of neoromanticism.[31] I will argue, however, that
the way out of this morass is not by the victory of one side over
the other but by the recognition that each has important contributions to make to living a good life.

The Challenge of Spirituality

Enlightenment theories about knowledge, ethics, and religion require reassessment because they have failed to provide a spiritual

vision of the good life. But that does not mean that all vestiges of the Enlightenment should be abandoned. On the contrary, even the most ardent critics of the Enlightenment ideas would be loath to forgo the many benefits that emerge from "enlightened" forms of scientific reasoning such as advances in transportation and communications technology, biomedical research, food production, and financial management. This might suggest that, although they have enabled us to view the Enlightenment project in perspective, critiques of epistemological concepts such as objectivity and the neutrality of reason should also be viewed with a certain amount of skepticism.

Nor would most of us be willing to forfeit the political and intellectual freedoms we enjoy that are rooted in Enlightenment ideas. These ideas protect our right, and provide the tools, to challenge even our most fundamental assumptions. Many people who seek spirituality today recognize the shortcomings of modernism. They have experienced a spiritual awakening, a call to provide in the modern social, economic, and political context what the Enlightenment ideology failed to offer—visions of the good life. But, they nonetheless appreciate the benefits of liberty and freedom of expression.

The problem is how to offer a compelling vision of the good while preserving the Enlightenment principles and values that are crucial to democracy. How is it possible in an open society to reengage the discourse of theology—to examine and adopt higher ideals—given that Enlightenment philosophy privatized discussions of the good life so thoroughly that theology cannot be shared and ideals not held in common? Robert Nozick points out that philosophers often face problems of this sort:

> How is it possible for us to have free will, supposing that all actions are causally determined? . . . How is it possible that we know anything, given the facts that the skeptic enumerates? . . . How is it possible for something to be the same thing from one time to another, through change? How is it possible for subjective

experience to fit into an objective physical world? How can there be stable meaning . . . given that everything in the world is changing? . . . How is evil possible, supposing the existence of an omnipotent omniscient good God?[32]

To answer such questions, philosophers search for deeper principles that can remove the apparent conflict and put their beliefs in alignment. Our task, therefore, is not to preserve old worldviews with new arguments; it is to reconstruct the possibility of spiritual vision by articulating the conditions that must be met for goodness to be meaningful today. This is the challenge of the new spirituality.

Meeting this challenge calls for an approach to theology that can frame our concept of a higher good within the context of an emancipated society. This is possible only if we break out of the Enlightenment dialectic of rationalism and romanticism in which the current discussion of spirituality has been framed. Instead of viewing thought and action, or knowing and doing, or reasoning and feeling, or epistemology and ethics as dichotomies, we need to understand them as complementary. We want not new modes of thinking, feeling, and living that are disengaged from one another, but renewed ways of feeling intelligently, thinking morally, and living thoughtfully. We require ideals that transcend our selves and our communities but that can guide both the individual and collective sides of our inner lives and our outward behavior. Such an approach embraces the conditions of ethical discourse as well as the democratic values they imply. It also lends itself to transmission and renewal through education understood as the study, practice, and celebration of goodness, not as a means to some other ends, but as an end in itself. I call it intelligent spirituality.

CHAPTER TWO

Spirituality and the Good Life

Out of my straits I called to the Lord. God answered by setting me free.

—Psalms 118:5

When the Israelites fled the Egyptian Pharaoh, the Hebrew Bible recounts that they did not have time for their bread to rise, so they baked it unleavened on their backs in the heat of the desert sun. Consequently, when the exodus is reenacted during the Passover festival, it is forbidden by biblical law to have any substance in one's possession that is or could become leavened. According to an ancient custom, the night before the festival begins, the house is to be searched by the light of a candle in order to illuminate even the darkest corners where old bread and cake crumbs may be found.

This search for old crumbs is sometimes compared to a spiritual quest. The Passover festival reenacts not only the exodus from Egypt but also redemption from slavery—the salvation of an entire nation. It also begins a period in the holiday cycle that culminates seven weeks later with the Feast of Weeks, commemorating the divine revelation at Sinai. Some see this spring cleaning as a symbolic cleansing of minds and hearts in preparation for the reception of God's message once again. If divine teachings are to set people free, then to receive them, the vestiges of slavery must first be thrown off.

In this interpretation, the Hebrew word for Egypt is understood to mean narrow straits.[1] Each year as the crumbs are removed, preparation is not only made to reenact the experience of slaves passing through the narrow Red Sea straits as they escape to freedom. It is also made to navigate the narrow straits of life, leaving behind the unproductive ways of being that enslave our souls. The search culminates in a reaffirmation of God's liberating vision, even in the hard-to-reach corners of our minds and hearts. Accepting this vision enables people to rediscover their freedom and reenter the Promised Land again each year.

In the previous chapter, we learned that the spiritual awakening of the past few years is a result of unproductive ways of thinking and living associated with the Enlightenment project; that our most cherished beliefs can be based on presuppositionless foundations unassailable by skepticism, that our conceptions of the moral life can be rationally justified, and that it is possible to erect a completely neutral society that embraces competing conceptions of the good life. Questioning these assumptions has destabilized the concepts of identity, community, morality, meaning, and transcendence that constitute our modern vision of life. Yet we also learned that the critical spirit, which led to the discovery of these difficulties, requires the sort of free society engendered by those very Enlightenment concepts.

Here are the narrow straits through which we must navigate if we are to reach the "promised land" of spiritual fulfillment: Where did the Enlightenment project go wrong? What did the Emancipation project get right? And how can a conception of the good life guide us in abandoning the former while preserving the latter? Like the candle used to search for crumbs, answers to these questions should illumine the distinction between those Enlightenment concepts to be discarded and those to be preserved as we reconstruct our commitment to a higher purpose.

Disenchantment with Enlightenment

Before we consider what Enlightenment politics achieved, it is important to understand why Enlightenment morality failed. Enlightenment moral theory focused on the analysis of moral reasoning without advancing a comprehensive account of how life ought to be lived. Indeed, most of Enlightenment moral thought prided itself on its independence from particular normative ethical traditions. It often claimed to be a "value-free" form of ethical deliberation. Although this attitude opens moral and religious thought to new intellectual challenges, it often leaves people in doubt as to how they ought to lead their lives.

Immanuel Kant, for example, offered an analysis of moral behavior as the exercise of one's rational duty to treat each person as an end rather than a means.[2] John Stuart Mill, an important nineteenth-century moral philosopher, argued that the ethics of behavior was to be justified according to its consequences. Among the alternative courses of action available, the most ethical would be the one that resulted in the greatest good for the greatest number of people.[3] John Locke held that the morality of a behavior was to be judged on the basis of a social contract to which one implicitly agrees when one accepts and enjoys the security of civilized society that such a covenant guarantees.[4]

If Enlightenment moral theory analyzed right action, modern religious thought rationally dissected the nature of correct belief. Rationalist followers of Kant contended that our most sacred beliefs could be grounded in a rational ideal that lay beyond our full comprehension, an ideal that all scientific thought strove to comprehend and all moral practice sought to emulate.[5] Pragmatic descendants of Mill, such as William James, claimed that religious faith should be embraced because it leads to the consequence of more meaningful, purposeful lives.[6] Covenant theologians argued that Jews and Christians are bound by faith commitments contracted between God and humankind centuries ago.[7]

Since no agreement could be reached on the correct rationale for either moral behavior or religious belief, romantic alternatives stepped in that attributed moral and religious intuition not to reasons but to feelings. Emotivism in moral philosophy suggested that there are no rational bases to ethical intuitions at all; they are the result of purely subjective emotions that are personal and private.[8] Friedrich Schleiermacher argued that religion is not related to rational ideals at all but is rather an expression of nonrational feelings.[9] Soren Kierkegaard went so far as to claim that religious commitments cannot be adduced by logical argument. They require a leap of faith that supersedes rationality. The moral claims of religion are above rationality and call for acceptance on the basis of faith rather than reason.[10]

Given the contestability of moral and religious commitments, it is no wonder that educational thought favored transmitting to the young that which was incontestable, namely, scientific knowledge and technical skill. The most influential twentieth-century conceptions of education deal not with what way of life is best but with what sort of knowledge will best prepare youngsters for adult life. Although John Dewey saw education as deeply connected to the democratic way of life, he understood democracy as a social extension of biological growth; so he thought that children ought to be taught the knowledge that best enables them to meet the needs they experience in their social environments.[11] Richard Peters considered education as the initiation into the traditional subject matter of the school curriculum the worth of which rests in their rationality.[12] His student Paul Hirst called them the "forms of knowledge."[13] When Benjamin Bloom and his associates published their influential taxonomy of educational objectives that distinguished cognitive from affective goals, there was little doubt which was to dominate life in schools.[14]

The Need for Holistic Ethical Vision

The problem with this reliance on the rational and the scientific is that it offers no understanding of the higher values on which to base morality, religion, and education. Suppose Kant is right that our ethical duty is to conform our behavior to a rational ideal. Whose rationality are we to follow? Kant believed that reason was part of the structure of consciousness, built into the very possibility of thinking. But suppose consciousness does not come in a single package but is influenced by culture and gender and genes. How can we make sense of our rational duty when the very idea of there being a single account of pure reason is called into question?[15] Alternatively, suppose we accept the utilitarian principle— "the greatest good for the greatest number." How are we to determine what counts as a good to be measured against the greatest number? Similarly, if we agree to abide by a social contract, which contract are we to follow? These same sorts of problems persist within modern religious thought as well. According to which rationality, whose conception of meaning, or what religious covenant should I conform my belief and practice?[16]

Nor does the emotivist solution resolve the dilemma; it transforms ethical and religious doctrines into matters that are so personal that they defy intelligent dialogue altogether. Yet even though we may not agree on the proper moral practices or religious attitudes to adopt, we appear able to understand one another well enough to deliberate, discuss, and debate our differences. How is this mutual understanding possible, if these matters are so subjective as to defy discourse altogether? "The problem with you religious guys," a professor of mine once quipped, "is that you say religious experience is ineffable and then go around 'effing' about it all the time." Even the question of what knowledge is most worth knowing—a query that has dominated educational discussion for so long—is unanswerable without some notion of what it means for something to be worthwhile in the first place.

In order to account for which rationality, or what measure of utility, or whose social contract, or how it is possible that we can communicate about moral and religious commitments, or why this is more worth knowing than that, we require not a piecemeal analysis of the elements of the moral life but a synthesis of the ethical whole, a vision of what life at its best can be. We need, in short, a holistic conception of the good. Yet it is precisely such a comprehensive vision that is missing from Enlightenment discourse. When the Humpty-Dumpty of medieval scholasticism was pushed off the wall by Descartes, modern thought became expert at analyzing the pieces, but failed to teach us how to put Humpty-Dumpty back together again.

The Culture of Narcissism

Consequently, we have become unsure about the ideals with which we should identify. Without a sense of the ideals to emulate, it has become unclear whether we should affiliate with any groups outside of those that share our most narrow, self-serving interests. Our sense of moral conduct has become greatly diminished because there seem to be no ideals to serve outside of our selves. We have come to discover meaning not in values that emanate from history, or tradition, or God, but from momentary and fleeting sensations that "feel good."

There seems to be nothing worthy of our devotion greater than our selves. Consider the magazines we find at our local supermarkets. Once we found *Life*, which offered a large and encompassing view of the world. Then we began to see *People*. People are a part of life, but our perspective is narrowed considerably when we limit our focus in this way. Soon we were asked to read *Us*, and then *Self*. I heard an entertainer comment recently that, "I expect the next popular magazine to be called *Me*. When I look inside, I will find only mirrors." Christopher Lasch calls this centering on the self the "culture of narcissism," after the figure in Greek mythology who fell in love with his own reflection and spent his days gazing at himself in the water.[17]

But moral, religious, and educational ideals cannot be found in the confines of the self alone. The very concept of an ideal suggests an appeal to something beyond the self, something higher, loftier, more elevated. To say that something is an ideal assumes that something else is not. To say that something is valuable, or meaningful, or preferable means that something else is not valuable, or meaningful, or desirable. Ethical terms must convey distinctions between better and worse, otherwise they convey no content whatsoever. To make these distinctions, there must be a dividing line—a standard—that distinguishes good from bad, right from wrong, better from worse. The very idea of pursuing a moral life means appealing to standards by which to measure the worth of that life. It is the absence of standards of value that has sent people searching for a vision of the good life. Modernism, they have come to realize, leads to a radical individualism that worships the self, and this turns out to be the worship of nothing at all.

The Rise of Instrumentalism

Whereas the Enlightenment has failed to provide a vision of life's higher purpose, the scientific and technological knowledge it engendered has been extraordinarily successful at enhancing the quality of our lives. From the easing of daily chores, to the increase in leisure time, to advances in health care and medical science, to the transformation of communication, travel, and entertainment, we have been enriched, enhanced, and empowered by advances in science and technology. These are significant accomplishments to be sure. But they have led some to equate scientific and technological thinking with the higher values that should guide our lives. This misconceives the nature of science and technology, which are about describing the way the world is rather than prescribing how it ought to be.

One consequence of this misconception has been to view either critical or instrumental reasoning as the ultimate moral ideal. Critical reasoning teaches us to identify good and bad reasons so that we can criticize or defend an idea. Instrumental reasoning involves identifying the means needed to achieve desired ends.[18] But, reasoning, critical or instrumental, cannot be the ultimate moral ideal. Rather, reasoning should be the tool we employ to arrive at our values. The fact that we focus on how, rather than what, to think about our most sacred aspirations and commitments only emphasizes that we do not know what they are.

Charles Taylor points out that as value options become increasingly vacuous and self-centered there are fewer and fewer of them. With fewer moral choices to make, we become less practiced and proficient at making them. Rationalization and instrumentalization of values, therefore, flatten our horizons of significance by severely limiting the choices at our disposal and our ability to make them. Idealizing reasons and techniques rather than the values they justify and engender leads to a problem on another score. It restricts the degree to which people will be willing or able to reach beyond the confines of their own instrumental self-interests to forge ties with others in communities of shared values and memory.[19]

"Christian Love"

In *Scandalous Risks,* one of several novels dealing with the Church of England in the twentieth century, Susan Howatch depicts Venetia Flaxton, a young woman searching for meaning. Set in the English town of Starbridge, home to a great medieval cathedral, amid the sexually charged atmosphere of the 1960s, the story edges toward a love affair between Venetia and the dean of the cathedral, Neville Aysgarth, who is old enough to be her father. One aspect of their complex relationship involves Aysgarth becoming Venetia's self-appointed "tutor." Together they examine John Robinson's *Honest to God,* a widely read book of modern theology. Robinson contends that the essence of Christianity is love, and that the formal institutions and mores of the Church are not necessarily the best or only guides to loving and being loved:

> We all need, more than anything else, to love and be loved . . . .
> We need to be accepted as persons, as whole persons, for our own sakes. . . . The universe, like a human being, is not a mathematical formula. It's only love that gives you the deepest clue to it. . . . "It's love that makes the world go round." That's what Christians have always said.[20]

The consequence of this view is that:

nothing can itself always be labeled as "wrong." One cannot, for instance, start from the position "sex relations before marriage" or "divorce" are wrong or sinful in themselves. They may be in 99 or 100 of 100 cases, but they are not intrinsically so, for the only intrinsic evil is the lack of love.[21]

Understanding and enacting Robinson's version of "Christian love" becomes the goal of Neville's "tutorial" sessions with Venetia. Unbridled by tradition and unbounded by communal norms, this perspective becomes the rationalization for their illicit liaison. This leads Venetia into extraordinary moral and emotional turmoil. She ends up having a mental breakdown because Neville has no intention of leaving his wife for her. Neville, for his part, nearly abandons the very Christian ideals that have given his life meaning and purpose.

Like critical rationality, the sort of love in which Venetia and Aysgarth engaged was missing moral context and ethical content. With love as the only vision of the good, no standards existed by which to judge whether the love between Venetia and Neville was right, or appropriate, or seemly. Their love was rooted in fantasy, self-indulgence, and narcissism. It led to contradiction and confusion. Robinson's purely subjective "Christian love" provided insufficient moral guidance for organizing a meaningful life.

Jewish Continuity

Similar difficulties are to be found in recent attempts by Jewish leaders to address the problem of Jewish continuity. In the late nineteen-eighties a number of key North American Jewish leaders became alarmed at the rapid rate with which Jews were abandoning their commitment to Jewish beliefs and practices and their affiliations with Jewish institutions. The continuity of the Jewish people in North America was threatened, they argued, because its educational system had failed. Most Jews who became adults during the seventies and eighties had been educated in synagogue-sponsored Sunday schools and in afternoon religious schools called Hebrew schools because of their emphasis on language. They usually met for no more than six hours of instruction per week.[22]

These schools were vastly unpopular. Due to limited resources and few opportunities for full-time, professional employment, few institutions properly prepared administrators and teachers for these schools. The curricula were loosely organized and aspired to accomplish too much while actually expecting very little. The students attended after a full day of secular public or independent school. They were tired and often uninterested. Under pressure to assimilate into the American secular or Christian "mainstream," parents rarely observed at home the Jewish customs discussed in school. They attended synagogue only occasionally. In many cases, the primary Jewish activity in a family was to transport the children to and from Hebrew school. The home and community, therefore, provided little support for the curriculum.[23] If only this educational system could be changed, it was argued, the chances of Jewish continuity could be increased. Education, in this view, is a means to Jewish identity for the individual and continuity for the group.

Like critical reasoning and Robinson's "Christian love," identity and continuity are ideals that are void of moral and spiritual content. Just as neither reasoning nor love can be a coherent ideal without a conception of the good life, so too identity and continuity are empty concepts without the context of a larger ethical vision. The burning questions are not whether, but with what, to identify; and not how, but why, to continue. Additionally, the transformation of education into an instrument for the production of identity and continuity lessens its moral significance. Education is not an instrument to produce these contentless outcomes. It must be a partner in conceptualizing the good life that makes identity and continuity compelling. The Jewish continuity crisis is not the result of a failed educational system. It is not only that educational institutions require reform; the community they serve cries out for spiritual renewal.[24]

However, education has been the subject of public criticism in the Western world for much of this century. It has increasingly been viewed as a solution to social, economic, and ideological problems. When economic growth is slow, we look to the schools. When the Soviets put a man into space before the Americans, we look to the schools. When we face endemic social problems, such as racism, we turn to the schools. When minority cultures experience alienation, we turn to the schools. When sexually transmitted diseases are on the rise, we turn to the schools. When people feel lonely and need acceptance, we turn to the schools. But the very idea that education consists in techniques that can be used to produce economic growth or to reduce racism or to foster love or to engender religious identity is a measure of the very spiritual crisis we are facing. Education is not a means to produce values—it is a value. But because of the moral vacuousness of our current crisis, we are entirely unclear as to what the substance of that value ought to be.

Moral Education

No where is this seen more clearly than in approaches to moral education designed for state schools in pluralistic societies. Lawrence Kohlberg's theory, for example, charts a middle course between values clarification, which views moral education as the clarification of student feelings about ethical concerns,[25] and socialization, which sees moral instruction as imposing accepted social norms on the young.[26] Values-clarification theorists criticize socialization on the grounds that, in Western societies, there is no agreement as to what norms ought to be taught in state schools. Kohlberg accepts this critique, but complains that clarifying student feelings about moral dilemmas does not offer them enough prescriptive guidance. He argues instead that the task of moral education is to improve how students think about morality. This is accomplished by challenging the conventional thinking characteristic of one stage of moral growth in order to stimulate movement to the next stage. According to this theory, the content of moral education is not to be found in substantive norms, about which there is indeed no public agreement, but in the improvement of moral reasoning.[27]

By transforming rationality into an ethical ideal, Kohlberg's approach to moral education falls prey to many of the difficulties associated with Enlightenment morality. Like Robinson's "Christian Love," and Jewish continuity, the highest stages of Kohlbergian moral development lack sufficient moral content. Moral reasoning is not an ideal of moral education but a means to consider which among the many alternatives available one ought to embrace. There can be no moral education, no education altogether, without a substantive vision of the good life, even in pluralistic public schools.

In his later work, Kohlberg recognized that his stages of moral growth presuppose such a vision. He called it "the just society." In such a society, the opportunity to pursue one's own vision of goodness is guaranteed, provided that it is grounded in principle rather than self-interest, and that it does not prevent others from pursuing alternative visions. This is a step in the right direction in that the social situatedness of ethical discourse is emphasized. However, this view confuses the Enlightenment's political framework that enables different visions to coexist within the same society with a conception of goodness sufficiently comprehensive to offer guidance in making life's most important choices.[28]

The Achievements of Emancipation

If the Enlightenment failed to provide comprehensive ethical vision, it nonetheless preserved the political and intellectual conditions necessary to engage in ethical discourse. The Kantian/Lockean program advanced a political framework in which several visions of goodness could live together, even if it offered no particular conception of the good to which people could devote their lives. The philosopher Karl Popper called the framework that preserved these conditions "the open society."

The Open Society

Popper contrasts his approach to Plato's influential political theory. In *The Republic,* Plato addressed the question: Who should rule in a just society? To this question there are essentially two reasonable answers: either the majority, or the best and the brightest. The problem with majority rule, argued Plato, is what he called the paradox of freedom—too much freedom yields too little. The majority can elect a tyrant who can take away their freedom and deny their right to rule. Plato did not think that average citizens should be enfranchised, because they may not understand these dangers. He conceived of justice as an absolute ideal and held that only those who understand that ideal—i.e. the best and the brightest— should govern. He called them the "guardians" or "philosopher-rulers."[29]

Popper's objection to Plato's theory is that it assumes the guardians' understanding and implementation of justice to be flawless. This ignores the essential fact that humans are fallible. In Popper's view, Shakespeare put it well when he wrote that "to err is human." We err not only in what we believe, but also in how we transform our beliefs into policy and practice. To place unchecked authority in the hands of the elite is to put at risk the rights and freedoms of the many by ignoring the fallibility of the few.

Popper says that Plato begins his discussion with the wrong question, namely, "Who should rule?" This question assumes that someone will have unchecked power, the only issue being who. The result is what Popper calls a "theory of unchecked sovereignty." He claims that the proper question is not "Who should rule?" but rather "How can society be organized to protect against the mistakes of those in power, even when they are the best and the brightest?" A political theory resulting from this question will always seek to constrain power. Popper calls this sort of doctrine "a theory of checks and balances."[30]

Checks and Balances

Unchecked power corrupts, was the message of Lord Acton. This is the fundamental principle of the Enlightenment political tradition established by Locke in his *Two Treatises on Civil Government*. The open society recognizes the fallibility of those in power, the capacity of its citizens for criticism, and their freedom to enact alternatives. This society, in short, celebrates and defends fallibility, critical intelligence, and freedom which, I argue below, are the conditions of ethical discourse.

An acquaintance once worked at a university in which the faculty sought to check the power of the administration in the area of academic affairs. This was accomplished by reorganizing the faculty into a legislative body with jurisdiction over curriculum matters. The chair of this body was to be elected by the faculty rather than appointed by the administration. When my acquaintance endorsed this new arrangement, the provost, who was appointed by the president to administer faculty affairs, questioned his position. "If you ever inherit my position," he said, "you will come to regret this new arrangement." "You're probably right," my acquaintance responded, "which is precisely why the faculty needs to elect its own chair."

My acquaintance eventually inherited his colleague's role as provost and came, just as predicted, to regret his enthusiasm for faculty empowerment. The faculty often questioned his authority and challenged his policies. They regularly called upon him to publicly justify the direction in which he was leading the institution. This made it more difficult to govern, but it is why checks and balances were so important. Churchill said it well when he quipped that democracy is the worst form of government, except for all the others. Only when colleagues are empowered to challenge their leaders can they expose mistakes and move closer to achieving just and worthwhile ends.

The Centrality of Inquiry

Cartesian skepticism lies at the heart of the open society. One of the most significant contributions of Descartes to modern thought was the willingness to question accepted dogma. He challenged us to conform our beliefs and behaviors to principles that can withstand criticism. According to this view, we do not despair at the fact that our opinions and attitudes may be wrong. We use this knowledge as a motivation to continually try to improve upon them. The Cartesian skeptic is not a person who is unable to believe or act, but rather one who strives to get closer to the truth. The assumption that I have the truth in my pocket is stultifying. It assumes that the beliefs that we hold and the lives that we lead are as good as they can be. This shuts down all hope of improvement and stifles the possibility of progress. Only a society committed to skepticism can empower its citizens to question the authority of those in power in order to seek a better way. Open society is founded on our capacity to inquire and to grasp the queries of others, even when we find the answers incomprehensible—to be mistaken and to learn from our mistakes. It is because of this capacity to learn from our mistakes that we can be moral agents.

I once attended a class in which the professor asked a friend to explain a difficult Hebrew passage. My friend read the passage aloud and translated it into English. The professor thanked him for his translation and asked for an explanation. My friend translated again. The professor complimented my friend on his translation and asked once more for an explanation. Once more my friend translated. In exasperation, the professor asked if my friend understood the point of the passage. Embarrassed, my friend responded defiantly that he did not. After thinking for a moment, the professor asked, "Do you understand the question that the author is addressing?" My friend smiled with pride and explained the question. "Good," retorted the professor, "now I know that you have prepared for class." Questions are often more important than answers, because they lead us down new and uncharted paths to reformulate our conceptions of admissible answers. Societies that restrict opportunities to question undermine the possibility for improvement that is the heart of ethical discourse and open society.

Nor is this commitment to questioning new to the modern temper. Already in the Hebrew Bible, Abraham the patriarch and Moses the prophet, among many others, challenge God.[31] When God comes to destroy the cities of Sodom and Gomorrah because of their sinfulness, Abraham protests: "Will You sweep away the innocent along with the guilty? . . . What if there are fifty innocent within the city, . . . Far be it from You . . . to bring death to the innocent as well as the guilty. . . . Shall not the Judge of all the Earth deal justly?" (Genesis 18:23–26). Abraham calls upon God to conform his own practice to principle.

Moses does so as well. When God's anger seethes after the Israelites have betrayed him by worshipping a golden calf, God seeks to destroy the whole people as he had done to all of humankind in the generation of Noah. But Moses intervenes:

> Let not Your anger, O Lord, blaze forth against Your people, whom You delivered from the land of Egypt with great power and with a mighty hand. Let not the Egyptians say "It was with evil intent that He delivered them, only to kill them off in the mountains and annihilate them from the face of the earth." Turn from Your blazing anger, and renounce the plan to punish Your people. Remember Your servants, Abraham, Isaac, and Jacob, how You swore to them by Your Self and said to them: I will make your offspring as numerous as the stars of the heaven. . . . (Exodus 32: 11–14)

Like Abraham, Moses questions God. He challenges the Divine to live up to His own principles and promises. The society governed by the consistent application of just standards rather than by the caprice of arbitrary authority defends the right of all moral agents to challenge those in power in order to preserve and improve upon our best understandings of goodness and truth. Cartesian skepticism is not antithetical to the biblical tradition, as both the followers and opponents of Spinoza supposed, it lies at the heart of the very biblical conception of moral agency so central to open society.

Moral Agency

"Open," "liberal," or "democratic" societies subscribe to political checks and balances and promote free intellectual inquiry. What makes them open is that they assume that their citizens are intelligent, and so protect their right to challenge accepted doctrine and practice. What makes these societies liberal is that they assume that their citizens are free to act as they choose, and so are responsible for their actions. What makes them democratic is that they assume that all people, even the best and the brightest, are fallible, and so seek to protect citizens against the mistakes of those in power. In short, societies rooted in the doctrines of checks and balances and free inquiry are made up of agents who are intelligent, free, and fallible. People who meet these conditions are called "moral agents" because they can choose a course of action intelligently and can change course should they deem it desirable.[32]

However, if ethical vision cannot emanate from the self alone, then a society of moral agents must be more than a community of individuals. It must be a community of communities, each espousing a distinct moral teaching, but also sharing in common with other ethical traditions a commitment to "preserve, protect, and defend" the status of all human beings as intelligent, empowered, and fallible moral agents. It is such a society, and the very notion of moral agency that it protects, that must be preserved as we navigate the search for spirituality. For the very idea of a concept of the good life that is missing from Enlightenment moral, religious, and educational thought is dependent on the idea of moral agency.

The Concept of a Good Life

We have said that children of the Enlightenment are searching for a concept of the good life. But what does it mean to have such a concept? To decipher the meaning of concepts like "good" and "bad" we need to understand how they differ from similar notions such as "right" and "wrong." Making these distinctions is sometimes called "mapping the conceptual terrain." We must also clarify the situations in which it makes sense to use these concepts. The rules that instruct us to use the term "good" in this situation and "right" in another can be thought of as the defining criteria of a concept. These criteria are often embedded in webs of belief that rest on a variety of assumptions. When we use concepts in daily life, thought, and speech, we instinctively employ these criteria and implicitly embrace the assumptions on which they rest. These are sometimes called the conditions of use, because using a concept in accord with criteria without accepting the relevant assumptions makes no sense. Mapping conceptual terrain, articulating the criteria that govern the use of a concept, and clarifying the conditions upon which it rests are the work of conceptual analysis. We can use these analytic tools to understand the concept of goodness.

There is a store in my neighborhood called "The Good Life." It caters to those who can afford the "better things," those trinkets and conveniences that lend an extra touch of class, indulgence, and privilege that are generally associated with the well-to-do. This use of the expression "good life" as connoting wealth, influence, materialism, and pleasure is quite common. It is a uniquely modern and capitalistic use of the concept "good"; but it is not how the term will be used here. This is the very sort of life that has led people to abandon modernism in search of a more fulfilling spiritual home. Not that there is anything inherently wrong with wealth, or influence, or material possessions; or that the moral life ought to be unpleasant. The point is that we need a conception of goodness to understand what is to count as valuable.

The concept of goodness can be conceived in terms of four criteria: (1) it is an ethical concept; (2) it is holistic; (3) it is pragmatic; and (4) it is synthetic. "Goodness," like the concept of "right," is an *ethical* concept in that it enables us to distinguish positive from negative value.[33] However, unlike "the right," which is often understood in contemporary ethics as an analytic tool used to rationally justify moral behavior, "the good" is *holistic*, envisaging the whole rather than analyzing its parts. It is also *pragmatic*; it is expressed in terms of concrete examples of excellence or virtues to be practiced, rather than in abstract rules or principles to be applied. Finally, goodness is *synthetic*. There are many different ethical traditions in the world. To say that a tradition is ethical means that, however it differs from others, it embraces certain basic assumptions without which the concept of ethics would make no sense. To say that goodness is synthetic means that it integrates the values of a particular tradition with those required of other traditions that wish to meaningfully refer to themselves as ethical. I call these assumptions "the conditions of ethical discourse" because our ability to engage in moral conversation is predicated upon them.

It is this holistic, pragmatic, synthetic sort of ethics that is missing from Enlightenment morality. Nevertheless, the assumptions that we must make for ethics to make any sense—the conditions of ethical discourse—are basic to the Enlightenment political framework that I have called the Emancipation project. Although Enlightenment morality may have missed the boat in terms of three criteria of goodness—holism, pragmatism, and synthesis—Enlightenment politics seems to have held onto one of them—the possibility of ethical discourse. The Enlightenment, in other words, was a moral failure due to the absence of a vision of the good life but a political success due to its political protection of the conditions that make ethical vision possible.

To better understand this distinction between the moral failure and the political success of the Enlightenment, it will be useful to discuss the first criterion of the concept of goodness—the conditions of ethical discourse. Chapters 3, 4, and 5 will consider whether some common conceptions of spirituality conform to these conditions. I argue that several of them do not.

The Conditions of Ethical Discourse

To say that goodness is an ethical concept presupposes that people have the capacity to *think critically, act autonomously,* and *make mistakes.* Ethical discourse makes no sense without these assumptions because people whose behavior is to be influenced by such discourse could be expected neither to understand nor to act upon it. Critical intelligence, free will, and fallibility, therefore, are the conditions on which meaningful ethical discourse is predicated. The conditions of ethical discourse, in other words, are also the attributes of moral agency.

Critical Intelligence

To engage in a meaningful moral conversation we must first have the capacity to understand the difference between good and bad, right and wrong, better and worse. Then, we must have the capacity to do that which we understand to be good or bad according to our own free choice. If we cannot understand the difference between positive and negative values, then our choices would be arbitrary. There will be no material difference between intentional choices and caprice. Our choices must be informed by a moral understanding based on our ability to discern positive from negative value. To be a moral being, in other words, entails intelligence.

This ability to distinguish good from bad is the root of critical thinking. Criticism involves the application of a standard. When we criticize a belief or behavior, we ask whether it meets the relevant standards according to which belief and behavior should be judged. In order to ascertain whether an attitude or an action conforms to the appropriate positive criteria, we must be able to distinguish them from negative ones. Formulating and applying these distinctions involves principles that can justify or explain why this is a better belief or behavior than that. These principles are often called reasons. Relations between them, such as whether one principle follows from, negates, or provides evidence for another, are properly defined by the field of logic. To think critically, or to act on the basis of critical assessment, therefore, is to think or act in accord with some conception of logic. To the extent that logic defines rational discourse, ethical deliberations entail a rational dimension.[34]

This is why a person can be held responsible for her behavior only if she can be supposed to understand the moral significance of her actions. An infant, for example, who has yet to acquire the maturity to distinguish right from wrong, cannot be held accountable for her actions. As a person grows, her capacity for understanding expands, along with her culpability for her actions. However, suppose a person is mentally diminished in some way, due to a serious birth defect or head injury, so that she cannot understand the moral significance of her behavior. We do not hold her accountable for her actions in the same way as we would a person functioning at normal capacity.

This is also why we can debate the advantages and disadvantages of different moral traditions using reason and logic, because critical rationality is a condition of ethical discourse. To engage in moral deliberations we must first be capable of understanding the distinctions, standards, principles, reasons, and logic that make those deliberations meaningful. It makes no sense to speak of arbitrary or unintelligent ethics.

Free Will

Free will is another prerequisite for moral discussion to make sense. The point of ethical discourse is to establish standards of behavior to be followed by those who embrace a tradition in which those standards make sense. This assumes that I can conform my practice to principle; I can take charge of my actions and behave according the ethical tradition I endorse. If my behavior is not controlled by my choices but determined by such external forces as history, society, chemistry, or the gods, then there is no point to ethical discourse. To influence my behavior we would need to alter the course of history, or change society, or modify my chemistry, or manipulate the gods.

The concept of morality presupposes that I can actually do good or evil, that I am the master of my own being, and responsible for my own behavior. It is for this reason that ethical discourse addresses me, and attempts to move me to act righteously; and it is for this reason that I can be held accountable for the choices that I make. In addition to intelligence, then, being a moral creature entails free agency. This is why ethical discourse presupposes the possibility of moral understanding, whereas the discourse of determinism requires only that the appropriate forces be properly manipulated in order to achieve the intended result.[35]

Fallibility
One consequence of these assumptions is that I can misunderstand and make incorrect choices. I can be wrong, both in what I believe and in how I act. In a word, I am fallible. This is the third condition of ethical discourse.

Human beliefs and behaviors are fallible because they are contingent; they could always be otherwise. It is not a necessary fact that I believe or behave as I do, but an accident of my choosing. Were I to have chosen otherwise, my beliefs or actions would be different. A particular line of reasoning or an especially moving series of events may have influenced me, but I could always have chosen to ignore that reasoning or remain unmoved by those events. Nor is it in my very nature to believe or behave in a certain way, for it is always possible to redefine my nature. If beliefs and behaviors could always be otherwise, then they are not necessarily correct. The choices I make can be wrong.

If it were necessarily the case that I believe or act as I do because of a certain line of reasoning or as a result of my nature, then it would not be me that determined my attitudes or actions, but logic or my nature. This contradicts the concept of free will, because my opinions and practices would be determined by logic or my nature rather than by me. How can I be held accountable for my beliefs and behaviors when an external agent determines them? Only if my choices are contingent—if it is possible that I might be wrong—

can it be said that I am in fact responsible when I get it right. To be the agent of my actions, it must be possible for me to miss the mark.

It follows that all learning entails the risk of failure. This is because learning is essentially a moral category. Learning to believe or do something means acquiring a cognitive or practical standard. It means understanding a criterion used in judging the adequacy of beliefs or practices; and this, as we have seen, lies at the heart of the moral enterprise. To learn means to get better at something and to do this we must apply a standard of value. If learning is a moral enterprise, then it requires the possibility that the learner might fail.

If I am unwilling or unable to risk failure, I will be incapable of benefiting from the opportunity to learn from my mistakes, to grow. Every time I get it right, I reinforce the path toward accomplishing worthwhile ends and I gain self-confidence as I experience the fulfillment of achievement. Moral progress requires risk because it depends on learning. I cannot learn to be good if I haven't the courage to chance being wrong. Living a good life is an achievement born of learning from failure and celebrating success. "If we are afraid to make mistakes because we have to maintain the pretense of perfection," writes Harold S. Kushner, "we will never be brave enough to try anything challenging. . . . We will never learn; we will never grow."[36]

I often tell novice educators that they will learn more from their mistakes than from their successes. Indeed, I am fearful of those who begin their careers too confident of their own ability to succeed. I once supervised an instructor who had a consistent problem with her students year in and year out. No matter how I tried to communicate that her behavior was causing the problem, she refused to acknowledge it. From her point of view, there simply was no problem. She responded as if her behavior belonged to someone else. Because she could not admit that there was a problem and could not own her behavior, she could not take responsibility for her actions. As a result, she could not decide to change, to grow, to learn. In this way she diminished her own moral agency; she limited her control over her own fate; and she eventually lost her job.

The unique moral significance of human beings follows from the assumption that we are moral agents. So long as we have critical intelligence and free will, and so long as there is the risk of failure, what we think and do matters. If any one of these is denied, then it makes no sense to speak of things mattering morally because it is the impersonal forces of chemistry, or history, or the gods that matter. They in turn are controlled not by moral choices but either by necessary conclusions that could not be otherwise, by empirical causes that are not likely to become otherwise, or by caprice. In each of these instances, there is no moral dimension to behavior. We matter, in short, because we are moral agents.

The Garden of Eden

In the biblical story of the Garden of Eden (Genesis 3:1–24), God creates a man and a woman and sets them in an idyllic garden. They are told they can eat the fruit of any tree in the garden but they are forbidden to eat of the tree of knowledge. A serpent entices the woman to eat of the forbidden fruit; the woman in turn persuades the man to do the same. To this God responds: "Now has the human become like one of us, knowing good and evil" (Genesis 3:22). Humans become like God, in this account, not when they do what they are commanded, but when they act on their own, even at the risk of experiencing evil. To *know* good and evil in the biblical sense is to have intimate personal experience with them. We become like God when we exercise our free will and gain a personal understanding of wrongdoing. We become like the biblical god by making mistakes. It is our moral agency that we share with divinity, our capacity to choose, to defy our creator, to make mistakes, to learn from those mistakes, and to gain moral wisdom as a result. God, in the biblical account, is a moral agent who has acquired moral wisdom through efforts to bring goodness into the world. We matter because we are like God and we are like God because we are moral agents.

Thus Maimonides wrote that the Eden narrative demonstrates how:

> the human species had become unique, there being no other species like it in the following respect, namely, that man of himself and by the exercise of his own reason knows what is good and what is evil and there is none who can prevent him from doing that which is good or that which is evil . . . . This doctrine is an important principle of the Torah and the commandments, as it is said, "See, I set before you this day life and good, and death and evil" (*Deuteronomy* 30:15); and again it is written, "Behold, I set before you today a blessing and a curse" (ibid. 11:26). . . . If God had decreed that a person should be either righteous or wicked, or if there were some force inherent in his nature which irresistibly drew him to a particular course. . . how could the Almighty have charged us through his prophets: "Do this and not that, improve your ways, do not follow your wicked impulses," when from the beginning of his existence his destiny had already been decreed, or his innate constitution irresistibly drew him to that from which he could not set himself free. What room would there be for the whole Torah?[37]

The biblical narrative beautifully captures the assumptions implicit in speaking of "moral agency" and "ethical discourse" that are preserved by Enlightenment political theory. Humans are not all-knowing but have the capacity for moral understanding. We are not all-powerful but can exert control over ourselves. We are not perfect but can learn from our mistakes. In all of these respects we are created in the image of the biblical Creator.

Democracy and Ethical Discourse

Democratic society depends on the conditions of ethical discourse and on the moral anthropology of the Hebrew Scripture which offered one of their earliest articulations. Without embracing a particular ethical vision, this sort of society aims to preserve the possibility of morality altogether. From this it does not follow that such a society is neutral. On the contrary, the conditions of ethical discourse are at the heart of free society. Responding to the moral failings of Enlightenment modernism without abandoning its political success, therefore, requires that we embrace critical intelligence, freedom, and fallibility.

Unfortunately, in the extreme forms in which they are often promulgated, many of today's most popular conceptions of spirituality deny the truth of one or another of these conditions. To address the failings of modernism, they tend to sacrifice the ethical assumptions embraced by liberal society. By rejecting our critical intelligence, freedom, or fallibility, as necessary conditions for spirituality, these responses threaten the conceptual heart of democracy. They also challenge the very possibility of ethical discourse required to formulate the visions of goodness that respond to our current spiritual crisis. The medicine turns out to be more infectious than the disease, the visions they offer more dangerous than the absence of vision they deplore.

Conceptions of Spirituality

When the Israelites approached the Promised Land at the end of their sojourn in the desert, they called Moses to appoint spies who would scout the land they were to enter. Of the twelve that were sent, ten returned with an exaggerated impression of what the people would encounter when they crossed the Jordan River. "The country we traversed and scouted is one that devours its settlers. All of the people that we saw in it are . . . of great size . . . . [W]e looked like grasshoppers to ourselves, and so we must have looked to them" (Numbers 13:32–33). In response to this report the people became frightened. They railed against Moses shouting, "If only we had died in the land of Egypt!" or "Why is the Lord taking us to this land to fall by the sword? . . . It would be better for us to go back to Egypt" (Numbers 14:2–4).

It is not surprising that the Israelites preferred the security of the slavery they knew to the insecurity of a freedom yet unknown.

In Egypt they were not free, they could not worship as they pleased or raise their children as they saw fit; but they were fed, and sheltered, and clothed, even if only in a very rudimentary way. As they approached the Promised Land, God's message of free will and moral responsibility was still very new, and the legal structures that Moses had put into place had only just begun to dismantle the slave culture they left behind. They were as grasshoppers in their own eyes, still slaves to the Egyptian taskmasters they so recently fled.

Like the Israelites, we too have been without a spiritual home, searching for values and vision in the moral desert of modernity. We are hungry for spiritual sustenance, for virtues to emulate and models of goodness to admire. The road to spiritual discovery is long and arduous. It is easy to be led off the track, to be frightened by the challenge, to think that a return to the old ways would be better than the uncertainty that lies ahead. The return to Egypt always looms as an attractive option. But in the final analysis Egypt and the ways of old are delusions. The slavery of Egypt will never quench our spiritual thirst.

We learned in this chapter that the search for spirituality begins with emancipation, with the recognition that we have the capacity to choose a good life as we have been given to understand it. The spiritual quest calls us to leave the slavery of Egypt behind, to navigate the narrow straits of Enlightenment failure by embracing Emancipation, to overcome our disenchantment with modernism through enjoying the achievements of open society. This capacity requires critical intelligence, the ability to understand our options and to consider their consequences. But it also entails fallibility, insecurity, and risk. We could fail. We might be wrong. We may not be good enough. We might be defeated. We might be grasshoppers not only in our own eyes but in the eyes of others as well.

The biblical text refers to the tendency of the ten spies to over-emphasize their insecurity as "slanderous." Not that it was false; the prospect of entering the land of Israel was daunting in the extreme. How would they deal with those already inhabiting the land? What would it mean to finally rule themselves rather than to be slaves? What if Moses' God was an illusion who would leave them enslaved to new masters worse than the old? The people had every reason to be afraid. The land was rocky and its inhabitants were entrenched and formidable.

This much of the spies' report was true. But it was also incomplete and distorted, which is why it was "slanderous." This skewed picture directed the people away from freedom and returned them to slavery. It did not build their confidence to take the risks ethical understanding requires. I am reminded of the parent who is forever chiding his children, telling them that they are unable to do this and should be afraid to try that, protecting them from the risk of failure that is required to succeed. Children raised in this way suffer insecurity that restricts their freedom to grow and flourish. They are denied the proper preparation for moral responsibility by being put down and told "It is too difficult, you cannot do it."

Several contemporary conceptions of spirituality are problematic in this way. Not that they are totally false; they point to vitally important truths about the spiritual life, yet build on exaggerations that place their own concerns at the center while distorting or omitting other equally important considerations. This leads away from embracing the conditions of ethical discourse and liberal society and toward a more restricted mechanized life that has fewer moral choices and less value content. We can identify these conceptions of spirituality by the"moral space," to use Charles Taylor's felicitous phrase, in which they "locate" goodness, the metaphoric places to which their spiritual journeys lead: (1) inside of us, (2) between us, and (3) beyond us.[38] I call them subjective, collective, and objective spiritualities.

Of course, many of the themes articulated within the current spiritual revival are intertwined with one another. They should not be identified with particular spiritual thinkers. Rather, they ought to be seen as strands of thought which may appear in one or another author but which may just as easily be found intermingled in the writings of a single person. Any attempt to untangle from the whole a subset of conceptual categories such as these will necessarily be incomplete, programmatic, and to some degree, arbitrary. I unravel the themes of subjectivism, collectivism, and objectivism because the extreme—and often incoherent—versions of these perspectives that tend to be popular in spiritual thought today are problematic in ways that undermine ethical discourse and democratic values. Recent epistemology, moral philosophy, and political theory can clarify these difficulties and point us in more productive directions.

The discussion of these conceptions in the coming chapters proceeds in four phases. First, I sketch some brief examples. These are not intended to be exhaustive but to illustrate the key issues that appear in the ensuing discussion. Second, I summarize some of the most salient recent arguments in favor of the conception in question. Third, I consider the strengths and weaknesses of these arguments in light of the conditions of ethical discourse outlined above. Finally, I ask what we can learn from each conception in view of this analysis. This paves the way for a more compelling account of spirituality in Chapter 6 that avoids the weaknesses and learns from the strengths of these conceptions.

In contrast to the ten spies whose troubling reports turned the Israelites back toward slavery in Egypt, two of the spies that Moses sent had a different perspective. "The land we have been sent to scout," said Joshua and Caleb, "is very good." (Numbers 14:8) "Let us go up at once . . . for we can surely succeed" (Numbers 13:30). Through the dangers inherent in freedom, they saw a vision of a good land, a better society, and a more elevated life. The question will be: How can we conceive of such a life today in the wake of the ensuing analysis of subjective, collective, and objective spiritualities?

CHAPTER THREE

Subjective Spirituality

You open the Book of Remembrance and it speaks for itself; every man has signed it with his deeds. The great Shofar [ram's horn] is sounded, a still small voice is heard.

—Prayer Book for the Days of Awe[1]

When Elijah of Gilead, the ninth-century Israelite prophet, was told that God would appear to him, he felt a powerful wind; but God was not in the wind. He then heard the thundering noise of an earthquake; but God was not in the earthquake. After this, he saw the flames of a great fire; but God was not in the fire. And then, he heard a still small voice. It was in that gentle whisper that Elijah finally heard the Holy One, speaking to him from beyond the mountain top (1 Kings 19:11–15).[2]

Elijah's gentle whisper may be among the most familiar conceptions of spirituality. It is "located" deep inside our souls. Existentialists, feminists, contemplatives, mystics, postmodernists, and new-age spiritualists reject the modern emphasis on reasoning and instrumental outcomes. They seek the good life in the inner depths of consciousness, in connectedness with other souls, and in hearing that still small voice that transcends all souls—in feeling, caring, and relating intimately with the divine. This sort of spirituality is highly subjective, personal, and individual. It always involves a turn inward but, for some, listening within also leads to looking outward and to reaching upward.

Subjective spiritualists have abandoned the cathedral churches and synagogues of the fifties and sixties in favor of smaller, more intimate communities that are less rule- and more relationship-oriented. They are dismayed by the hierarchical structure of religious and educational organizations, and seek institutions that are more egalitarian and less authoritarian. Some also express nostalgia for times in the distant or not so distant past when communities are believed to have been more personal and life is thought to have been less frenetic and fragmented. They mourn a loss of wholeness brought on by modernity, in which religion, family, work, community, and leisure, seem to be at war rather than in sync with one another.

Turning Inward

I want to unravel two strands of thought within this orientation. One path engages the inner life in order to transcend it. This approach eschews both narcissism and solipsism—the idea that I am alone in the world. The other embraces both self-centeredness and loneliness by identifying the good exclusively with that which is felt naturally within.

Transcendental Subjectivism

The first path is already found in Plato. In the *Republic* he develops the idea that goodness entails an inner life which balances urges for survival and pleasure with love and companionship, and discipline and reason.[3] In the *Phaedrus,* Plato suggests that balancing the soul in this way enables a unification with the ultimate good.[4] This imagery of spirituality as cultivating a balanced inner life that leads to unification with the godhead took root in both Judaism and Christianity. This was especially so among mystics who sought to develop proper methods for disciplining the soul in such a way that it could become one with the Creator and Master of the Universe.[5] The first strand of contemporary spiritual thought consists in a revival of these ancient and medieval mystical themes. Let us reflect on a Christian, a Jewish, and an existentialist example.

The Contemplative Tradition
Consider the Catholic contemplative tradition. The monastic mystic Thomas Merton articulated a version of this tradition that spoke not only to American Christians but also to an international following of believers and seekers of all kinds.[6] He points out that:

> Every one of us is shadowed by an illusory person: a false self. . . . My false and private self is the one who wants to exist outside the reach of God's will and God's love—outside of reality and outside of life. And such a self cannot help but be an illusion. . . . For most people in the world, there is no greater subjective reality than this false self of theirs, which cannot exist. . . . All sin starts from the assumption that my false self, the self that exists only in my own egocentric desires, is the fundamental reality of life to which everything else in the universe is ordered.[7]

A person can only discover his true self by receiving the gift of God's infinite love and mercy within and then beyond the deepest, innermost point of his being.

> The secret of my identity is hidden in the love and mercy of God. . . . Ultimately the only way that I can be myself is to become identified with Him in Whom is hidden the reason and fulfillment of my existence. Therefore, there is only one problem on which all my existence, my peace and my happiness depend: to discover myself in discovering God. If I find Him I will find myself and if I find my true self, I will find Him.[8]

This discovery is accomplished in contemplation, which is "the highest expression of man's intellectual and spiritual life":

It is that life itself, fully awake, fully active, fully aware that it is alive. It is spiritual wonder. It is spontaneous awe at the sacredness of being. It is gratitude for life, for awareness of being. It is a vivid realization of the fact that life and being in us proceed from an invisible, transcendent and infinitely abundant Source. Contemplation is, above all, awareness of the reality of that Source.[9]

Contemplation is also the response to a call: a call from Him Who has no voice, and yet, Who speaks in the depths of our own being; for we ourselves are words of His. But we are words that are meant to respond to Him, to answer Him, to echo Him, and even in some way to contain Him and signify Him. Contemplation is the echo. It is a deep resonance in the inmost center of our spirit in which our very life loses its separate voice and re-sounds with the majesty and the mystery of the Hidden and Living One.[10]

Contemplation, however, is not "the fruit of our own efforts. It is the gift of God Who, in His mercy, completes the hidden and mysterious work of creation in us by enlightening our minds and hearts, by awakening in us an awareness that we are words spoken in One word, and that Creating Spirit (*Creator Spiritus*) dwells in us, and we in Him."[11] Nor does contemplation involve narcissistic centering on the self. "Instead of worshipping God through His creation," writes Merton, "we are always trying to worship ourselves by means of creatures. But to worship our false selves is to worship nothing. And the worship of nothing is hell."[12] Instead, contemplation leads us to a life of service to others. "A man cannot enter into the deepest center of himself and pass through that center into God, unless he is able to pass entirely out of himself and empty himself and give himself to other people in the purity of selfless love."[13]

The New Kabbalists

Among Jews, this revival is seen in the dramatic reemergence of the Jewish mystical tradition known as *Kabbalah*. In academic circles, the revival began with the work of Gershom Scholem.[14] In popular circles it began with the writings of the first chief rabbi of Israel, Abraham Isaac Kook. Scholem's work gave *Kabbalah* intellectual legitimacy and made it accessible to rabbis and lay people untrained in the arcane Aramaic terminology of Jewish mystical writings. Kook, on the other hand, gave it new spiritual power by interpreting the return to the land of Israel, even among secular, antireligious Zionists, in light of the redemptive urges of Jewish messianism.[15] In Israel, this mystical resurgence has taken a decidedly nationalistic and sometimes fundamentalist direction.[16]

In North America, however, it has occasioned the publication of an abundance of popular explications of Jewish mystical themes for liberal audiences.[17] In an exceptionally lucid example of this genre, Perle Besserman explains that since it is so intertwined with Jewish history, the key concepts of *Kabbalah* ("received" tradition) are best explained chronologically.[18] In order to capture the most significant themes of this revival, we need not discuss ancient and medieval Jewish mysticism, which would in any event require the explication of highly technical terms, concepts, and texts. It will suffice for our purposes to begin with antecedents to modern *Hasidism* in the thought of the Rabbi Isaac Luria.

In the sixteenth century, a community of Kabbalists emerged in the Galilean town of Safed under Luria's leadership. Luria developed an interpretation of kabbalistic teachings that responded to the destruction of the Spanish Jewish community in the fifteenth century—a catastrophe experienced in his generation no less intensely than the Holocaust has been experienced in ours. According to this interpretation, in the beginning everything was God. In order to create a world God first had to contract himself to make room for beings that were not God, and then to transform divine No-thingness into material existence. The vessels through which God attempted to accomplish this transformation could not contain the divine glory, and so they burst asunder, leaving shreds or *klipot* of divine essence scattered throughout the universe.

The world, in other words, was created in a cosmic catastrophe, and the scattered sparks of divinity were lodged within human souls. To repair this fragmented and broken world we must seek to discover the *or ganuz*—hidden holy spark—that lies within each of us, in order to reunite us with our Creator.[19] The *mitzvot* (commandments) which God revealed in the *Torah*, constitute a blueprint for accomplishing this *tikkun* (repair). This Lurianic myth was so influential that it led to a messianic revolution in the seventeenth century, in which thousands believed Shabbatai Tzvi to be the messiah who had come to redeem the Jewish people and reunite the scattered *klipot*.[20]

These themes were renewed once again in Eastern Europe during the eighteenth century by Israel ben Eliezer of Miedzyboz, who became known as the *Baal Shem Tov*—master of a good name. In response to the dry legalistic Talmudic learning of his day, the *Baal Shem Tov* established a mystical tradition devoted to celebrating the joy in Judaism and to meditating upon Lurianic teachings. Known as *hasidim*, or pious ones, the followers of the *Baal Shem Tov* avoided the false messianism of the Sabbatean rebellion by punctilious adherence to the letter of Jewish law. At the same time they invested charismatic powers in righteous leaders, or *tzadikim*, who could trace their spiritual lineage to the *Baal Shem Tov*. It is through discipleship, or identification with the *tzadik*, that the *hasid* discovers his hidden light in order to achieve *deveikut* or attachment to the Creator.[21]

Lawrence Kushner, a well-known contemporary interpreter of this revival, explains the message of this tradition, albeit with a somewhat modern, individualistic slant, in language that echoes Merton.[22] "Each person lives according to a unique teaching or *Torah*. God too has a *Torah* that defies public communication. It is communicated directly from the "Self of the Universe" to the self of one who receives it." What we know as the *Torah* scroll is but a symbol, a reminder in human language of the word of God. It should not be taken at face value but read in light of *Kabbalistic* and *Hasidic* teachings in order to uncover its secret meaning.

Ultimately, as our understanding of and devotion to the scroll of *Torah* develop, our own individual *Torah* increasingly comes to resemble God's *Torah*. Until finally, at the moment of our death, the two become one, our *Torah* becomes God's *Torah*. But a person need not wait until his or her final moment. There is one other way. It is called *teshuvah,* letting go of one's old self, returning again to the Source. When we "make" *teshuvah* we remember the Source of our innermost selves and our purpose in creation. We are renewed as in days of old. The old ego slips away and we remember that we are creatures. . . .

At such moments the unitary Source of all being is revealed to us again. We realize that on our deepest levels what we want and what God wants have been the same all along. . . . Our desires to behave contrary to God's *Torah* have only been self-deceptions, contrary to what we really want. This is why they were unsatisfying, unfulfilling, elusive. At our core we want what God wants. The "way" of creation is within us.[23]

Relational Existentialism

Martin Buber's existentialism can be understood in part as an attempt to capture key themes of this *Hasidic* tradition in a philosophical language accessible to a wider audience.[24] Buber taught that we experience God through subjective moments of relationships. He called these "I-Thou" relations, because they entail accepting the other as is, with no objective other than pure encounter. He contrasted these subjective moments with instrumental ones in which people use others like objects to achieve their own predetermined ends. Buber called such instrumental interactions "I-It" relations, because the other is treated as an object.

God, in this view, is "eternally thou"—a being who never uses others but always accepts them as they are. Buber was opposed to expressing our relations with the divine by means of rituals because he believed that God cannot be manipulated, controlled, or reduced to formula, but only met in moments of pure subjectivity in which there are no means and no ends, only acceptance. At those moments, Buber wrote, "the other fills the firmament."[25]

Buber was a relational theorist in that he "located" the good in the moment when two subjects meet, rather than in a radical subjectivism that leads to narcissism and solipsism. His subjectivism does not lie in an obliteration of the role of the other—on the contrary, meeting the other in relation is constitutive of his vision of the good. Buber's subjectivism lies, instead, in his insistence that this meeting takes place "inside" of us. The other presents herself to me in consciousness. She is received within; and any effort to "objectify" that other, to have her stand "outside" of me by means of formulas, or rituals, or analysis, or empathetic projections, instrumentalizes the moment and transforms it into an I-It association.

Feminist philosopher Nel Noddings, who was greatly influenced by Buber, describes this process of receiving the other in her notion of "engrossment" or "feeling with" the other:

> The notion of "feeling with" that I have outlined does not involve projection but reception. I have called it "engrossment." I do not "put myself in the other's shoes," so to speak, by analyzing his reality as objective data and then asking, "How would I feel in such a situation?" On the contrary, I set aside my temptation to analyze and to plan. I do not project: I receive the other into myself, and I see and feel with the other. I become a duality. I am not thus caused to see or to feel—that is, to exhibit certain behavioral signs interpreted as seeing and feeling—for I am committed to receptivity and that permits me to see and feel in this way. The seeing and feeling are mine, but only partly and temporarily mine, as on loan to me.[26]

Radical Subjectivism

Many of the mystical connotations that made their way into Buber's thought were already present in late eighteenth- and early nineteenth-century romantic reaction to rationalism, especially in German and French philosophy and British poetry.[27] However, un-

like the ancient and medieval mystics, and unlike Buber and Noddings, early modern romantics such as Jean-Jacques Rousseau identified the inner life more with nature than the other—whether
human or divine. This moved them away from a conception of the
moral life that is in step with the designs of a transcendent God and
towards a focus on the self as the primary source of moral ideals.
Charles Taylor writes that for Rousseau:

> Goodness is identified with freedom, with finding motives for
> one's actions within oneself. Although drawing on ancient
> sources, Rousseau is actually pushing the subjectivism of mod-
> ern moral understanding a stage further. . . . The good is dis-
> covered partly through a turning within, consulting our own
> sentiments and inclinations. . . . the definition of that inner
> voice of my true sentiments *define* what is good: since the elan
> of nature in me *is* the good, it is this which has to be consulted
> to discover it.[28]

It is this more radical subjectivism that is reflected in postmodern and new-age spirituality. The French postmodern philosopher
Michel Foucault, for example, is known for an extreme subjectivism that is centered in the self. In his view, morality has to do
less with following rules of action and more with constructing the
self out of ingredients found within, through "self-reflection, self-
knowledge, self-examination . . . the decipherment of the self by
oneself."[29] Foucault calls this "the cultivation of the self."[30] He
writes: "By spirituality I mean . . . the subject's attainment of a certain mode of being and the transformations that the subject must
carry out to attain that mode of being."[31] Spirituality, in short, entails the creation of myself out of myself. There are no givens, no
foundations, no external objects, no social determinants; only pure
creativity. "What matters," he says, "is to create the conditions
whereby we can all be artists of our own lives."[32]

Foucault's American colleague, Richard Rorty, points out that our
capacity for "self-cultivation" is a consequence of "the contingency

of selfhood."[33] The self, in this view, is not a necessary product of heredity. Nor does the self depend unequivocally on the structure of mind, or on history, culture, or family. It is an accident of creativity, a contingent product of our own construction that could have been and always can be other than it is. The good life is to be found in the creation of this contingent self, in the construction of personal identity.

This sort of subjective spirituality has made its way into the popular literature of contemporary spirituality as well. David A. Cooper writes as follows in his guide to spiritual practice, *The Heart of Stillness:*

Our efforts in practice are toward revealing the enormous potential that already exists within us. . . . There is nothing to acquire outside our selves and we do not have to be transformed into a new breed.[34]

Cooper quotes the Ramana Maharishi:

Truly there is no cause for you to be miserable and unhappy. You yourself impose limitations on your true infinite Being, and then weep that you are a finite creature. . . . [Y]ou are really the infinite Being, the Self Absolute. You are always that Self and nothing but that Self.[35]

Inwardness Defended

Three arguments are currently employed to defend spiritual subjectivism. Just as there are at least two strands of subjectivism in contemporary spirituality, one less self-centered than the other, there are also two versions of these arguments, one more extreme than the other. The more extreme versions support radical, solipsistic subjectivism, while the less extreme versions uphold the more temperate variety.

The Expressive Argument

The expressive argument claims that modern rational discourse does not allow for expression of the full breadth, or even the most vital dimensions, of human experience. As Merton put it: "Contemplation is always beyond our own knowledge, beyond our own light, beyond systems, beyond explanations, beyond discourse, beyond dialogue, beyond our own self."[36] Any vision of the good life, therefore, must be represented in nonrational, nondiscursive modes of expression such as religious ritual, literature, the arts, or the contemplative life itself.

The less extreme version of this claim suggests that rational discourse tells only part of the human story. What does logic have to teach about love, or the miracle of birth, or the awe and wonder of nature, or the amazement of color and texture and sound, or the mystery of the divine? Other nondiscursive modes of expression—metaphor, poetry, the arts, religious ritual, pageantry, life itself—are required to refine our understanding of the miraculous and the amazing.[37] When these experiences and the forms of representation required to express them are ignored, our lives are impoverished at the very least, and perhaps also stilted, meaningless, and even misguided.[38]

The more extreme version of this argument claims not only that the modern emphasis on rational and objective discourse inhibits us from experiencing, understanding, and telling part of our story, it in fact tells no part of the story accurately at all. This is because modern discourse assumes that the knowledge we can most readily and legitimately express is based on that which is given externally, outside of us. But nothing can actually be known at all about that which lies outside of us. We can only have knowledge about phenomena as they present themselves in consciousness. Indeed, the life-worlds we inhabit are not given but constructed by us. Hence, conceptions of the good life cannot be based on reasons, experiences, laws, or rituals that are given from without by such agents as historical traditions or divine commands. Rather they must be constructed from within, out of the life-worlds we have come to share with others nearby who present themselves in consciousness.[39]

The Prescriptive Argument

The prescriptive argument questions the value of modern rational discourse as a source of moral insight. In Noddings's words, "Obedience to the law is simply not a reliable guide to moral behavior. One must meet the other in caring. From this requirement there is no escape for one who would be moral."[40]

The less extreme version of this argument holds that the predominately male preoccupation with justifiable rules is not a reliable guide to moral behavior. Rather, a different, female voice teaches that goodness is rooted not in reasons but relationships, not in cognition but in affect, not in formulas but in feelings, not in conduct governed by rules but in interactions characterized by caring. It is not that rules teach us nothing about justice and fairness or that reasoning is irrelevant to the moral life. Rather, justice and fairness are not primary but secondary moral concepts that often mislead when employed in the absence of a caring affect. Any adequate conception of the good, on this account, must begin with the cultivation within a person of the feeling of having been cared for. On this basis, rules and rituals can be used as guideposts to a good life, but not as a rigid road map, because a compelling vision of goodness must respond to concrete, unique people, who have their own feelings and attitudes, and who live in specific and unpredictable circumstances.[41]

The more extreme version of this claim holds that language is completely indeterminate. There are no rules that govern its use, no reliable guides to understanding anyone. We can make words and texts mean whatever we want them to mean. Since language is not governed by rules but by anarchy, it is impossible to conceive of a moral vision that could be made up of general principles of conduct. However one understands these principles, others might always understand them in radically different, even contradictory, ways. The very idea of a vision of the good life that expresses more than my own momentary desires is impossible. Not only is my vision of the good constructed from within, but my understanding of another's vision is a product of my own construction as well. Goodness is not partially subjective, it is wholly and radically so. When it comes to choosing how to live, we are all unavoidably alone.[42]

The Argument from Discovery

The argument from discovery holds that the very good we seek is not given objectively, in a manner that can be discursively described and formally prescribed. It is discovered through the very process of self-exploration. We receive the life we were meant to lead by turning inward. As Merton put it:

> When I consent to the will and mercy of God as it "comes" to me in the events of life, appealing to my inner self and awakening my faith, I break through the superficial exterior appearances that form my routine vision of the world and of my own self, and I find myself in the presence of majesty . . . . this is a majesty we do not *see* with our eyes and it is all within ourselves . . . . Our true self is, then, the self that receives freely and gladly the missions that are God's supreme gift. . . . Any other self is only an illusion.[43]

The less extreme version of this position holds that by giving up the false ego that deludes us, we can discover the true self that God intends us to become. The subjective turn, in this view, is but a path to the discovery of a truth that lies beyond but which is discovered within.

The more extreme version of this argument is that we discover the self by turning inward because this discovery is itself a creative process. We are constantly creating and recreating ourselves out

of the contingent bits of life that are presented to us in consciousness. There is neither a false nor a true self to be discovered, no
person we were meant to be, but only the contingent self that we
have become, and those who are yet to emerge from the creative
processes in which we are currently engaged. Goodness is not given.
It is constructed.[44]

The Ethics of Subjectivity

The more extreme versions of these arguments overemphasize the
formless and spontaneous side of the inner life. This leads them
to conflict with each of the conditions of ethical discourse: critical
intelligence, freedom, and fallibility. They are consequently not as
compelling as the less extreme versions. To see why, let's look
again at the extreme arguments.

Inwardness and Critical Thinking

According to the critical-thinking condition, ethical discourse requires that we have the capacity to make meaningful choices. This
requires that we are able, within limits, to understand our options
and their consequences, that we have moral intelligence. The extreme versions of these arguments undermine the possibility of
distinguishing between positive and negative values, since there
are no standards to which I might appeal to evaluate my construc-
tions. What is good for me is good for me, according to this account, and what is good for another is good for the other. There
are no criteria according to which I can legitimately say that this is
good for you or you can say that this is good for me.

We cannot even tell whether a person's use of the concept
"good" is consistent from one instance to the next, since all understanding is constructed internally and there is no way of entering into another's consciousness. In fact, it is impossible to tell
whether internally constructed claims about the good life are true,
since they may be true for one but not for another. Even if it is

claimed that the standard for judging the truth of these claims is found within a community, it could not be assumed that such a community exists outside of my consciousness. I could only rely upon the community that I experience within, which need bear no resemblance to any community that exists outside of my own subjectively constructed reality.[45]

To complicate matters, the claim made by the extreme subjectivists that all moral statements are subjective must necessarily be subjective, and the claim that they are all constructed must necessarily be constructed. But this is impossible. To say that a position is "subjective" or "constructed" means that it is true for *some* people in *some* places *some* of the time; but the statement that *all* moral positions are subjectively constructed claims to be true for *all* people in *all* places at *all* times. Put simply, the proposition that *all* truths and values are subjectively constructed is itself not a subjective or constructed assertion. If this claim is true, then subjectivism must be false, and only if it is false can subjectivism be true. Since no doctrine can be simultaneously both true and false, subjectivism is incoherent.

Students often complain that the standards teachers use in evaluating their essays are subjective. If another teacher were to assess their writing, the mark would not be the same. A student once challenged the grade a teacher awarded on this basis.

"Your opinions about how an essay is to be written are subjective," the student said to the teacher. "They are based on your feelings alone. Another teacher would have given this paper a better grade."

"On what basis do you say this?" asked the teacher.

"All opinions of this kind are subjective," responded the student, "because there are no 'objective' ideals against which to judge good writing."

"I see," said the teacher. "Does this mean that your opinion that 'all opinions about writing are subjective,' is also a subjective opinion?"

"I suppose it does," responded the student.

"Then aren't you engaging in just the behavior you accused me of when you complained that I employed 'subjective' standards in evaluating your essay?"

"What do you mean?"

"Aren't you imposing your 'subjective' opinion about the 'subjectivity of opinions' on my assessment of your paper?"

"I suppose I am," retorted the student.

"In other words, your view that every opinion is 'subjective' is also a 'subjective' opinion."

"That seems to be the case."

"So following your own thinking, there is no reason for me to accept your critique that my standards of assessment are 'subjective', since the opinions upon which you base this critique are themselves 'subjective'."

"I guess so," answered the student, now beginning to feel a bit uncomfortable.

"Then your grade stands," the teacher concluded. "Since you claim that my approach to assessment is 'subjective' but admit that the opinions upon which you base your claim are also 'subjective', I can't make any sense out of what you could possibly mean by the complaint of 'subjectivity'."

"I see your point," the student said in disappointment.

The incoherence of the extreme subjectivist claim that moral vision is based on how one feels, then, appears to undermine the possibility of there being standards to distinguish between positive and negative values. But are there not subjective standards for moral choices that are affective rather than cognitive? Can I not choose to do or observe what "feels right"? In the extreme case in which this is intended to mean how one feels at any given moment, the answer is no. The formlessness and spontaneity of this conception of subjective feeling denies the very notion of standards to differentiate between positive and negative values, since standards must, at the very least, be consistent from one application to the next. However, according to this approach, in doing what "feels right," I am not behaving consistently according to a standard but following the spontaneous inclinations of the moment. By definition these are mine and mine alone. They require no commitment to consistency.[46]

The inward dimension of spirituality cannot be wholly capricious or unintelligible, as the extreme subjectivists suggest. The very concept of ethics requires that feelings associated with the good life conform to communicable and understandable standards. They must be, in a word, intelligent.

Inwardness, Freedom, and Fallibility

Since the extreme subjectivist account undermines the possibility of critical moral intelligence, it also conflicts with the other two conditions of ethical discourse: freedom and fallibility. For choices to be free, they must be based on understanding of the positive and negative consequences of alternatives. Otherwise, these choices are no different than rolls of the dice. Without moral intelligence, therefore, the sort of free choice required for moral discourse is impossible. Nor can any sense be made of the idea of moral fallibility on this account, since there is no way to judge whether a person has done wrong; and if there is no difference between right and wrong, the whole idea of ethics makes no sense.

The extreme subjectivist account of spirituality neither addresses the moral crisis of modernism nor embraces the achievements of free society. Searching for the good wholly within our selves is a prime example of the centering on the self that Christopher Lasch called the "culture of narcissism."[47] There can be no good life centered solely on the self since the very idea of goodness requires that we appeal to standards that lie beyond the self in history, tradition, community, or God. The inward turn so popular among current spiritual seekers does not lead away from the emptiness and meaningless of modernism but returns us to it.

Nor does this doctrine point in the direction of emancipation. Freedom is not synonymous with capriciousness or the license to do whatever I desire whenever I see fit. Freedom requires commitment to a discipline, some way of distinguishing right from wrong, some standards that transform our choices from rolls of the dice into intentional and thoughtful decisions aimed at worthwhile ends. Seen in this light, freedom is dependent on intelligence, on moral understanding, disciplined emotions, and thoughtful behavior. Like the troubling reports of the Israelite spies, spirituality as radical subjectivity does not point us in the direction of this sort of freedom but returns us to an enslavement to caprice over which we can exert no control.

Discovering the Self in Transcendence

This is not to say, however, that the attention to the inner life can be ignored in our search for spirituality. The less extreme versions of these three arguments are compelling, if sometimes overstated. There *are* important dimensions of the human experience about which reasoning and everyday discourse can say very little of value. The very idea that we can understand anything at all is a miracle, since, as we have seen from the skepticism of the radical subjectivists, it could be otherwise. Philosophical analysis may help to explain the fact that we are often able to understand one another, but it cannot give proper expression to our wonder at being able to do so.

That the reality of contemplation lies beyond all forms of communication, however, does not mean that mystics cannot share their experience of the divine with others in the public arena. From the fact that there is no substitute for personal encounter with God in discovering one's true self, it does not follow that the path one has taken cannot be illumined through metaphor, symbols, rituals, exercises, and even discourse that point the way for others. Indeed, absent a community of discourse or tradition within which to interpret one's mystical experience, it will be impossible to tell whether what one has encountered is the divine, an aberration, or even the Devil himself. Kabbalists relied heavily on their communities to share spiritual exercises that lead to encounter with the divine.[48] Merton was also aware of this need. The solitude required for contemplation, he writes:

is not and can never be a narcissistic dialogue of the ego with it-self. Such self-contemplation is a futile attempt to establish the finite self as infinite, to make it permanently independent of all other beings. And this is madness. . . .[49]

There is no true solitude except interior solitude. And interior solitude is not possible for anyone who does not accept his right place in relation to other men. . . . Solitude is not separation . . . . We are all members of one another and everything that is given to one member is given for the whole body.[50]

Similarly, to say that justifiable rules are no reliable guide to moral behavior is to take the point too far. According to some feminists, for example, doing what "feels right" means behaving in a caring manner. But when one cares for a lover, a friend, or a student, one is not only doing what "feels right" at the moment but also behaving in accord with how one has learned to feel, how we are supposed to feel. These feelings are not capricious, form-less, or unanticipated. They are intelligent, and can be learned, communicated, and understood.

Children often rely on the examples set by their parents when developing relations with a lover or mate; and they tend to fol-low the lead set by their teachers when nurturing relationships with their students. The attraction to a potential lover or friend may be spontaneous at the outset, and all teachers find some stu-dents more likable than others. However, once the initial attrac-tion has been transformed into a lasting relationship, the cultiva-tion of a caring affect involves disciplining one's feelings according to norms learned from experience and by example. Indeed, how would it even be possible to understand the concept of caring, were it not for criteria to inform us which relations are caring and which are not? Surely these linguistic criteria become guidelines for moral conduct when applied to human behavior.[51]

Any adequate conception of the good needs to nurture the ex-pression of emotion and to celebrate feelings concerning our most cherished commitments. It needs to cultivate not only the capacity to express these feelings by means of literature, poetry, the arts, and religion, but also the ability to feel them—to encounter the good directly in experience. This grows from appreciating and engaging in these forms of artistic and religious expression. Learning to emulate ethical ideas is *certainly not* a purely cognitive affair. It requires the disciplines necessary for direct encounter with "being itself" and for expressing our innermost feelings as we confront that brute reality. These feelings can point the way toward a good path only in the context of community or tradition. Indeed, outside of such a context, they can be dangerous.

The sages speak of four among them who entered paradise by engaging in direct, mystical encounter with God. Simeon ben Azzai "looked and died"—according to some interpretations, he committed suicide. Ben Zoma "looked and was smitten"—he became mentally ill. Elisha ben Abuyah, called *aher* or other, "cut the shoots,"—he became an apostate, perhaps embracing gnosticism. Only Rabbi Akiba "entered in peace and left in peace," enlivened by the encounter and awakened with renewed faith in his Creator. Akiba is said to have been so well grounded in the traditions of his people that he was the only one of the four adequately equipped to interpret the experience and integrate it into his way of being.[52] The experience of Akiba's colleagues brings to mind people who lose their minds and their very lives from experimentation with ecstatic experience through drugs.

The task of a moral ideal is not to validate every encounter or desire but to facilitate experiences and desires that will enable us to lead the lives we were meant to lead, according to some adequate conception of the good discovered in the context of a community or tradition. Spirituality is not about just any encounters or feelings; it is about those that are disciplined, not arbitrary or capricious, by the intelligence inherent in the very idea of goodness, and drawn from the communities in which that intelligence is given expression.

When Elijah heard the still small voice, it murmured, "What are you doing here, Elijah?" He answered, "I have been zealous for the

God of hosts, because the children of Israel have forsaken Your covenant, thrown down Your altars, and slain Your prophets with swords; and I alone am left, and they seek to take my life as well." The voice responded to Elijah, "Go! Return to your path" (1 Kings 19:11–15). The message of Elijah's gentle whisper was to return to his path as a prophet, to recommit himself to the life he was meant to lead, to become the best version of himself he was capable of being.

But to hear that voice, and to find that path, he needed to stand within a tradition of prophecy. Otherwise, he would have no way of distinguishing between God's voice and his own less elevated wishes, desires, or memories. Indeed, where did Elijah hear God speak within his soul? According to the text, it was while standing for forty days and forty nights on Mount Sinai, where Moses had stood before him (1 Kings 19:8). The question is: Even if community and tradition are necessary conditions for discovering the good life, are they sufficient? Or, just as the radical subjectivists find themselves isolated within themselves, might we not also end up traveling in increasingly dogmatic circles within the insularity of our communities?

CHAPTER FOUR

Collective Spirituality

You shall be to Me a kingdom of priests and a holy nation. . . .

—Exodus 19:6

When the Israelites entered the wilderness of Sinai, God called Moses to say to them, "You have seen what I did to the Egyptians, how I bore you on eagles' wings and brought you to Me. Now then, if you will obey Me faithfully and keep My covenant, you shall be My treasured possession among all the people. Indeed, all the earth is Mine, but you shall be to Me a kingdom of priests and a holy nation" (Exodus 19: 1–6).

The idea that one people is chosen, or chooses, to embody particular spiritual values has led some to "locate" the good within the bonds of group solidarity. In the contemporary quest for spirituality some people have looked to collective identity. Unable to find meaning in the larger society because it is too big or too diverse, they sometimes look for a smaller community in which they can feel at home and can cultivate a sense of belonging. Some of these communities share the faith commitments of a religious tradition, others share ties of a more secular nature.

According to this account, the good is to be found in the frameworks to which we belong: ethnicity, culture, nationality, religion, gender, sexual orientation, linguistic community, or socioeconomic class; or artistic, literary, scholarly, or scientific tradition. Liberation theologians, secular Zionists, religious experientialists, critical theorists, multiculturalists, post-Zionists, and even "reborn" evangelical Christians and "returning" orthodox Jews yearn for connections with their fellow human beings or with God. They seek the reassurance that comes from having one's most important convictions reinforced by close friends, respected colleagues, and a collective relationship with the divine. This reassurance is found in the ideological ties that bind us to the communities to which we belong. It is found, in other words, in solidarity with those whom I count as part of my group.

The Politics of Spirituality

The notion of solidarity has had its greatest impact in social and political theory. To some, it may not seem that the search for meaning in collective ties relates to the same spiritual urges as the sort of subjective spirituality described in the previous chapter. They might question the relevance of concepts such as solidarity and collectivity to a discussion of the current spiritual revival. This would be especially true on a narrow account of spirituality that sees it primarily as a mystical or religious concept such as the sort of Christian perspective that links spirituality to faith commitments unbound by nationality or ethnic heritage. Yet the same need to fill modernity's moral void that motivates a mystical turn inward often drives the contemporary search for community and political association. Some express this in terms of a desire for "fellowship" or "communion."

In fact, for most Jews and Moslems, and for many Christians as well,[1] the lines between communal, political, and religious association are not easily drawn. Although Islam obviously entails faith commitments that transcend national and ethnic boundaries, it has historically been closely associated with Arab ethnic and national aspirations.[2] Judaism, too, involves religious beliefs and behaviors, but there are communal, ethnic, and political dimensions to Jewish identity that cannot be ignored. The renaissance of Jewish life taking place today can only be understood in light of the rise of the State of Israel out of the ashes of the Holocaust and the historic emergence of Jewish power at the end of the twentieth century in both Israel and North America. Similarly, the rise of both Islamic and Jewish fundamentalism cannot be understood outside of their national contexts. In all of these cases, religious, ethical, and political associations are so intimately intertwined that the group itself often becomes a source of spiritual sustenance and a "location" of ethical vision.

Additionally, many people are searching for the good outside of institutional religions, in neighborhoods, ethnic communities, political movements, identification with the poor and oppressed, and even national patriotism. These "secular" rebellions against modernity are no less spiritual, I want to argue, than those involving a return to some form of traditional religion or mystical experience.[3] They exhibit many of the same conceptual contours and evidence many of the same dangers as more religiously oriented versions of this phenomenon.

To exclude these journeys from the discussion of spirituality is not only to make unproductive and divisive distinctions between groups of people otherwise on parallel paths. It is also to risk missing a large portion of the phenomenon under examination, and hence to misconceive the very nature of the topic under discussion. The challenge of spirituality today involves empowering individuals to choose a good life in light of the moral failures and political successes of modernity. To ignore the political dimensions of spirituality, therefore, not only uproots the concept from its current historical context but also fails to address key problems and opportunities presented by the revival itself.

Two Conceptions of Collectivism

To illuminate this political dimension of spirituality, it will be useful to unravel two strands of thought, one more radically collectivist than the other. According to the first, group solidarity provides a gateway for discovering and a context for interpreting a good that transcends the confines of any particular community. For moral conversations to make sense, we must agree that such a transcendent good exists, even if we cannot agree on its nature.

According to the second strand, the collective actually defines the nature of the good; there are no moral ideals whose value transcends group consciousness. There is no objective knowledge or higher moral truth untainted by bias and expectation: nothing against which to judge the veracity of such knowledge or the value of such ethics. What we take to be facts are determined by the cognitive frameworks within which we inquire, and what we take to be moral givens are determined by the assumptions of the ethical theory we embrace. All commitment is ideological. There is no overarching, nonideological framework against which ideologies can be judged. The very fact that a community shares my moral vision is sufficient for its legitimacy.

Both strands of thought embrace the notion that goodness is intimately connected to context. This idea is already found in Plato's *Republic*,[4] which otherwise tends toward the first strand, and in Aristotle's *Nichomachean Ethics*,[5] which otherwise leans toward the second. Both philosophers argue that problems of morality as they affect the individual cannot be separated from problems of political association. Ethics and politics are not independent of one another, therefore, but supplement each other by treating common issues from different points of view. They also agreed that justice was the ultimate virtue of the *polis* or state.

Plato defined justice in terms of a relationship between intellectual, mercantile, and working classes that reflected the balance he required within a well-ordered soul. So Plato appears to have believed that justice is a virtue of human beings independent of and antecedent to the well-ordered *polis*. Indeed, Plato held that a prerequisite for leadership of the *polis* was an understanding of the essence of justice, which is eternal and unchanging. Ethical ideals, on this view, transcend the collective. They inform and drive communal will rather than being a product of it.

Aristotle, on the other hand, "represents a tradition of thought, in which he is preceded by Homer and Sophocles, according to which the human being who is separated from his social group is also deprived of the capacity for justice."

> A human being stands to the *polis* as a part to its whole, in a way analogous . . . to that in which a hand or foot stands to the body of which it is a part. . . . detach a hand from its body; it then lacks both the specific function and the separate capacity of a hand; it is no longer in the same sense a hand. . . . What is it that a human being is deprived of, if radically separated from the life of the *polis*? . . . . law and justice which only the *polis* affords. . . . Separated from the *polis*, what could have been a human being becomes a wild animal. [6]

According to this more radical position, moral ideas are meaningless outside the context of community. There can be no assumption of transcendent ideals around which a community is galvanized. Rather, moral vision is the product of the communal experience itself.

A version of the Platonic view finds its way into scholastic political theory such as that of Maimonides and Aquinas. Both defined community in terms of common commitment to religious and natural laws that are independent of the collective. Both interpreted the role of the prophet as a religious and political leader in light of Plato. And both conceived of the right to rule in terms of an unsolicited, sometimes even unwanted, divine call. Maimonides understood adherence to the divine commandments contained in the Jewish Scripture as preparation for the sort of philosophical contemplation that would position one to receive such a call.[7] Aquinas, on the other hand, understood philosophical discourse as preparation for adherence to a religious discipline outlined in the Christian Bible that would enable one to hear God's call.[8]

Like its subjectivist counterpart, the more radical approach to solidarity emerges in nineteenth-century European romanticism;

not so much in the reaction against Kantian reason as in the socialist rebellion against capitalism and instrumental reason. Here again, Rousseau is a pivotal figure. Unlike Locke, who viewed the social contract as an agreement among autonomous moral agents with competing conceptions of the good, Rousseau understood that contract as a consensus of what he called the "general will." According to Rousseau, moral ideals emerge naturally within us and are molded by our social surroundings. Those who share a common background and social context, therefore, develop a common view that reflects collective consciousness. The political task is to discover the collective view concerning any relevant issue.[9]

Rousseau never went so far as to claim that the will of the people is determined entirely by social context. This was Karl Marx's contribution. Marx rejected the idea advanced by Adam Smith that in a free market each rational person would be permitted to pursue his own best interest.[10] Owners may be able to pursue their interests because they have the power to do so, but workers cannot, because those who own the products of their labor withhold power from them. Knowledge and religion are tools used by owners to manipulate the consciousness of the workers into believing that they are not really oppressed and alienated from the fruits of their own labors. Neither reflects an objective truth that is not influenced by the interests of those who control the means of production. Instead, building on Rousseau's conception of the collective will, Marx argued that knowledge and religion are expressions of political ideologies that serve the interests of those in power. There is no such thing as truth or goodness, only ideology. The good life is to be found in the inevitable defeat of the ideologies of the owners by those of the workers.[11]

Transcendental Collectivism

I call the more moderate position that follows Plato transcendental collectivism, because it views the community as embodying a vision of the good that originates and receives legitimization beyond its boarders. Consider some instances that influence the current spiritual revival: liberation theology, secular Jewish spirituality, religious experientialism, and modern orthodoxy.

Liberation Theology
In Christian theology, the notion of solidarity has had its greatest influence among Latin American liberation theologians. Gustavo Gutierrez, for example, understands theology as critical reflection on praxis—practice leading to social change. The criticism employed here, as in other neo-Marxist doctrines, is not epistemological but economic, cultural, and political. Liberation theology seeks to uncover hidden ideological presuppositions that theologians bring to their work. This theology involves a "preferential option" or "solidarity with" the poor.[12]

The motivation for this identification with the poor is well illustrated at the opening of Leonardo and Clodovis Boff's *Introducing Liberation Theology:*

> A woman of forty, but who looked as old as seventy went up to the priest after Mass and said sorrowfully: "Father, I went to communion without going to confession first." "How come, my daughter?" asked the priest. "Father," she replied, "I arrived rather late, after you had begun the offertory. For three days I have had only water and nothing to eat; I'm dying of hunger. When I saw you handing out the hosts, those little pieces of white bread, I went to communion just out of hunger for that little bit of bread." The priest's eyes filled with tears. He recalled the words of Jesus: "My flesh (bread) is real food . . . whoever feeds on me will draw life from me" (John 6:55,57).[13]

Because of its commitment to praxis, social criticism, and solidarity with the poor, Liberation Theology offers a new theological paradigm, a new way of doing theology. Instead of expecting pastoral activity to flow from theological doctrine, the doctrine of liberation theology grows out of reflection on praxis. The criteria for evaluating its success, therefore, are not theoretical but rooted in its contribution to the class struggle that will overcome the domination and oppression of the poor. The path toward this end is not developmental but revolutionary. Based on prophetic denunciation of injustice, liberation theology calls for a revolutionary new social and economic system in Latin America.

Although this utopian aspiration tends to reduce religious eschatology to political revolution and social change, liberation theologians refuse to divorce religion and faith from the concrete social, political, and economic conditions in which people live. In the final analysis, argues Leonardo Boff, the universal Church must be relativized according to the realities of local communities and the needs of the poor. The result is not politicization of the Church. The historical alignment of the Latin American Church with those in power makes clear that the Church has often been politicized. The question is: On whose behalf does the Church exercise its political influence—its own or that of the poor and marginalized?[14]

Liberation Theology inherited many relativistic concepts from Marxism such as its understanding of the relation between ideology, power, and class interest. Nevertheless, its vision of goodness draws on a profound faith in God, who is discovered through action leading to social change. Additionally, its solidarity with the poor echoes the Israelite prophets, who cried out against injustice and oppression in God's name. Its revolutionary methods are grounded in the strength of the collective, but its moral vision responds to nothing less than a call from heaven.

The Secularization of Jewish Spirituality

In the previous chapter, we saw how the redemptive impulse of messianism is a powerful driving force in Kabbalistic spirituality. Secular Zionism, the movement to reestablish a Jewish polity and culture in the ancient homeland of the Jewish people, capitalized on the spiritual power of messianism by seeking to restore the Jewish people to its national homeland and heritage. Given the problematic state of European Jewry at the turn of the twentieth century, this could not be accomplished without political revolution. Like liberation theology, this movement learned its revolutionary rhetoric from Marx and its ethical vision from the prophetic call for justice and egalitarianism. These ideals were concretized in small collectives known as *kibbutzim*, which for many years represented the highest realization of Zionist ideals. With the decline of socialism and the economic success of Israeli capitalism, some of these ideals have eroded, such as each working according to his ability and receiving according to his needs. Consequently, a rediscovery of the spiritual meaning of Zionism that is afoot in Israel today is parallel in many respects to the spiritual renewal in North American Jewry.[15] To understand this revival, we require some background.

Prior to Enlightenment and Emancipation, European Jews lived as an autonomous religio-political community within larger principalities, kingdoms, and mercantile republics. Enlightenment and Emancipation challenged not only the intellectual tenets of Jewish faith but also the political authority of its autonomous communal structure. No longer could the political identification of the Jew with the Jewish polity be assumed, because he now was to owe allegiance to the modern nation-state as a citizen. However, acceptance into emancipated society, when offered, often carried the price of assimilation and loss of Jewish identity. Zionism addressed this problem by taking redemption out of the hands of the rabbis and reconceiving the Jewish redemptive impulse in political and cultural terms. This brought about nothing less than a secularization of Jewish spirituality through an amalgamation of Judaism and nineteenth-century European nationalism.

Labor Zionists such as Berl Katzenelson and A. D. Gordon employed Marxist categories to analyze the Jewish condition of their day. Diaspora Jews, they argued, live under the rule of nations in which they are marginal, dominated by cultures of which they are not a part. Even when they acquire power or wealth, it ultimately serves the ends of rulers or people alien to them. Under these conditions, Jews are alienated from the products of their labor. This can only be rectified if the Jews return to their historical homeland and undertake a spiritual rebirth through laboring on their own soil. Katzenelson wrote:

> Precisely because we fully recognize the catastrophic state of the world in which we live, because we see the need for the most fundamental overturn, because we know that at the door of every new social system the sins of the old are waiting to enter—therefore we insist that revolutionary efforts . . . are worthless unless they are accompanied by renewed and improved constructive energies. . . . Our revolutionary constructivism cannot confine itself only to the economic field; it must embrace our entire life and stamp its imprint upon our culture and our milieu. . . . No true revolution is conceivable without intense spiritual life.[16]

Ahad Ha'Am defined this "spiritual life" culturally rather than religiously. He saw in Hebrew language and literature a historic Jewish repository of humanistic ethics that could form the basis of a secular spiritual ideal for the citizens of the new Jewish state.[17] Religious Zionists have recently criticized secular Zionism, claiming that it lacks meaningful values to transmit across the generations. This critique confuses political Zionism with both labor and cultural Zionism.

Political Zionism has not contributed higher ideals to Jewish secularism. Its leaders have been content to focus their efforts on the establishment and growth of a Jewish state as a solution to the political powerlessness and vulnerability of the Jewish people.[18] Both Labor and Cultural Zionism, however, have striven not only for the establishment of a Jewish state but also for a renaissance of Jewish culture that would infuse the new society with higher ideals. The claim that secular Zionism lacks values may be true of political Zionism, therefore, because it views the Jewish state as a nation like any other. But it may not be as applicable to labor and cultural Zionism, which are on the defensive today because of the failures of socialist and modern thought to which they attached themselves. However, they posses rich sources of moral vision to be reconstituted for a new situation.

The task of labor and cultural Zionism today is precisely the challenge faced by the current spiritual awakening, to offer meaning and moral vision in a postmodern age without forfeiting the political successes of Enlightenment.[19] The revival of cultural Zionism in Israel today is attempting in some small measure to address this challenge through a rediscovery of classical Jewish texts. Throughout the country, study groups and institutions of higher learning are exploring biblical and rabbinic material as sources of national cultural values.

Mordecai Kaplan translated Ahad Ha'Am's ideas into the American context when he argued that Judaism is a religious civilization committed to a common monotheistic, ethical heritage. In this theology, Kaplan naturalized divinity as the force for good in the universe, and understood the divine commandments of the Hebrew Bible and rabbinic tradition as the folkways of the Jewish civilization. He also expanded the mission of the synagogue from a house of worship alone to a house of study and community assembly. This synagogue center, as Kaplan called it, was the hub of Jewish civilization in the Diaspora.[20] Kaplan's views captured the rationale behind two generations of American Jewish commitment to survival and solidarity. Some of the heirs to Kaplan's collectivism gather in small prayer- and study-groups known as *Havurot,* which are also associated with the new Kabbalism discussed in the previous chapter. Some larger synagogues have co-opted the idea of *Havurot,* in order to create a greater sense of family and belonging among its members.[21]

Religious Experientialism and the New Orthodoxy
Among religious experientialists, Abraham Joshua Heschel defended belief in God by thinking of those who profess a traditional faith as one large community.[22] Those who do not live within a

religious framework have no way of evaluating the meaning or truth of divine existence. God is discovered within the experiences of awe and wonder of which we are made aware through "the main aspects of religious existence: religious worship, learning, and action."[23] "All *mitzvot* are means of evoking in us an awareness of living in the neighborhood of God, of living in the holy dimension. They call to mind the inconspicuous mystery of things and acts, and are reminders of our being stewards, rather than landlords of the universe. . . . All *mitzvot* first of all express reverence."[24]

Understanding of God, therefore, is not attained by means of scientific or logical reasoning, "by calling into session all of the arguments for and against Him, in order to debate whether He is a reality or a figment of the mind. . . . Speculation does not precede faith. The antecedents of faith are the premises of wonder and praise. Worship of God precedes affirmation of His realness. We *praise* before we *prove*. We respond before we question."[25]

> Thus, the certainty of the realness of God does not come about as a corollary of logical premises, as a leap from the realm of logic to the realm of ontology, from an assumption to a fact. It is, on the contrary, a transition from immediate apprehension to a thought, from a preconceptual awareness to a definite assurance, from being overwhelmed by the presence of God to an awareness of His existence. . . . Our thought is but an after-belief. . . . (o)ur belief in His reality is not a leap over a missing link in a syllogism but rather a regaining, giving up a view rather than adding one, going behind self-consciousness and questioning the self and all its cognitive pretensions. *It is an ontological presupposition.*[26]

One joins the community of the faithful, then, by embarking on a path that leads one to "regain" an awareness of God, whose existence is independent of and antecedent to any particular community's way of attaining that awareness. The community of religious experience is essential for finding one's way to God; but the nature of God's being is neither defined by nor dependent upon any particular path. Heschel argues that God seeks our devotion, not in order to exist, but in order to achieve a moral mission in the universe.

Joseph Soloveitchik, a leading figure in American modern orthodoxy, reconciled the secular and religious communal impulses by conceiving of two antithetical tendencies within human nature. The Hebrew Bible contains two stories depicting the creation of human beings. In Genesis 1, male and female are created together in the image of the Creator at the climax of creation. They are enjoined to "be fruitful and multiply, fill the earth and master it" (1:28). This story depicts the creation of Adam the First—a modern, secular, scientific person of the technological age who seeks control and dignity. According to Soloveitchik, Adam the First requires community in order to fulfill the creative impulse embedded in his very nature.

> Adam the First is never alone. Man in solitude has no opportunity to display his dignity and majesty, since both are behavioral social traits. Adam the First was not left alone even on the day of creation. He emerged into the world together with Eve, and God addressed himself to both of them as inseparable members of one community.[27]

Indeed, his very success as a master of nature is only possible in a collective context:

> Distribution of labor, the coordination of efforts of the many, the accumulated experiences of the multitude, the cooperative spirit of countless individuals, raise man above the primitive level of natural existence and grant him limited dominion over his environment. What we call civilization is the sum total of a community effort through the millennia.[28]

According to Genesis 2, "The Lord God formed man from the dust of the earth, and He blew into his nostrils the breath of life: and man became a living being" (2:7). Since it is "not good for man to be alone," God fashioned a "fitting helper for him" out of one of his ribs (2:18). The man responded by saying, "This one at last is bone of my bone, and flesh of my flesh," and the text observes: "Hence a man leaves his father and mother and clings to his wife, so that they become one flesh" (2:21–24).

This is a second Adam, who is charged not with mastery and control but with cultivating and caring for the garden in which he is placed (2:15). Insecure, afraid, and alone in the world, he seeks not dignity and domination but intimacy, love, and redemption. He is overwhelmed by God, who is not discovered through scientific experiment or logical proof, but is an ever-present, driving force in his life. "Adam the Second, in the midst of his sense of failure to transcend finitude and make real contact with other mortal creatures, surrenders himself 'unreservedly' to God, expressing his commitment through sacrificial action which carries no promise of reward or success."[29] He discovers the nature of the sacrifices required of him in a covenental community of caring.

Because they are both part of divine creation, Soloveitchik views these two human impulses—the secular push for dominion and dignity, and the religious inclination toward intimacy and redemption—as equally important. He suggests two modes of interaction between them: oscillation and reclamation. On the first model, one moves back and forth between the two communities, often feeling alienated from one while seeking fulfillment within the other. According to a second approach, one seeks to retrieve a dimension of holiness within the creative world of Adam the First by reconciling its value to the world of Adam the Second.[30]

For example, Soloveitchik reclaims the holiness of secular Zionism by observing that God established not one but two covenants with the Jewish people. The first was already agreed upon in Egypt: "And I will take you to be my people, and I will be your God" (Exodus 6:7). The second was contracted at Mount Sinai: "Then he took the record of the covenant and read it aloud to the people. And they said, 'all that the Lord has spoke we will faithfully do'" (Exodus 24:7–8). The first of these, he calls a covenant of destiny. The Jewish people is tied to a common destiny by virtue of history, family, ethnicity, and political community. Anti-Semites do not hate on the basis of religious pedigree. In this respect, the Jewish people is one community.

However, on a deeper level, this common destiny is the product of a second covenant. Soloveitchik calls this the covenant of purpose. It is the historical willingness of the Jewish people to accept a common way of life, revealed by God in the *Torah* that has created its common destiny. It is this common teaching that called the Jewish people into being. Without a covenant of purpose, the covenant of destiny cannot be sustained, because it has no meaning.[31] Ultimately, the Jewish collective does not define its own mission; its transcendent purpose is discovered through the study and practice of divine revelation.

Radical Collectivism

Liberation theology, labor and cultural Zionism, religious experientialism, and the new orthodoxy all understand the collective as committed to a common moral vision that precedes, and even generates, communal bonds. In contrast, radical collectivism conceives of that vision as constructed by and inseparable from the social group.

Rorty's Universal Solidarity

In contemporary thought, it is probably Richard Rorty who popularized the term "solidarity," at least among intellectuals. Whereas Marx sought to cultivate a universal human solidarity by means of a victory of the oppressed over the oppressors, Rorty endeavors to create a sense of identification with the whole of humanity through diminishing the significance of difference. This is accomplished by expanding our conceptions of who is to be counted in our conception of "us." He holds that the task of solidarity is to develop this sense of "us," of who is included when speaking intentionally and self-consciously of "we." Following philosopher Wilfred Sellars,[32] he calls these "we-intentions" and argues that the challenge is to make them as expansive and inclusive as possible. The goal is to cultivate "the ability to see more and more traditional differences (of tribe, religion, customs, and the like) as unimportant when compared with the similarities with respect to pain and humiliation—the ability to think of people wildly different from ourselves as included in the range of 'us'."[33]

In order to properly assess the degree to which goodness can be "located" in collective solidarity, we must determine whether we are speaking of identification with the whole of humanity, as Rorty argues, or with particular groups, as Marx maintains. I contend that the particularistic understanding of solidarity is more compelling than the universalistic one. It is precisely Rorty's unending openness that has left many people with a sense of emptiness, of not knowing who they are supposed to be, or what they should believe, or how they ought to live. The infinite "us" is a collective of empty "I"s. Without reference to ideals outside the self, the unique feelings that people may want to express will lack not only intelligible content but also the communal context in which to express it. If everyone's ways are "our ways," then there is no basis on which to choose between the available options of belief and behavior. If everyone is "us," then no one is "us," because the very idea of including someone in a "we-intention" requires that we also exclude someone else, otherwise there would be no difference between the concepts of "us" and "them" or "we" and "they."

In one sense, of course, Rorty is correct. Every human has the potential for moral agency and ethical discourse. In this case, the "us" refers to humankind and the "them" to creatures incapable of moral agency. But if this is the end of the story, there could be no way to move beyond the potential to do good, to the actual ability to do so. This requires a concrete account of goodness that can be found only in the collective context. In order to experience solidarity with the whole of humanity, we must identify with a particular moral community.

Critical Theory

One example of this sort of reasoning builds on the Marxist observation that truth and goodness are products of socioeconomic class. According to this view, people experience solidarity not only in the framework of class-consciousness but in the context of any intersubjective community that shares values, beliefs, behaviors, and languages. The contemporary German philosopher Jürgen Habermas construes reason and ethics as "grounded" in "domination-free communication" rather than in the self. The good life, in this view, is to be found in a community of discourse, in those with whom we share bonds of communicative solidarity.[34] For example, a disciple of Martin Buber was enamored of his theology but found meaning in a traditional prayer community that had little use for Buber's views. The disciple was known to say, "I can't pray with those to whom I can talk, and can't talk to those with whom I can pray." In Habermas's terms, Buber's student was caught between two communities of discourse.

Like Rorty, Habermas seeks to expand the limits of those to be counted in our communities of discourse. To this end, he argues that we should increase the number of communities committed to "domination-free" interaction, who communicate to understand rather than to control. However, unlike Rorty, Habermas seeks universal solidarity through a heightened rather than a diminished sense of the significance of difference, by "grounding" ethics in particular intersubjective communities of discourse.

Multiculturalism and Post-Zionism

One application of this sort of neo-Marxist criticism has led to a "deconstruction" of the American undergraduate curriculum. Since knowledge is a product of cultural interest, the knowledge often chosen for instruction in American colleges and universities is a reflection of the white, Anglo, male culture that has dominated the academy for more than a century. Those who do not identify with this culture, but who are required to study its curriculum in order to achieve economic and social status, are thereby alienated from their own cultural heritages. To alleviate this form of cultural oppression, and to empower those who identify with cultures that are neither white, nor Anglo, nor male, a multiplicity of cultural heritages must be represented in the college curriculum. Indeed, proper preparation for a world free of cultural domination demands exposure to a variety of cultural traditions other than one's own.

A similar application of cultural criticism has emerged lately among those writing about Jewish secularism, both in Israel and North America. They argue that Zionism created several forms of cultural domination: of European over non-European Jews, of Israeli Jews over Israeli Arabs, and of Israelis over non-Israeli Palestinians. For Israel to live up to its democratic potential, it is argued, it must move past Zionism to a post-Zionist phase that eschews the domination and oppression of others, and that allows a multiplicity of cultures to flourish.[35]

Solidarity Defended

The view that the good is found within the bonds of collective and communicative solidarity is usually based on two claims. One holds that (a) goodness and truth are functions of the frameworks (cultures, languages, religions, traditions, or theories) within which we reason. The second (b) contends that it makes no sense to criticize one framework on the basis of another. Statement (a) has been called the thesis of relativism and statement (b) the critical immunity thesis. Those who accept the thesis of relativism but reject critical immunity are weak relativists. Those who believe that critical immunity follows from the thesis of relativism are strong relativists.[36] Weak relativism is consistent with transcendental collectivism. Strong relativism is required to sustain radical collectivism.

Transcendental collectivism is more compelling than the more radical alternative because weak relativism is more appealing than its stronger counterpart. To see why, let us reflect on these two versions of relativism and their relation to collective spirituality.

Goodness and Truth Are Functions of Framework

Both transcendental and radical collectivists claim that truth and goodness are functions of the collective frameworks in which they are conceived. Liberation theologians, for example, follow Marx in claiming that the religious ideology of those in power is presented as truth when in fact it represents the interests of the wealthy. There is an alternative religious perspective that is grounded in the experience of poverty. Similarly, cultural Zionists such as Ahad Ha'Am as well as the followers of Mordecai Kaplan hold that Jewish civilization has produced a unique system of values that offers a compelling vision of how to live.

Likewise, Heschel claims that for the religious person the existence of God is not a hypothesis to be tested according to the criteria of scientific inquiry, rather it is a presupposition of religion. This can only be so because religion and science are rooted in radically different conceptual frameworks. The truth of each is dependent upon the assumptions relative to their respective frameworks. Since the notion of a hypothesis is taken from the scientific, rather than the religious, framework, it cannot be used to understand or assess religious ideas such as God.

This sort of reasoning is also present among radical collectivists. Multiculturalists claim that the writings of particular cultural, ethnic, linguistic, gender, or sexual lifestyle communities deserve to be widely read in colleges and universities because they represent unique value perspectives. In the terms of Habermas's discourse ethics, multiculturalists argue that white, Anglo males do not share "domination-free communication" with people of color, non-Anglos, and women. The dominant groups—Anglos, whites, males—are more powerful and seek to impose their views on those weaker than they—non-Anglos, people of color, women.

Criticizing One Framework on the Basis of Another Makes No Sense

Even though they hold that truth and goodness are functions of framework, transcendental collectivists assert that there exists a higher vision of the good, even if we disagree over its content. Such a transcendent vision makes it possible to debate the relative desirability of several conflicting sets of values. Liberation theologians hold not only that the poor have their own unique perspective, but also that this is a better position than that of the wealthy and powerful because it is in tune with divine justice.

So, too, labor Zionists such as Katzenelson and Gordon thought not only that egalitarianism had deep roots in the prophetic tradition but also that this tradition was preferable to the capitalist orientation that allocated wealth on the basis of power. Indeed, some Zionist thinkers followed the prophets in conceiving a Jewish state as a light unto the nations. In Soloveitchik's terms, the covenant of purpose drives the covenant of destiny; there is a Jewish collective *because* there is a transcendent Jewish mission. Similarly, when Heschel argues that it makes no sense to critique religion on the basis of science, he is asserting a preference for an intellectual position that admits the legitimacy of religious faith over one that does not.

However, Heschel may take an additional step that is clearly embraced by more radical collectivists. He apparently holds that the way of life drawn from religious tradition is unassailable by scientific reasoning. It is only subject to critique according to its own internal assumptions.[37] Multiculturalists clearly adopt the thesis of critical immunity when they argue that the literatures of people of color or women cannot be adequately assessed according to Anglo, white, male assumptions and literary standards.[38]

Using Habermas's analysis again, those with less power—non-Anglos, people of color, women, and perhaps religionists—seek protection from the "hegemony" of "dominant cultures" by arguing that it makes no sense to criticize one framework on the basis of another. The discourse of the "dominant cultures," on this view, does not share relevant standards of reasoning with the less powerful "dominated cultures" that could be used as a basis for critique. Radical collectivists tend to believe that critical immunity—the idea that one framework cannot be criticized on the basis of another—follows from the thesis of relativism—the idea that truth and goodness are functions of framework. There are three reasons commonly used to defend this assumption. One holds that language, concepts, rituals, and symbols only have meaning in context.[39] A second contends that key concepts cannot be translated from one framework to the next.[40] The third assumption asserts that our perceptions of reality and what we are prepared to count as evidence are determined by framework.[41] Let us consider each of the arguments in favor of these claims before we assess their strengths and weaknesses.

Concepts Have Meaning Only in Context
According to the first claim, each framework—science, religion, culture—has its own language. The meaning of these languages is understandable only within the relevant context. Science is meaningless within the religious framework. It simply makes no sense to speak of God as a hypothesis. Similarly, to impose criteria of the predominantly white, male, Anglo-American academy on the selection of curriculum materials drawn from nonwhite, female, or non-Anglo cultures is to rely on concepts that have no meaning within these alternative frameworks. It is literally nonsense to criticize one context on the basis of another *because the concepts of one make no sense within the other.*

Concepts Cannot Be Translated from One Framework to Another
It might be asked whether it is possible to translate the key concepts from one framework into another, from science into religion, or from Anglo into non-Anglo culture. Couldn't the appropriate standards then be applied to decide whether God exists or whether a certain non-Anglo author should be studied? According to the second claim, the answer is no, because frameworks are so distinct

from one another that the most essential concepts cannot be translated. Any translation to another context does them so much damage that they are rendered incomprehensible. The scientific concept of "hypothesis" has no counterpart in religion into which it might be translated; and the concept of God has no parallel in science. Religion cannot be criticized on the basis of science, according to this view, *because the key concepts cannot be translated from one framework to the next.*

Perceptions of Reality Are Determined by Framework
In response, one might ask why translation is impossible. Don't the languages of these different frameworks describe a common reality that exists outside of the frameworks themselves? Don't science and religion both depict the world in which we live, and don't Anglo and non-Anglo writers describe common life experiences? According to the third claim, the answer is no, because that which we posit as real or suitable to be used as evidence is also a product of a framework. W. V. O. Quine called the observation that our perceptions of reality are products of frameworks, "ontological relativity," where the term "ontology" refers to what we believe to be real.[42] Scientific concepts cannot be used to critique religion or Anglo criteria of excellence be used to evaluate non-Anglo literature *because the very realities they reflect are determined by the frameworks used to describe them.*

The Ethics of Solidarity

One can see why the bonds of solidarity offer an attractive place in which to "locate" a vision of the good life. It appears extraordinarily safe and protected, because one's most basic commitments are not subject to critiques from opposing camps. This is one reason why "reborn" Christians and "returning" Jews often rely on this sort of thinking to understand and defend their new-found religiosity. What these individuals usually want is relief from the insecurity and vulnerability of modern life in which everything is assessed and evaluated—one's work, one's beliefs, one's behavior, one's politics—and in which nothing is secure, or protected from doubt, or from change, or from fragmentation. Spirituality as solidarity provides the migrant from modernism a haven, a refuge. It offers a home, to borrow Peter Berger's felicitous phrase, for a homeless mind.[43] This may also be why this sort of thinking is attractive to analysts of domination such as critical theorists and critical pedagogues. It provides a kind of intellectual protection against the onslaught of alien ideas in a world where being powerless, or at least less powerful, offers little protection elsewhere. But how real is this protection if the strong relativism that this view embraces undermines the very conditions that make ethical discourse possible?

The Critical Thinking Condition

Radical collectivism parochializes critical intelligence so completely that it renders the concept meaningless, since one group's intelligence is another's nonsense. The distinctions that ethical discourse guarantees between right and wrong, better and worse, good and bad, valuable and worthless are obliterated. What is right within one framework is wrong within another. What is good is also bad, what is valuable is also worthless. This obliteration of distinctions leads to incoherence. If strong relativism is true, it must be false, since relativism of this kind is itself an absolute claim. Like extreme subjectivism, strong relativism is incoherent.

The idea that extreme subjectivism and strong relativism are incoherent is not easy to grasp. To clarify, let's look at an example used by philosopher of religion D. Z. Phillips. It makes no sense to condemn child sacrifice when practiced in a tribal culture, he claims, because we have no concept of what such a sacrifice means in that culture.

> If I hear that one of my neighbors has killed another neighbor's child, given that he is sane, my condemnation is immediate. . . .

But if I hear that some remote tribe practices child sacrifice, what then? I do not know what sacrifice means for the remote tribe in question. What would it mean to say that I condemned it when "it" refers to something I know nothing about? If I did condemn it, I would be condemning murder. But murder is not child sacrifice.[44]

The meaning of religious practices, according to this view, is relative to culture, and to rip a practice out of its natural context renders it literally meaningless. How can we criticize what we don't comprehend?

How are we to understand this position? If we say that the meaning of child sacrifice is relative to a conceptual framework such as a culture, then should we not also say that the meaning of *condemning* child sacrifice is also relative to a conceptual framework? If so, it follows not only that we ought not to condemn religious practices outside of their own conceptual contexts, but also that we ought not to condemn the condemnation of these practices outside of their own conceptual contexts. In other words, relativists such as Phillips ought not chastise nonrelativists for condemning such practices as child sacrifice. This creates a paradox. According to the strong relativist position, it appears to be both acceptable and unacceptable to condemn child sacrifice.

It is this paradoxical situation that renders strong relativism incoherent. All views turn out to be both true and false and all values both good and bad. The very distinctions between positive and negative value that are required to make sense of moral deliberations are obliterated. This renders ethics meaningless.[45]

The Freedom Condition

Additionally, strong relativism undermines our freedom to choose between alternative religious, moral, cultural, or intellectual frameworks. Since each of us can only understand what is meaningful within our own framework, we cannot understand alternatives, either from within our own preexisting frameworks or by means of translation. The only way we can move from one framework to another is not by intentional, willed choice but by caprice or epiphany. I suddenly see the light, recognize something of significance in the alternative, view the world in a new way. But nothing I can do will prepare me for this epiphany. This is random, not intelligent, choice.

The Fallibility Condition

Nor does the condition of fallibility fare any better, since this sort of relativism rejects the possibility of external criteria against which to evaluate traditions or theories. Since only internal criteria are allowed, and evidence is determined by those very criteria, the only way a doctrine might be rejected is on the basis of internal inconsistency. Frameworks that reject the value of consistency cannot be evaluated at all.

What's left of the ethical discourse is neither intelligence, nor freedom, nor fallibility, but raw power. The most powerful group dominates. Since one group can never understand or be persuaded by the position of another, the only way to overcome this domination is through the exercise of power. This is why Marx called for armed struggle and revolution. In his view, relief from oppression can only be won at the barrel of a gun. But it is only in the context of moral discourse that the very outcry against oppression makes sense. When neo-Marxist multiculturalists and critical theorists who accept strong relativism decry oppression and cultural domination, their outcry has no basis other than in raw power alone. Since they have rejected the conditions that give meaning to ethical discourse, their objections have no moral bite.

Radical collectivism fails to offer a conception of goodness to fill the void left by the crisis of modernism because it undermines the possibility of ethical discourse. Instead, it favors an a-moral conception of the human condition according to which might rules rather than right, and history, society, culture, or ideology determines our behavior. Humans are absolved of responsibility for their actions, denied their intrinsic moral worth, and robbed of the hard-won freedom of the Emancipation. Enslavement to history, or environment, or human taskmasters wins the day.

Criticism and Community

Up to this point, we have addressed the inability of the strong relativistic account of spiritual collectivism to offer ethical vision. But can the argument for strong relativism withstand criticism on its own merits? If it could, we would have to conclude that the search for spirituality as an ethical pursuit is misguided. The return to slavery is not the wrong direction; it is the only, the necessary, one. This, however, is not the case. The argument for critical immunity and strong relativism is the product of a series of exaggerations. Our task is to discern the grains of truth embedded in this argument in order not to throw out the intersubjective baby with the strong relativist bath water.

Are Concepts Only Meaningful in One Context?

Consider first the claim that language only has meaning in particular contexts. There is truth to this. According to Wittgenstein, words are tools we use to express concepts that are part of our daily lives. The meaning of words consists in the criteria that govern their use. They make sense in a particular context.[46] But from this it does not follow that words have meaning only in one context, or that they have only a single meaning in any given context. Language is a very flexible tool and the many contexts of our lives overlap, such that we often draw on terms learned in one context to understand another. To ask whether God exists in the same way as neutrons or quarks is not an unintelligible question. It is even an important one. It helps us to get clear about just what sort of existence it is that we attribute to God.

Heschel was right, of course, that those who thought that the unprovability of God's existence tells the whole story of faith have a foolishly narrow understanding of both religious experience and scientific inquiry. But he was wrong to delegitimize the question. Heschel understood the practices of religious community as a pathway to discovering the God that lies beyond the collective. However, by embracing a version of critical immunity, he comes close to relativizing this God so completely that it would be difficult to discover in such a deity a vision of goodness that can arbitrate between competing values.

If God is relative to religious experience of the faithful, should divinity not also be relative to the specific traditions in which the faithful discover God? But, if the meanings of these traditions cannot be translated from one community to another, how can we know whether the deity discovered within one faith bears any relation to that found in another? This is not the transcendent God Heschel set out to defend but a collection of parochial deities that reflect the narrow interests of isolated groups. As such, it is not the sort of higher good that enable us to escape the quagmires of strong relativism. Heschel's relativistic defense of faith in a transcendent God beautifully illustrates the difficulties in using radical relativism to defend transcendental collectivism.[47]

If Heschel, who appears to sit on the border between transcendental and radical collectivism, falls prey to confusion as a result of the assumption that concepts and standards have meaning only in context, this view must surely raise questions for clearer instances of radicalism. Concerning the inclusion of non-Anglo literature in the curriculum, for example, accepted criteria of literary or intellectual excellence by no means exhaust the relevant indices according to which the worth of a particular work might be judged, but neither are they completely irrelevant.

Can Concepts Be Translated from One Framework to Another?

The same can be said for the claim that concepts cannot be translated from one framework into another. Surely some concepts cannot be translated from one context to the next. But from this it does not follow that nothing is translatable, or that we are frozen within our own frameworks because of our inability to translate the ideas of another into our own. This is false on the face of it. Works of literature, poetry, and philosophy are translated between cultures every day. Yes, something is lost in the translation, but not everything. Hence, the idea that scientists cannot understand religion or that scientific concepts cannot be translated into religiously relevant categories is simply not true.

Consider the historian's use of critical methodologies to reconstruct the Dead Sea Scrolls (which include the oldest known copies of the Hebrew Bible) or the archeologist's use of carbon dating to identify the age of artifacts found in the Qumran caves (where the scrolls were found). These are examples of applying scientific concepts to the study of religion. One can choose to reject this sort of application for reasons of religious conviction but not on the grounds that the ideas are untranslatable.

Multiculturalists would also do well to heed this critique. Indeed, one of the most valuable criteria that might be employed in the selection of literature from non-Anglo sources for the curriculum could be their accessibility to the general public. The stories of Job and Boethius—who suffered despite their basic goodness—were written in cultural contexts very different from our own. But the problem of evil that they address affects us today and allows their stories to speak across time, place, language, and culture.[48]

Is Perception Determined by Framework Alone?

The claim that perception is determined by framework also offers a valuable insight that has been exaggerated. Of course our perceptions are influenced by the expectations we draw from our cultural, religious, linguistic, and intellectual frameworks. But from this it does not follow that these expectations determine what we see. To draw that conclusion, we would have to suppose that there were no other influences on our perceptions other than single frameworks such as religion, culture, or scientific discipline. But we all live within multiple frameworks, and experience many influences in the life of a day.

Suppose that there was no physical reality that imposed itself upon us, which seems more the fantasy of skeptical philosophers than the experience of daily life. There are nonetheless many factors that influence our perceptions including family background, psychological makeup, intellectual capacity, artistic talents, physical handicaps, gender, and sexual orientation. It is patently absurd to suppose that religion, culture, ideology, or academic training alone determine perception. From the idea that no observation is completely neutral, it does not follow that all evidence is completely determined by framework. Ontology—what we believe to be real—may be relative, but only in the weak sense that it is influenced, not determined, by perception.

Can Frameworks Be Criticized?

With regard to the immunity of frameworks from criticism, it is true that any conception of goodness must begin with some assumptions, and that these will be found within the confines of some framework or another. From this it does not follow that we cannot criticize one set of assumptions on the basis of another. This guts the very concept of criticism altogether. What could it possibly mean to criticize my views only on the basis of my own assumptions? Unless I contradict myself, my views will always pass muster.

Genuine criticism involves precisely what the critical immunity thesis precludes, testing my ideas against the criteria of alternative perspectives. To embrace this, I need not require an agreed upon neutral framework within which to judge all opposing views. I need only be willing to engage in a process of genuine dialogue with another point of view in order to enrich my own.[49] The possibility for such dialogue depends not on an agreement as to what such a neutral framework consists in, but merely on the idea that there is a higher good, at least in principle, and that our divergent views all seek to depict some aspect of it. To paraphrase Karl Popper, dialogue requires us to believe both in the possibility of truth and goodness and also in the proposition that no one has the truth in their pocket.[50]

Protecting religions, cultures, and intellectual traditions from criticism is not only impossible and unjustifiable; it is also undesirable. The results of confronting differing perspectives with one another are often fruitful and exhilarating. On the other hand, the consequences of isolating conceptual frameworks from competing points of view is stultifying and limiting. Conceptual protectionism of this kind ends not in open but closed societies, in which ideas are censored and freedom of expression thwarted. This leads away from the freedom of the Promised Land and back to the slavery of Egypt.

The bonds of solidarity constitute a significant, but not exclusive, location of goodness. It is not, after all, the perspective of the poor, the marginal, and the alienated that ought to be embraced. We require rather a conception of the good that views oppression and domination as unacceptable and that empowers us to resist it, both within our own consciousness and in society as a whole. To adopt such a perspective we need to avoid strong relativism and embrace fallibilism; we must be prepared to admit the possibility that our community's tradition could be wrong and another's right. This calls for faith in the possibility of a higher good, even if we disagree over its content. As opposed to the strong relativism of radical collectivism, let us embrace theologies that articulate visions of a higher good that transcend the parochial confines of particular communities and traditions even as they speak in the languages of those communities and traditions. Theologies of this kind accept the idea that every conception of the good worthy of the name ultimately attempts to give expression to the genuinely worthwhile.

That the Israelites became a "kingdom of priests and a holy nation" was not a consequence of any inherent merit they possessed. Rather, this distinction was contingent on the people faithfully obeying their covenant with God. In Hebrew, the word for holiness also means distinctive or set apart. What enabled this people to become holy—set apart, unique—was its ability to see beyond themselves, to recognize a divine hand in their salvation.

They came to understand that redemption depends neither on the self nor on the collective alone, but also on a vision of the good that transcends both. The question is: Can such a transcendent good be embraced without also succumbing to dangerous forms of dogmatism?

CHAPTER FIVE

Objective
Spirituality

When Moses had ascended the mountain, the cloud covered the mountain. . . . Moses went inside the cloud and ascended the mountain; and Moses remained on the mountain for forty days and forty nights. . . .

—Exodus 24:15–18

And let them make Me a sanctuary that I may dwell among them. . .

—Exodus 25:8

When Moses ascended Mount Sinai to receive the Ten Commandments, the people became restless and uncertain. Moses' God was abstract. The Israelites had seen the redemption, how plagues had been delivered upon the Egyptians, and how they had drowned while the Israelites crossed to freedom. But they had not seen God. They had no direct way of knowing that their deliverance was the result of divine intervention into history. So they turned to Aaron, Moses' brother whom God had appointed to be Moses' spokesperson, and they said, "Come, make us a god who shall go before us, for that man Moses, who brought us from the land of Egypt—we cannot tell what happened to him" (Exodus 32:1). In response, Aaron collected gold jewelry from the people and made it into a molten calf. When the people saw the calf, they cried, "This is your god, O Israel, who brought you forth from the land of Egypt" (Exodus 32:4).

When God and Moses became aware of these events, they became enraged. How could the people have so completely misunderstood the events that had led to their redemption as to think that a molten object could be the source of their salvation? God was so angry at this stiff-necked people that he laid plans to destroy them, and only relented upon Moses' plea. According to the Sages, it was the inability of the people to distinguish between the golden calf and genuine divinity that led to the building of the tabernacle in the wilderness. This holy sanctuary, and the ritual sacrifices that would take place within it, would symbolize God's presence among the people so they would not need to worship false gods. They would not worship a molten calf but would sacrifice a real calf to its Creator. Theological concepts such as God and goodness are abstract and lend themselves easily to misunderstanding. Symbols are also not precise forms of communication. Since they often take on an aura of holiness all their own, it is especially easy to confuse the symbol with that which it symbolizes.

This sort of confusion has often been found within a third conception of spirituality. Advocates of this orientation "locate" goodness in "objective" or outward existence. Rationalists, traditionalists, and people of many religious faiths sense a voice that calls from beyond inner or collective experience with a message of how we ought to live. Like transcendental subjective and collective spiritualists, objectivists believe in a reality—rationality, tradition, or God—that lies outside of themselves, their communities, and even the confines of space and time. They recognize a transcendent dimension to ethical vision, an ontological substance to the good, an "object" of their faith. However, because objectivists share an aversion to subjectivism and relativism, their path to the good life entails an emphasis on outward expression by means of rules, traditions, or rituals, even if it also involves inwardness or community.

This trend encompasses what might be thought of as the outward dimension of transcendental subjective and collective spiritualities, for example, those elements of kabbalistic and existentialist thought that understand public religious ritual as facilitating experiences that lead to the divine. However, this attitude also includes those who emphasize outwardness as the primary path to the good, even to the exclusion of inwardness and solidarity.

To clarify the problems and opportunities presented by this attitude, it will once again be useful to unravel two strands of thinking, one less extreme in its objectivism than the other. I refer to the less extreme case as "fallible objectivism."[1] People who embrace this position recognize the existence of a transcendent reality that is the source of ethical vision. Some call it "the Absolute." Paul Tillich called it "the ground of being."[2] But they also make a rigorous differentiation between that reality and the diverse ways in which it has been understood and depicted. They recognize the limits of human language and symbolic expression, and so assume the fallibility of any particular concrete representation of transcendence. Rather than retreating to what they perceive to be a false sense of certainty, they embrace doubt and openly question even the most sacred manifestations of this reality.

I refer to the more extreme cases of this orientation as "dogmatic objectivism." In this line of thinking, there is a tendency to treat spiritual vision as if it were an inanimate "object"—external fixed, unbending, essentially unmoved by the forces of history, and unresponsive to the emotional stresses and strains of inner life and communal consciousness. In the wake of the failure of modern morality, and in response to the dangers of radical subjectivism and collectivism, they seek a more "authentic," less compromising version of the good that offers clear and unambiguous guidelines for living. In a world clouded with ambiguity and dominated by rapid social and intellectual change, advocates of this approach seek security in that which is certain, eternal, unchanging.

Two claims can be differentiated within this attitude: (1) that there is an "object" of faith, an ontological reality or transcendental content to the good, and (2) that the spiritual quest ought to be represented outwardly in public, observable forms such as rules, texts, symbols, or rituals. These forms of representation are often poetic in that they capture aspects or characteristics of their subject matter through allusion, comparison, imagery, or metaphor. It is not always easy to separate the poetry from its subject matter, the symbol from the symbolized. Consequently, conceptions of the "object" of faith, or "content" of the good are often closely tied to the attitudes about the forms in which they are represented.

Fallible objectivists see the "content" of the higher good as dynamic and developing. Even when they refer to this "objective" dimension of spirituality as "Absolute" or "Ultimate," the intention is not to connote stasis or rigidity, which are limiting concepts, but rather endless or infinite growth, evolution, and fermentation. Additionally, they strive to differentiate between this "content" and depictions of it, for example, by understanding these representations as subject to human finitude, limitation, and fallibility. Dogmatic objectivists, on the other hand, tend toward a rigid view of the higher good, often represented in inflexible and infallible doctrines, texts, symbols, or rituals. They also embrace a closer tie between the higher good and its forms of representation, for example, understanding texts, symbols, and rituals to be the unambiguous expression of an unbending divine will.

Turning Outward

We will consider some historical examples of the tenets that unite fallible and dogmatic objectivists before we turn to illustrating their differences.

As we saw in the biblical story of the golden calf and the building of the tabernacle, the outward turn has deep roots in Hebrew Scripture. That the God of the Bible speaks from beyond this world is evident from the very first lines of Genesis, when God spoke and the world was created. The excruciating attention to the details of the tabernacle in Exodus and to sacrificial cult in Leviticus make clear that the external expression of ethical vision and relations with the divine are part and parcel of biblical religion.

Plato, too, understood the good to emanate from beyond worldly experience. This can be seen in his doctrine of ideal forms which holds that the material world is but a partial and shadowy instantiation of eternal forms or essences that exist in the realm of ideas. This doctrine is beautifully illustrated in Plato's well-known parable of the cave. The parable depicts people staring at images illuminated by a distant light on the wall of a cave. Someone finally follows that light to discover that what he had thought to be reality was but a shadow of a much clearer world that exists beyond the cave. This world outside the cave, according to Plato's parable, is the realm of ideas where true unchanging reality is to be found.[3] For Plato, the path to discovering this reality is not through religious ritual but through what he called dialectic, which entails following the rules of reason to their inevitable conclusion.[4]

Although they turned inward to discover the divine voice calling within, mystics such as Isaac Luria and John of the Cross placed a strong emphasis on religious ritual as a way to discipline the powerful and often dangerous urges captured in the kabbalistic tradition. Similarly, even though scholastics such as Maimonides and Aquinas conceived a role for the collective and its leadership in the cultivation of a good life, they also linked Platonic dialectic with the religious rituals defined in their respective scriptures as ways of externalizing the path to divine goodness.

Fallible Objectivism

Consider now three instances of fallible objectivism. The first draws on Israelite prophecy, the second on the Protestant existentialism of Paul Tillich, and the third on the Jewish existentialism of Franz Rosenzweig.[5]

Israelite Prophecy
Perhaps the earliest instances of fallible objectivism can be found in Israelite prophecy. For example, before the Temple in Jerusalem was destroyed by the Babylonians in 586 BCE, the prophet Isaiah (57:14–58:14) challenged the ritual practices of his day:

Cry aloud, hold nothing back; shout as loud as a *shofar* blast. Tell
my people their transgressions, tell the House of Jacob their
sins. . . . Behold, on the day of your fast you pursue business
as usual, and oppress your workers. Behold you fast only to
quarrel and fight, to deal wicked blows. Such fasting will not
make your voice audible on high.

Is this the fast I have chosen? Is this the affliction of the soul?
Is it to droop your head like a bulrush, to grovel in sackcloth
and ashes? Is that what you call fasting, a fast the Lord would
accept?

This is My chosen fast: to loosen all the bonds that bind men un-
fairly, to let the oppressed go free, to break every yoke. Share
your bread with the hungry, take the homeless into your home.
Clothe the naked when you see him, do not turn away from
people in need. Then cleansing light shall break forth like the
dawn, and your wounds shall soon be healed. Your triumph
shall go before you and the Lord's glory shall be your rearguard.
Then you shall call and the Lord will answer, you shall cry out
and He will say, here I am.

Clearly, the prophet experiences God as an "objective" reality,
who speaks to him from beyond the heavens. But the prophet
does not reject the role of ritual as is sometimes supposed by religious liberals and secularists. Much as Moses challenged the worship of a golden calf, Isaiah questions the atonement fast of his day.
Isaiah teaches that it is a mistake to suppose that these rituals will
magically produce atonement for sin. Rituals cannot atone for sin,
they can only lead us to take the steps required to repent. The task
of the fast, in Isaiah's view, is to teach solidarity with the poor and
the downtrodden, to inspire action, to motivate us to change the
world, beginning with ourselves. In other words, the purpose of
sacrificial *rites,* to cite Shalom Spiegel, is to teach us about basic
human *rights.*[6] To miss this point is to worship the ritual, just as the

Israelites worshipped the calf. Ritual has a teleological purpose; it teaches us how God intends for us to live and thereby leads us to discover a purpose to our existence. We were not created to perform ritual but to learn from it.

This view of ritual is consistent with a dynamic view of divinity that is found in the earliest stages of Israelite religion. When God sent Moses to confront Pharaoh, for instance, He said:

> I appeared to Abraham, Isaac, and Jacob as El Shaddai, but I did not make Myself known to them by My name YHWH. I also made My covenant with them. . . . I have now heard the moaning of the Israelites . . . and I have remembered My covenant. Say, therefore, to the Israelite people: I am YHWH. I will free you. . . . I will redeem you. . . . I will take you to be My people and I will be your God. (Exodus 6:2–7)

In the biblical mentality, a name often conveys essential information about the person or thing named. That God changes His name suggests that He is not static but responds and changes in relation to others. He related to the patriarchs in one way, and to their descendants in another. God adapts. We have already encountered two additional instances of God changing course in response to humans, Abraham at Sodom and Gomorrah (Genesis 18:16–33) and Moses after the incident of the golden calf (Exodus 32:9–14). Consider another case:

Korah led two hundred and fifty compatriots in rebelling against the leadership of his cousins Moses and Aaron. The rebels said to the leaders: "You have gone too far! For all the community are holy, all of them, and the Lord is in their midst. Why then do you raise yourselves above the Lord's congregation" (Numbers 16:3). Moses responded by saying, "Truly, it is against the Lord that you and all your company have banded together" (16:11). When the Lord finally appeared on the scene, He became enraged and said to Moses and Aaron, "Stand back from this community that I may annihilate them in an instant!" (16:21). But they fell on their faces to plead for mercy on behalf of the innocent. They said: "O God, Source of the breath of flesh! When one man sins, will You be wrathful with the whole community?" (16:22). So God relented, and punished only the rebels (16:23–25).[7] This God is not unbending but subject to influence based on the divine-human encounter.

Protestant Existentialism

Another example of fallibilism in objectivist spiritual thought can be found in Paul Tillich's Protestant theology. Tillich uses the term "faith" to capture the commitment to a vision of the good life we have been discussing. He conceives of faith as "the state of being ultimately concerned." The claim of ultimacy can be made in the name of a national group or a god. However, whatever the object of this concern, "if it claims ultimacy it demands the total surrender of him who accepts this claim, and it promises total fulfillment even if all other claims have to be subjected to it or rejected in its name."[8] Thus, he holds that faith as ultimate concern "happens at the center of the personal life and includes all of its elements."

> Faith is the most centered act of the human mind. It is not a movement of a special section or a special function of man's total being. They are united in the act of faith. But faith is not the sum total of their impacts. It transcends every special impact as well as the totality of them and it has itself a decisive impact on each of them.[9]

Tillich touches on the first aspect of objectivism—that there is an "object" of faith or ontological content to goodness—under the heading "the source of faith." As a "centered act of the personality," he points out, there is an objective meaning to faith. "The ultimate concern is concern about what is experienced as ultimate. . . . There is no faith without a content to which it is directed."[10]

This "objective" side of faith can be understood as the flip side of the "subjective" aspect of spirituality that we saw in Merton and the new Kabbalists. The term "ultimate concern," Tillich claims,

"unites the subjective and the objective side of the act of faith"—
"the faith through which one believes" and "the faith which is
believed." Tillich continues:

> In terms like ultimate, unconditional, infinite, absolute, the dif-
> ference between subjectivity and objectivity is overcome. The
> ultimate of the act of faith and the ultimate that is meant in the
> act of faith are one and the same. This is symbolically expressed
> by the mystics when they say that their knowledge of God is the
> knowledge that God has of himself. . . . In the act of faith that
> which is the source of this act is present beyond the cleavage be-
> tween subject and object. It is present as both and beyond both.[11]

He touches on the second aspect of objectivism—that the "object" of faith or goodness requires outward expression—by reference to "acts of faith." "There is no way of having the content of
faith except in the act of faith," Tillich explains, and this act is
expressed in symbols of the divine. "All speaking about divine
matters which is not done in the state of ultimate concern is meaningless. Because that which is meant in the act of faith cannot be
approached in any other way than through an act of faith."[12]
Religious rituals such as reciting a traditional liturgy or entering a
ritual bath are acts of faith; they are symbolic behaviors that enable us to express our ultimate concerns.

Even though Tillich anchors his analysis of faith in terms like
ultimate, unconditional, and absolute, he does not understand
faith to be contingent upon an unquestioning certainty. He claims,
rather, that "an act of faith is an act of a finite being who is grasped
by and turned to the infinite. It is a finite act with all the limitations of a finite act, and it is an act in which the infinite participates
beyond the limitations of a finite act."

> Faith is certain in so far as it is an experience of the holy. But
> faith is uncertain in so far as the infinite to which it is related
> is received by a finite being. This element in faith cannot be re-
> moved, it must be accepted. And the element in faith which

accepts this is courage. . . . In the courageous standing of uncertainty, faith shows most visibly its dynamic character.[13]

We can be certain of our subjective experience of faith, our passion toward that with which we are ultimately concerned. "But
there is not certainty of this kind about the content of our ultimate
concern, be it nation, success, a god, or the God of the Bible. . . .
their acceptance as matters of ultimate concern is a risk and therefore an act of courage."

The risk to faith in one's ultimate concern is indeed the greatest risk man can run. For if it proves to be failure, the meaning
of one's life breaks down; one surrenders oneself, including
truth and justice, to something which is not worth it. One has
given away one's personal center without having a chance to
regain it.[14]

And every risk entails doubt. "Faith includes courage. Therefore, it can include doubt about itself." This doubt is not that of the
skeptic or the scientist who questions whether a proposition is true
or false. It is rather an existential doubt that is aware of the element of insecurity in every existential truth.[15]

Tillich queries whether the doubt implicit in every act of faith is
incompatible with "a community which needs creedal expressions
of the concrete elements in its ultimate concern." He concludes
that communities that attribute "infallibility" to human interpretations of the content of faith become static and embrace a "non-
questioning surrender not only to the ultimate . . . but also to its
concrete elements as formulated by the religious authorities." We
must fight, Tillich argues, against the idolatrous implications of this
kind of static faith.

How can a faith which has doubt as an element within itself be
united with creedal statements of the community of faith? The
answer can only be that creedal expressions of the ultimate concern of a community must include their own criticism. It must

be obvious in all of them—be they liturgical, doctrinal or ethical expressions of the faith community—that they are not ultimate. Rather, their function is to point to the ultimate which is beyond all of them. This is what I call the "Protestant principle," the critical element in the expression of a community of faith and consequently the element of doubt in the act of faith.[16]

Jewish Existentialism

If the interdependence of faith and doubt is so closely tied to Protestantism as Tillich suggests, does this mean that his analysis of the risk of failure inherent in the act of faith applies only to Christianity? Does the obligation to observe God's commandments as finite law preclude traditional Jews from doubting whether the good can be discovered though religious observance? If we take seriously the thought of Franz Rosenzweig—an influential twentieth-century Jewish existentialist and colleague of Martin Buber—the answer appears to be no.

In a famous letter to Martin Buber, later published as an essay entitled "The Builders: Concerning the Law," Rosenzweig responds to Buber's opposition to ritual.[17] Recall that Buber opposed religious ritual as an expression of or a way to a spiritual vision of the good because he believed that it stifles the spontaneous element in I-Thou relations, transforming them into instrumental I-It associations. Rosenzweig praises Buber's philosophy of education. According to Buber the task of Jewish education is not to communicate knowledge inherent in some arbitrary conception of that which is essential to Judaism. Rather, it is to transform the learning (*Lernstoff*) of subject matter into a *teaching* (*Lehre*) that becomes a guidepost for living. The key to this transformation is Buber's concept of inner power.

This is what Buber demands when he asks the learner to stake his whole being on learning the subject matter at hand, "to make himself a link in the chain of tradition and thus become a chooser, not through his will but through his ability. We accept as teaching what enters us from out of the accumulated knowledge of the centuries."[18]

The way to teaching leads through what is "knowable." . . . But the teaching itself is not knowable. It is always something that is in the future, and he who asks for it today in his very question may offer a partial answer to be given to someone else tomorrow, and certainly affords the larger part of the answer to be given today to the questioner himself.[19]

This being the case, Rosenzweig asks Buber, should not the same analysis apply to observance of the law? Ritual practices, like knowledge, are not inherently meaningful. We cannot know when we first entertain the possibility of observing them whether they can become genuine guideposts for our lives. But, as is also the case with knowledge of a religious tradition, we can never sense whether they can become ours unless we first engage them by actually doing them. The educational task is to transform a subject matter to be learned into a teaching for life. Similarly, the spiritual task is to transform law (*Gesetz*) into commandment (*Gebot*), to infuse the external observance of the law with "inner power" so that we can hear God reaching out to us through His commandments.

Parker Palmer captured the essence of Rosenzweig's distinction between law and commandment when he wrote that "we often confuse authority with power, but the two are not the same. Power works from the outside in, but authority works from the inside out."[20] In Rosenzweig's view, laws are imposed upon us by means of the coercive tools of power, they are *enforced* by those with the ability to cause others to conform. Commandments, on the other hand, call to us with the authority of God's voice. The will to perform them emanates from a place deep within our souls where our true selves touch the divine.

And this effort to transform the law entails the very existential risk about which Tillich spoke—the risk of staking one's whole life on infusing the "law" with the inner power or authority of "commandment," only to discover that this represented the wrong path. This can only be overcome by the courage to take the risk of observing the law accompanied by a vigilant and ongoing questioning of whether that law is truly becoming a guidepost for a good life.

Rosenzweig holds that we must differentiate "between what can be stated about God and what can be experienced about God."

What can be stated objectively is only the very general formula "God exists." Experience, however, goes much further. . . . (I)t is incommunicable, and he who speaks of it makes himself ridiculous. Yet everyone knows that though unutterable it is not a self-delusion. . . . It is man's own experience—totally inexpressible—that is the fulfillment and realization of the utterable truth.[21]

For Rosenzweig, the way to discovering this inner truth is by embracing the outward performance of Jewish law. "The Law," he wrote, "is analogous to the wealth of experience." Only that experience is relevant which, in the act of being undergone, holds for him who is undergoing it.[22] In contrast to Merton and the Kabbalists, the path to transcendence begins not by turning inward. Rather, Rosenzweig would have us begin with outward performance of religious observance, and allow that experience to lead inward, toward God's gentle but commanding voice.

Thus, although little can be said directly of God, the relationship between humans and the divine is a dynamic one. "There are no rigid boundaries in this relationship," Rosenzweig wrote, "except the boundary between what can be expressed and what cannot be expressed." What can be expressed in traditional observance, "marks the beginning of our way," and in the immediacy of the "theo-human reality of the commandment"—the moment when people and God meet in religious observance. Even if we cannot "express" God, we can "address" God.[23]

This does not lead to doubting the existence or nature of God but to questioning whether the law of traditional Judaism is in fact that which God intended. In this connection, Rosenzweig wrote, "our doubt must be a genuine doubt, which willingly listens to reason and is as willing to be swayed to a 'yes' as to a 'no.'"[24] The only way to satisfy this doubt is through the courage to risk the possibility that God can indeed be found through the performance of Jewish law.

Dogmatic Objectivism

If fallible objectivism expresses the transcendental side of moderate subjective and collective spiritualities, dogmatic objectivism emphasizes outwardness at the expense of inwardness or solidarity. According to one such view—the fundamentalist or ultraorthodox approach—the source of goodness is the literal word of God. A second example places a traditional canon at the moral center, not as an evolving set of documents that respond to current needs but as a permanent set of texts, ideas, and questions representing fixed values. A third approach places scientific and logical reason at the center of the good life, not merely as a set of skills to be mastered but also as a character trait, ideal, or moral value. On the face of it, these views are more disparate than those collected under the headings of subjectivity and collectivism. Nevertheless, they share a tendency to rigidify the good, however they conceive it, to assume that it can be understood in terms of mechanical formulas, strict rules, and unambiguous certainties.

Ultraorthodoxy and Fundamentalism
People often turn to ultraorthodoxy and fundamentalism in a variety of faiths because they perceive the West to be in decline as a result of individualism and relativism. "The core of Western society can be expressed in one word," wrote one such person, "the individual. He is king. Whatever he likes, whatever is good for him, whatever he finds pleasurable, is the center of the Western value system."[25] Another points out:

> The Western world, once the bastion of religious civilization, under the influence of Enlightenment and the subsequent plethora of secular ideologies to which it gave birth, has slowly

been losing its own justification for existence. The crusading, temporal dogmas which once inspired the soul of Western man appear . . . to be running out of gas. No longer do peoples of America and Western Europe look forward toward . . . spreading the doctrines of secular democracy, progress, technology. . . . An alienated Moral relativism has descended upon the world.[26]

The ultraorthodox response to these challenges involves a total reversal of "failed" Enlightenment thinking, a complete rejection of modernity.

The ultraorthodox community, because of its rigidity and extremism, meets the . . . need for certainty and consistency. . . . (F)irmness and resoluteness in what is considered to be truth is more desirable than tolerance, openness, and balance. . . . (I)dentification with a dogmatic and rigid community, which has been unwilling to entertain compromise, is highly attractive. . . . It is an extreme movement, founded upon an absolute decision, worked out in a total way in the daily life of the individual who has undertaken it.[27]

Abraham Joshua Heschel described one aspect of this attitude as "religious behaviorism." It stresses, he wrote, "external compliance with the law and disregards the importance of inner devotion. It maintains that . . . there is only one way that the will of God need be fulfilled, namely outward action."[28] This often leads to an emphasis on punctilious ritual practice, and strict adherence to a rigid moral code.

Hayim Soloveitchik explains how the return to orthodoxy has contributed to this phenomenon. The Judaism of his youth, Soloveitchik says, was learned by imitation. One was initiated into the tradition by watching how one's parents, grandparents, and aunts and uncles practiced their faith. However, if one was not raised in a traditional household, observance had to be acquired by some other means.

A plethora of texts on ritual observance addressed to returning Jews have been published in recent decades. They emphasize measurement. How much, they ask, must one do to fulfill one's obligations according to God's law? If the law states that one must eat a measure of bread the size of an olive upon reciting the relevant blessing, precisely what size must that olive be? Returning Jews feel the need to establish traditional credentials lacking from their upbringing by proving that their observance fulfills the letter of the law. This lends itself to a religious competitiveness, where the more the observance, and the greater the precision, the greater the assumed spiritual connection to God.[29]

It is not that those who adhere to this sort of literalism completely eschew the inner and communal aspects of the spiritual life. Indeed, mystics of many faith traditions have made their way to fundamentalism. However, the quality of the spiritual life in this context is not evaluated in terms of its inner or communal "power" but by reference to strict acceptance of officially sanctioned doctrine and quantifiably stringent observance of religious and moral codes.

This sort of literalist attitude is found within several traditions. Christian fundamentalism, for example, is a conservative American Protestant movement that has battled the liberal influences of modernism since the late nineteenth century. The movement has emphasized as fundamental to Christianity the literal and absolute inerrancy of scripture, the imminent and physical second coming of Jesus Christ, the virgin birth, resurrection, and atonement. One distinguishing feature of fundamentalism has been its attempt to advance its literalist agenda in the public arena. In the 1920s fundamentalists opposed evolution because they believed that Darwin's views on the origins of life were irreconcilable with the Bible. Antievolution crusaders lobbied for legislation against the teaching of Darwin's theories in public schools. Tennessee passed such a statute. In 1925, John T. Scopes, a science teacher in the small town of Dayton, allowed himself to be used as a defendant against the charge of having taught evolution.

In the 1970s creationists campaigned for the teaching of Genesis whenever evolution was taught in the public schools. This was followed by an attempt to mandate the teaching of "creation science" in public schools as an alternative scientific paradigm to evolution. During this period, the Moral Majority emerged under the leadership of Baptist minister Jerry Falwell. As a fundamentalist citizens organization, the Moral Majority crusaded against a variety of political initiatives that, in its view, contradicted scripture. These included legalized abortion, homosexual rights, and the women's equal rights amendment.[30]

Islamic fundamentalists not only understand their reading of sacred scripture as expressing God's unambiguous intentions, they also interpret authenticity and piety in terms of extreme, measurable stringency. Strict adherence to the religious dictates of the Koran and uncompromising commitment to its moral code are the touchstones of this fundamentalist legacy.

Traditionalism as Objective Spirituality
Another example of this sort of rigid thinking emphasizes the role of tradition in the quest for goodness. According to this view, tradition is contained in a clearly circumscribed body of texts—a "classical" canon of definitive documents. The good life is to be discovered through studying these texts and practicing their teachings. In extreme cases, both the texts of the canon and the meanings attributed to them become somewhat rigid.

One instance of this line of thinking is found within the so-called Great Books tradition in American higher education. This movement began under the leadership of Robert Maynard Hutchins[31] and his colleague Moritmer Adler[32] at the University of Chicago in the 1930s. It was based on a critique of pragmatism and progressivism in American educational and spiritual life. Hutchins rejected the narrow vocational view of education attributed to the progressives, arguing instead that its task was to introduce people to a vision of the good life. This life was to be discovered, he argued, in the study of the classical works of Western civilization. Reading these classics would initiate the student into what he called the "great conversation" about fundamental values, and enable the student to make critical life-choices based on a rich historical tradition. Participation in this conversation—reading and discussing the Great Books—was the very heart of the good life as Hutchins saw it. Education, in this view, entails a lifelong pursuit of the good through engagement with this classical tradition.

So far so good, but the list of books, and hence topics, questions, perspectives, and subject matters, that could be included in this canon became rigid. There were, it was argued, essentially only one hundred Great Books that must be read for a person to be properly initiated into this tradition. Alternative works such as those that allowed the perspectives of women or people of color into the conversation were not considered. Nor was there room for changing the list due to recent developments in the arts, humanities, or sciences. To be educated, and have any chance at a genuine spiritual life, it was *this* conversation that must be entered and *these* books that must be read.³³

The revival of this tradition in the 1980s is indicative of the search for stability in a world overrun by subjectivism and relativism. In his best-seller *The Closing of the American Mind* Alan Bloom notes with consternation this pervasive belief in relativism:

There is one thing a professor can be absolutely certain of: almost every student entering the university believes, or says he believes, that truth is relative. . . . The relativity of truth is not a theoretical insight but a moral postulate, the condition of a free society . . . the modern replacement for the inalienable natural rights that used to be the traditional American grounds for a free society.³⁴

The danger they have been taught to fear, Bloom continues, is not error, but intolerance and absolutism—and the fear of absolutism results in the elevation of relativism into an absolute virtue. Relativism, Bloom notes with disdain, "is necessary for openness;

and this is the virtue, the only virtue, which all primary education for more than fifty years has dedicated itself to inculcating."

> Openness—and the relativism that makes it the only plausible stance in the face of various claims to truth and various ways of life and kinds of human beings—is the great insight of our times. The true believer is the real danger. The study of history and of culture teaches that all the world was mad in the past; men always thought they were right, and that led to wars, persecutions, slavery, xenophobia, racism, chauvinism. *The point is not to correct the mistakes and really be right; rather it is not to think that you are right at all.*[35]

Bloom reviews both a history of the modern American university and current alternatives in the undergraduate curriculum. He then notes that "the only serious solution is one that is almost universally rejected: the good old Great Books approach in which liberal education means reading certain generally recognized classic texts, just reading them." This is not to say that questions and inquiry are unimportant. However, the content and form of questions to be encouraged are to be drawn from the texts themselves. Let the texts "dictate what the questions are and the method of approaching them." We should not force them into "categories we make up," or treat them as "historical products" but should try to read them "as their authors wished to be read."[36] Bloom concludes:

> The real community of man is the community of those who seek the truth, the potential knowers, that is, in principle all men to the extent that they desire to know. But in fact, this includes only a few, the true friends, as Plato was to Aristotle. . . . Their common concern for the good linked them. . . . They were absolutely one soul as they looked at the problem. This according to Plato, is the only real basis for friendship . . . . The other kinds of relatedness are only imperfect reflections of this one . . .

gaining their only justification from their ultimate relation to this one.[37]

Scientism as Objective Spirituality

A third, less obvious, example of this tendency claims that, in an era when people are searching for values, the rationality of science and formal logic must be recognized as the ultimate source of value and moral virtue. When coupled with a simplistic view of science or logic, the result is an uncritical, dogmatic form of rationalism. Some call it "scientism."[38] It is not a genuinely scientific perspective but a tendency to place blind faith in a caricature of science. M. Scott Peck calls this "the religion of science." Scientists sometimes suffer, he points out, "from a kind of tunnel vision, a . . . self-imposed psychological set of blinders which prevents them from turning their attention to the realm of spirit."[39] Peck considers it to be "a mark of maturity in scientists," if they are aware, "that science may be as subject to dogmatism as any other religion."[40] Mechanical thinking rarely brings out the best in either science or religion. "[J]ust as it is essential that our sight not be crippled by scientific tunnel vision," Peck continues, "so also is it essential that our critical faculties and capacity for skepticism not be blinded by the brilliant beauty of the spiritual realm."[41]

I once had a student who was a science teacher. When I introduced the concept of indoctrination, she was quick to point out that science instruction was always nonindoctrinary because of its reliance on evidence, whereas the inculcation of religion was the classic case of indoctrination because the doctrines it called us to believe could not be proved. If more people could learn to think like scientists, she claimed, we could solve many of the world's problems and lead better lives. The good life was to be discovered, in her view, in the dynamics of scientific inquiry alone. She was surprised when I pointed out that whether or not something is an instance of indoctrination depends less on whether the subject matter is science or religion and more on whether the subject matter in question is taught so as to enable understanding, encourage intelligent decision-making, and recognize fallibility.

Outwardness Defended

Just as the good life requires subjective and communal components, it also depends upon a vision emanating from beyond the
self and the community. Indeed, our critique of subjectivism and
relativism rests on the need for a transcendent dimension in the
quest for the good life. The arguments in favor of a transcendent
dimension in moral discourse follow the arguments against radical subjectivism and relativism. In their extreme forms, both of
these undermine freedom, critical thinking, and fallibility because
the ideas they represent are incoherent. If we are not to fall prey
to these quagmires, we need to approach the inner life and the
community as pathways to a value and vision that lie far beyond
them. Without a sense of the transcendent, we can never move beyond the limitations of our own individual or collective conceptions
of the good to a vision that is more reliable and less muddled.

Despite the problematic nature of postmodern, subjectivist and
neo-Marxist, relativist attacks on objectivity, these critiques have
left a chink in the armor of objectivism. If there is an objective basis
for moral judgments to which we are to appeal in our spiritual
journey, where is it and why is there so much disagreement about
it? Clearly, this is because each of us can only view life through the
prism of his or her own experience, which will always be colored
by the lenses of culture, language, history, and environment.
There is no neutral vantage point from which to look down without bias upon proposed moral theories. If there is a transcendent
higher good which all visions endeavor to emulate, we cannot
agree on what it is.

This leaves us in a bind. We cannot overcome the difficulties of
radical subjectivism and relativism without a transcendent vision,
yet the postmodern and neo-Marxist critiques appear to render
this intellectually impossible. Tillich called the anxiety that results
from this untenable situation "spiritual" or "existential" despair.[42]
To overcome this impasse requires faith communities that nurture
visions of a higher good. Without the idea that something lies beyond our own limited perspective, there is no reason to hope for

an improved life or to strive for a better tomorrow.[43] To use the kabbalistic imagery, to discover purpose in life we require the dream that our fractured world can be repaired, that we can make a difference, that the universe can be made whole once again, re-united with its Creator and reawakened to the majesty and splendor of creation.

It is the possibility that there may be a better way, or a more complete picture, that motivates us to challenge our current circumstances and to strike out on new and uncharted paths. Yet not only do we dream of improving our own lives and the lives of others, we occasionally even realize those dreams. This can only happen when we speak openly and communicate with others about those dreams, when we express our faith in a higher good in forms that enable it to be grasped by others. There is no one fixed way to communicate ideas and feelings having to do with transcendence. As we give voice and shape to our hopes and aspirations, the images, metaphors, rituals, and explanations in which we express them will surely grow and develop. Our conceptions of spirituality may become more refined or change; and transcendence itself may evolve. But without a community of meaning and memory in which to share ideas and images of that which lies beyond us, and without the outward tools with which to communicate within that context, our images are likely to become stale and our ability to transform dreams into reality frustrated.

Kant called the transcendent motivator of hopes and dreams, and the initiator of evolution in how we express them, a "regulative principle." It calls us to have faith in a higher good which (or who) enables us to engage in conversation about moral vision and to strive to actualize it in our lives, even if we disagree over its nature and content. The problem with outward spirituality, then, lies not in its effort to seek a picture of a larger whole that lies beyond the self and the community, whether in God, tradition, or reason. The danger lies in the tendency toward a dogmatic view of that transcendent whole which *is* subject to the postmodern and neo-Marxist critique. In other words, fallible objectivism is more compelling than its dogmatic counterpart. It is dogmatic and not fallible objectivism that renders ethical discourse meaningless.

The Ethics of Objectivity

Advocates of dogmatic objectivism have made an important contribution to the current spiritual revival by bringing into public view the dangers of radical relativism and subjectivism that flow naturally from the Enlightenment project. And there is much to be admired in their call for renewed commitment to clear and unambiguous moral rules, texts, and teachings. However, in the search for clarity and certainty, their solutions become as problematic as the dangers they decry. Since the three examples we have considered are so disparate, we will evaluate the moral viability of each separately asking whether and to what extent these are consistent with the conditions of ethical discourse: critical intelligence, freedom, and fallibility.

When Religion Becomes Dogmatic

Unquestioning devotion to the unambiguous word of God is problematic. To be sure, there is nobility to the deep spiritual passion, grandeur to the total dedication, and sweetness to the naive faith inherent in this sort of holistic piety. Moreover, of the three cases of dogmatism we have been discussing, religious extremists have been the most strident in their critique of subjectivism and relativism. Nevertheless, fundamentalism and ultraorthodoxy do not offer a promising medicine for the moral disease of our age; for by rejecting the achievements of free society, these doctrines fail to resolve the moral crisis of modernism.[44]

Afraid of external influences and unwilling to allow questions, those who adopt these views tend to rule by total submission of mind and will rather than by intelligent choice. Power over the follower's life is often given to charismatic or "infallible" leaders who presume to represent the unbending will of God. In the name of dogmatic morality, these leaders undermine the intelligence, free will, and fallibility of their followers. This can result in a mechanized, routinized way of life in which the uniqueness of each person is diminished in favor of rigid uniformity. It can also lead to insularity, chauvinism, and xenophobia that limit concern for those who are different and to a flight from moral responsibility that calls for the performance of travesties in the name of a false sense of impending salvation.

When coupled with political aspirations, this sort of religious extremism has serious consequences. Among Moslems the combination of religious and political extremism has led to an emphasis on *jihad* or holy war and to the elevation to hero status of suicide bombers and others who take innocent lives in order to further an Islamic-nationalist agenda. Christian fundamentalists have also embraced violence—such as the bombing of abortion clinics—on the ground that it results in holy ends. Nor have ultra-orthodox Jews been immune from the use of force against those who oppose their views—witness the pillaging of innocent Moslem worshipers in the ancient city of Hebron or the assassination of Israeli prime minister Yitzhak Rabin by Jewish religious nationalists. This trail of bloodshed is not a necessary consequence of religious extremism, but it is, unfortunately, an all too common one.

The claim of the religious right—the American "Moral Majority" or the Israeli ultraorthodox—to moral and spiritual superiority over secular humanism is unfounded, therefore, not because religious beliefs are false but because, like narcissistic secularism, religious extremism makes no sense. Representatives of the religious right claim to offer an ethical vision, but when subjected to careful scrutiny it becomes clear that they adhere to assumptions that undermine the very possibility of ethical discourse. Whether or not the followers of Jerry Falwell are a majority in the United States is an empirical question, but in no sense can they be said to be a *moral* majority since the views they espouse tend to deny the fundamental importance of moral agency. Similarly, the ultra-orthodox claim that Israeli secularism lacks values to teach its children, however accurate, is a bit like the pot calling the kettle black, since ultraorthodoxy tends to reject the very assumptions that enable values and moral norms to make sense altogether.[45]

These are not the Israelites liberated from bondage, or the self-conscious moral agents of democratic society. The ten spies were afraid to put their trust in God. As a result, they were left with little trust in themselves. Religious extremists begin with too little trust in themselves, which ultimately leads to estrangement from God. They are afraid to risk the insecurity of freedom that enables self-confidence born of achievement. In place of the spirituality of freedom, they prefer the emptiness of slavery, which is not the life the biblical God calls them to lead.[46] Unfortunately, the public too readily associates this sort of extremism with the whole of institutionalized religion, when it in fact represents only a small minority. People consequently search for spirituality outside of organized religion, when answers may be waiting in nearby churches and synagogues of a more moderate mentality.

When Tradition Becomes Dogmatic

Similar criticism can be levied against an unbending view of tradition, whether legal, literary, religious, or ethical. If tradition cannot be questioned, if it is infallible—or the canon unassailable—then intelligence and free will are undermined. Tradition, rather than God, forces my hand and requires me to believe or behave, or to read and discuss, in accordance with its rigid demands. This mechanical form of decision-making limits rather than enhances moral possibilities.

Absolute Truths, another of Susan Howatch's novels about the Church of England, tells the story of Charles Ashworth, bishop of Starbridge. Charles is an unbending traditionalist. His opposition to extramarital sexual relations is so well known that Cambridge undergraduates call him "anti-sex Ashworth." He becomes a leading spokesman for the Church's uncompromising opposition to the new sexual morality of the sixties.

Ashworth's sexual attitudes were forged by an experience as a young canon. He was sent to investigate Alexander Jardin, a married bishop who had become convinced that taking an adulterous second "wife"—Lyle—was preferable to divorcing his first. Ashworth rescues Lyle from the affair. The two are then married, and when she give's birth to Jardin's son Ashworth adopts the lad, naming him Charlie, for himself. Ashworth believes that his adopted son is his divine reward for rescuing Lyle, which gives him the right to control Charlie's destiny. A second son, Michael, follows who becomes jealous of the attention Ashworth lavishes on the older half-brother.

Yet Charlie does not enjoy this attention. Although he is not told of the adoption until his late twenties, Charlie senses that he is different from his younger brother. Whereas Michael follows his own rules, the older brother feels that he must meet Ashworth's exacting demands. When Charlie finally learns of his true father, he becomes insecure and petrified of being abandoned by the only family he has known. Rather than becoming his own person, he conforms to his adopted father's expectations. Michael, on the other hand, secure in his father's love but still jealous of his older brother, seeks his father's attention through a variety of very public sexual liaisons.

Lyle dies, and in her diary Ashworth learns that his rigid adherence to "absolute truths" is injuring his sons. Charlie is insecure and afraid, due to Ashworth's uncompromising understanding of reward and punishment. Michael is angry and estranged, due to his father's unbending dedication to the Church's sexual morality. Ashworth's family is in shambles because of his arrogant adherence to tradition, his unwillingness to consider the possibility that he might be wrong, his insistence on understanding morality in terms of rigid rules rather than as a basis for intelligent judgment. To demonstrate his love for Michael or to allow Charlie the freedom he requires, Ashworth needs to approach morality more intelligently and less mechanically.[47]

When Science Becomes Dogmatic

When people place uncritical faith in scientific research methodologies to discover truth, and in rational discourse to articulate
their vision of the good, they ultimately limit the intelligence and
free will of the moral agent by denying the possible fallibility of scientific or rational method.[48] Rationality, on this account, becomes
a dogmatic caricature of science and logic. Rather than understanding them as tools to serve ends greater than themselves, empirical and a priori reasoning are transformed into objects of worship and devotion. Instead of serving as checks on our conceptions
of the good, helping to distinguish between that which is more and
less worthwhile, reasoning is misconceived as an end in itself.

When taken to an extreme, rationality can become dogmatic and
unintelligent. If my beliefs or behavior are necessary consequences
of premises that I take to be absolute, they cannot be wrong. I am
forced by the demands of science or logic to behave and believe in
this way. Refusing to do so would be heresy, a matter of ignorance
or irrationality, but not of judgment. On this account, choosing rational belief and behavior is not an intelligent but a mechanical act.
The choice is not based on the exercise of intelligent judgment but
determined by the *force* of reason that compels me to behave and
believe rationally. Michael Crozier called this "the arrogance of
reason"; Reinhold Niebuhr called it "pride of the intellect," which is
derived from "ignorance of the finiteness of the human mind."[49]

"Why," writes Robert Nozick, "are philosophers intent on forcing others to believe things. Is this a nice way to behave toward
someone?"

> I think we cannot improve people that way—the means frus-
> trate the ends. . . . A person is not most improved by being
> forced to believe something against his will, whether he wants
> to or not. The valuable person cannot be fashioned by commit-
> ting philosophy upon him.[50]

Nor can the valuable person be fashioned by committing science, or logic, or any other sort of reasoning upon him. People can only become better if the possibility of doing so is sustained by embracing the conditions of ethical discourse. Moral decisions are contingent, not necessary. They could always be otherwise. We must be careful not to adopt too rigid a view of the role that rationality plays in moral decision-making and to recall that for a decision to be an ethical one, a moral agent must exercise intelligent rather than mechanical judgment. Reasons are rarely if ever as definitive as a rigid view of rationality would have it, and most conclusions, whether descriptive or prescriptive, require a large dose of judgment that renders them more intelligent than mechanical.

Toward Integrated Personalities

If radical subjectivism and collectivism might be seen as representing the romantic side of the affective-cognitive split, dogmatic objectivism tends to embrace its rational side, sometimes in surprising ways. Probably the most influential instance of this rational tendency in the twentieth century has been a philosophical movement known as "positivism." According to this view, the most stubborn problems of philosophy such as the existence of God, the nature of the soul, the demands of ethics, and the possibility of knowledge can be reduced to problems of scientific thinking or formal logic.[51] The criteria against which all truth should be judged is either the empirical verification of scientific method or the a priori reasoning of logical analysis. If God's existence cannot be demonstrated empirically or logically, then not only does intellectual integrity demand that we reject religious faith, but the very meaning of the concept of divinity is called to question. If the existence of the soul, or the psyche, or the mind cannot be verified, then its study is not truth preserving science but pseudo-science—an unreliable impostor. If ethical claims cannot be empirically verified or logically demonstrated, they must be matters of mere emotions and unreliable subjectivity.[52]

It is easy to see how scientism is influenced by this trend. The connection of traditionalism and fundamentalism to positivism is less apparent. On the one hand, both of these attitudes recoil at the progressive consequences of positivism such as its willingness to abandon the religious convictions of the past if they fail to meet rigorous rational criteria. Traditionalism and fundamentalism tend, instead, to embrace a nostalgic, romantic view of the past. On the other hand, if we look closely at these attitudes we can see that they attempt to repel the consequences of positivism not by highlighting pure feeling or nonrational political power, but by incorporating pseudo-scientific rigor in the form of rigidity within their own value frameworks. They become more "positivist" than the positivists. Their starting point, however, is not the scientific world of space, time, and logic, but the worlds of tradition and faith. Once one has passed the threshold of a particular canonical or religious community, there is a kind of relentless logic that grabs hold and won't let gò. There is a rigorous and mechanistic flavor to the return to tradition and faith. However romantic and nostalgic this return may be, it nonetheless shows signs of strong positivist influence with dogmatic leanings.[53]

But, the good life is found neither in radical relativism, extreme subjectivism, or dogmatic objectivism. These accounts leave us locked in the dialectic between rationalism and romanticism, between reasoned or rigid conclusions and emotionally motivated actions. This Enlightenment dichotomy results in a deeply conflicted personality that is divided against itself, with thoughts, feelings, and actions at war with one another.

The spiritual task is to become people who are integrated rather than conflicted. Of course, emotions influence actions, but feelings and behavior can also be thoughtfully disciplined. Only the integrated personality can lead a good life on any adequate account of the good, because the very idea of goodness requires that we imbue emotion and activity with intelligence in order to generate moral choices that lead us to follow ethical ideals. In short, we require softer versions of all three "locations" of goodness combined, so that each can be tempered by the others. Subjective feeling must give way to communal consciousness, which in turn must be grounded in a fallible form of transcendence—a nondogmatic higher good—that embraces the possibility of criticism.[54]

When God commanded Moses to build a sanctuary in the wilderness, he offered a reason. "Let them build me a sanctuary *that I may dwell among them*" (Exodus 25:8). The point of the sanctuary was to enable the Israelites to discover God's vision of how to live. The text here is intentionally ambiguous. The Hebrew for "among them" in this context also means "within them." God is to dwell both among the people as a whole and also within the individual members of the Israelite community. The building of a sanctuary allowed the Israelites to respond to the spiritual crisis brought on by the building of a golden calf. To meaningfully address the spiritual crisis of our time we too need to build sanctuaries that will enable us to discover our best selves in communities that embrace transcendent visions of the good. The question is: Who will pray in them, in what sorts of communities will they reside, and what sort of God will be worshiped within?

CHAPTER SIX

Intelligent Spirituality

There is a people that dwells apart, not reckoned among [that does not conspire against] the nations . . . . How fair [goodly] are your tents, O Jacob, your dwellings, O Israel.

—Numbers 23:9–10, 24:5

You shall not hate your kinsman in your heart. . . . Love your neighbor as yourself. . . . . The stranger that resides with you shall be to you as one of your citizens; you shall love him as yourself; for you were strangers in the land of Egypt, I am the Lord your God.

—Leviticus 19:17–18, 33–34

In the last stage of their journey to the Promised Land, the Israelites camped on the border of Moab, which filled its king, Balak, with dread. He summoned the prophet Balaam to curse the Israelites, hoping that this would prevent his people from defeat. Balaam insisted that he had the power only to bless those whom God viewed as blessed and to curse those whom God wanted cursed. When he finally lifted his voice, he offered a blessing: "There is a people that dwells apart, not reckoned among [that does not conspire against] the nations. . . . How fair [goodly] are your tents, O Jacob, your dwellings, O Israel" (Numbers 23:9, 24:5).

These words capture the three ingredients of a conception of the good life that remain from our discussion in Chapter 2. In addition to being ethical, we said that a conception of the good life must also be holistic, pragmatic, and synthetic. People that share a vision of goodness "dwell apart" from others by virtue of their common commitment to it. Ethical vision is also pragmatic; it saturates our beings in the "tents" and "dwellings" of our communities through the daily practice of virtue.

However, if we become so different from one another that our distinctions become divisive, that we "conspire against" those who do not share our views, then we deny the moral agency of others. This is why the Hebrew Bible distinguishes between the obligation to "love one's neighbor" (Leviticus 19:18) and to "love the stranger" (Leviticus 19:34). It is natural to feel affection for those whose values I share; but it is easy to despise the person who does not see things my way, who "dwells apart" from my crowd. Goodness requires that we respect views different from our own, provided our humanity is recognized as well.

In other words, ethical vision is not only *holistic* and *pragmatic*, but also *synthetic;* it enables creative interaction with those who are different, as long as they embrace the conditions of ethical discourse. Unfortunately, today's most influential conceptions of spirituality contradict these conditions, which results in enslavement to caprice or dogmatism, rather than in the free choices characteristic of open society. Our current spiritual crisis requires that we "locate" ideals neither inside of us, nor between us, nor beyond us, but in the integration of all three.

This calls for *intelligent* spirituality which entails discovering ourselves in learning communities devoted to a higher good. The intelligent core of goodness enables the exercise of freedom by making choices meaningful; and this allows the dichotomies of modernism to be left behind without undermining democracy. Let us return to the remaining criteria of goodness: holism, pragmatism, and synthesis, to see why this is so.

Whole Choices

A wise person once said: "You can give someone a choice between an apple and orange, but if she has tasted neither an apple nor an orange, she will not be able to make a very informed choice." All understanding is limited, but to participate in only part of a communal existence—to observe a few rituals, use a phrase or two in the language, occasionally read a story or appreciate a work of art or musical performance once in a while—is to be impoverished. The more we are involved with a community, the greater our capacity to gain insight into its form of life and to make informed choices concerning whether this way is right for us. This is why a conception of the good needs to be holistic, to offer a whole, integrated life, that enables the possibility of intelligent moral choice.

One such conception advocates acquiring *authentic identities* in *learning communities* that teach *visions of a higher good*. This view embraces the ethical conditions of freedom, critical intelligence, and fallibilism. It also moves beyond the Enlightenment dichotomy between rationalism and romanticism by blending the positive aspects of subjectivism, relativism, and objectivism. "Authentic identity" constitutes the inward dimension of spirituality. Concern for solidarity is expressed in the notion of "learning communities." The need for looking beyond self and society is addressed in terms of "visions of a higher good."

Authentic Identity

In contrast to the narcissism that is the darker consequence of the Enlightenment mentality, Charles Taylor suggests that modern individualism can offer a higher ideal. Narcissism tends to an incoherent subjectivism that aims for fulfillment of self, "neglecting or delegitimating the demands that come from beyond our own

desires or aspirations."[1] This leads to affiliations that are strictly instrumental and to disintegration of common grounds for collective
living and communication.

However, individualism need not lead to this centering on the
self. Following Lionel Trilling, Taylor uses the term "authenticity"
to denote an alternative ideal.[2] He argues that I can define a stand-
point for myself that is not trivial, "only against the background of
things that matter . . . only if I exist in a world in which history,
or the demands of nature, or the needs of my fellow beings, or the
duties of citizenship, or the call of God, or something else of this
order . . . matters crucially."[3] Authenticity teaches that "there is a
certain way of being that is *my* way. I am called upon to live my
life in this way, and not in imitation of anyone else's."[4] But, this "is
not the enemy of demands that emanate from beyond the self; it
presupposes such demands."[5]

The old rebbe Zusia is said to have been found crying on his
deathbed. When his students inquired why he was crying, he responded that he was worried about what he would be asked when
he met his maker. "I will not be asked why I was not a better
Moses," Zusia told his students. "To this I might have an answer. I
will be asked, instead, why I was not a better Zusia. And to this I
have no response."

Learning Community

Authentic identity—the sort that centers not on the self but on being
the best that one can be—requires a conception of goodness that
emanates from beyond the self. One source is what we will call
learning community. To understand this idea we need three distinctions: between (1) unintelligent and intelligent behavior and belief, (2) training and teaching, and (3) mechanical and genuine
learning.

Unintelligent behaviors and beliefs are mechanical. To do or believe them we need not form intentions, make decisions, attribute
or interpret meaning, or draw conclusions. On the other hand,

intelligent behaviors and beliefs require us to do one or more of these mental acts. Our hearts beat mechanically but feelings of love or anguish require interpretation and understanding. Spelling is routine, writing poetry intelligent.

We train people to behave and believe mechanically but teach them to do so intelligently. We train students to count but teach them to do algebra; we train them to recite the alphabet but teach them to read. Teaching, in other words, always involves mental activity. It requires an attempt to communicate understanding to a student. Teaching entails intelligence.

Mechanical or rote learning is generally accomplished by means of training. Genuine learning, on the other hand, requires the sort of understanding associated with teaching. For this reason, teaching and learning *always involve* the risk of failure. The student can miss the point. If she chooses not to learn, or lacks sufficient preparation or capacity, she can get it wrong. Teaching and genuine learning entail the possibility of criticism.[6]

Teaching and Learning as Moral Activities
Because teaching involves understanding, it reinforces the intelligence and fallibility required for ethical discourse. Teaching, then, is a moral activity, not in the sense that it entails endorsing a particular doctrine, but in the sense that it strengthens the moral agent within, empowering students to make moral choices more intelligently on their own. Genuine learning is likewise a moral activity; it entails acquiring the skills necessary for moral agency.

In contrast, training is a-moral; it is mechanical and does not entail the sort of understanding necessary for moral discourse. The line between teaching and training is not always easy to discern. Teaching often relies on prior training in order to achieve the desired understanding. To do algebra, one must be able to count; to read, one must know the alphabet. When training leads to teaching, it participates in the process of moral development. However, if training continues when teaching is in order, it is sometimes called indoctrination. Instead of empowering students to act independently on the basis of their own understandings, we promote mechanical responses. This thwarts the process of moral development because it undermines the capacity of students to act as moral agents and renders ethical discourse meaningless.[7]

Community, Morality, and Meaning
Since understanding requires context, genuine learning and teaching must take place within frameworks that provide it. These are often called *learning communities*. Lee S. Shulman suggests that communities such as these often share the following characteristics: (1) The subject matter studied is generative; it generates new understandings. (2) The learning is active through experimentation and inquiry, writing, dialogue, and questioning. (3) Learners can become reflective about why their way of thinking and practice is desirable. (4) There is collaboration among learners and between learners and teachers. And, (5) the processes of activity, reflection, and collaboration are nurtured within a community that values such experiences and creates opportunities for them to occur.[8]

Learning communities teach scientific, artistic, literary, or religious disciplines; ethnic, national, or cultural values; or gender-related or sexual lifestyle commitments. However, they share a commitment to intelligent understanding, to distinguishing between ways of believing and behaving that are preferred and non-preferred, better and worse, desirable and undesirable. It follows that learning communities are always moral communities—because they offer contexts in which ethical discourse makes sense—and that authentic identity is found in learning communities—because they provide standards to judge who the better me can be. Robert Bellah and his colleagues describe this sort of community:

> Communities . . . have a history—in an important sense they are constituted by their past—and for this reason we speak of a real community as a "community of memory," one that does not forget its past. In order not to forget that past, a community is involved in retelling its story, its constituent narrative, and

in doing so it offers examples of men and women who have embodied and exemplified the meaning of the community. . . . The
stories that make up a tradition contain conceptions of character, of what a good person is like, and virtues that define such
a character. . . . If the community is completely honest, it will
remember stories not only of suffering received but of suffering
inflicted—dangerous memories, for they call the community to
alter ancient evils. The communities of memory that tie us to
the past also turn us toward the future as communities of hope.
They carry the context of meaning that allow us to connect our
aspirations for ourselves and those close to us with the aspirations of a larger whole and see our own efforts as being, in part,
contributions to a common good.[9]

Morality and meaning, however, cannot be self-centered. They
must be about us, not only about me, about how we as moral agents
relate to one another in the context of community. Whatever else
they teach, then, learning communities must embrace some form
of relational ethics. This involves caring for those within my community as well as those beyond it. This is sometimes called an ethic
of "care" or "relation."[10]

It is the imperative to care for people and ideals that forms the
foundation of a meaningful life. If meaning in general requires
public rules, then meaning in life requires concern for that which
lies outside of me; and if a meaningful life is one that has purpose,
then caring for others or for collective ideals is one of life's intrinsic ends. However, if this ethic is not to fall prey to unacceptable
forms of subjectivism or relativism, it needs to be part of a grander
scheme, one that transcends not only the self but the community
as well.

A Higher Good

Philip Phenix understands transcendence as "the experience of
limitless going beyond any given state or realization of being."[11]
According to Phenix, transcendence is inherent in the very nature

of consciousness. Built into our experiences of time, place, and value is a recognition that our own perspective is necessarily limited. There is always another time, a broader place, and a better formulation of an idea. Transcendence is the wellspring of hope and creativity because it leaves open the possibility that there is always another, better way to consider any possible situation.

There is a natural tendency to believe that our own moral and religious convictions are based on some sort of bedrock, some absolute good or ultimate truth in the dogmatic sense. John Dewey called this tendency the "quest for certainty."[12] Yet, believing that one has discovered the absolute truth or ultimate good in this limiting sense closes off the possibility of something better that is an outgrowth of our own creativity. This suppresses doubt and undermines intelligent questioning. The quest for transcendence need not reject doubt; however, it can embrace and encourage it. To see the possibility of that which lies beyond, I must be willing to doubt and question that which lies at hand. Transcendence need not be the partner of restriction; it can be the handmaiden of possibility.[13] I therefore prefer to speak of a *higher*—rather than an *absolute* or *ultimate*—good. It is, to use Sarah Lightfoot Lawrence's felicitous phrase, good enough, at least for now. [14]

The search for transcendence involves what Kant called a regulative principle. It regulates our belief in the value of our current perspective by encouraging us to recognize that every point of view is limited, that every framework is fallible, that even my most basic beliefs and practices could turn out to be wrong.[15] But if the quest for transcendence yields only the fallibility of my current view, it has yet to guarantee the moral content and sense of purpose necessary for learning communities to reach beyond subjectivism and relativism.

The Jewish philosopher Hermann Cohn once gave a talk on Kant's Idea of God as regulator of truth and goodness. God, according to Cohen's understanding of Kant, is that idea which lies beyond our ability to describe how the world actually is or to prescribe how it ought to be. God exists in the moment when the ideal and the real merge, when things are the way they ought to be. By assuming the existence of such an ideal, we are motivated to pursue it. We are also guaranteed that our pursuit will not be in vain. Although we may never attain this ideal, our efforts are made meaningful by the possibility that we can always come closer to it. After the lecture, an old man approached. "Herr Professor," he said, "I very much enjoyed your lecture. I have only one question for you. Where in all of this philosophical discussion of rational ideals is the God of Abraham, Isaac, and Jacob?" Cohn, the story goes, had no answer for the old Jew but the tears in his eyes.[16]

Transcendence must speak to the heart of the old Jew, as did the God of Abraham, Isaac, and Jacob; and of Sarah, Rebecca, Rachel, and Leah. It must provide something worthy of life's devotion, a vision of goodness worth worshiping. For some, the grandeur, otherness, expansiveness, and infinitude inherent in transcendence are transformed into a divinity who is a source of mystery, awe, and wonder. Encounter with such a deity defies discourse. Rudolf Otto called this the *Mysterium Tremendum*.[17] Others such as Plato have depicted the transcendence in rational terms as the ultimate ideal that we strive to emulate.[18] Still others find higher ideals in more worldly pursuits such as tolerance, respect for persons, and caring.

A Fallible God
Consider the God of the Hebrew Bible as a model of such a higher good. Under the influence of Plato and Aristotle, much Christian and Jewish theology has viewed this God as perfect—omniscient, omnipotent, benevolent. However, the biblical God does not come across as perfect. God created the world in order to transmit a vision of the good, but when He discovered that Noah's generation was corrupt, He became angry and flooded the world (Genesis 6:9–8:19). Afterwards He had second thoughts: "Never again will I doom the world because of man, since the devisings of man's mind are evil from his youth; nor will I ever again destroy every living being, as I have done" (Genesis 9:21). There had to be a better way to teach people to be good. So God chose Abraham and Sarah as disciples to learn about goodness. Teaching about goodness turned out

to be harder than expected. Abraham's cousin Lot lived in a corrupt city, so God set out to destroy the city where Lot lived. As we saw in Chapter 2, Abraham protests:

> Will you sweep away the innocent along with the guilty? What if there should be fifty innocent people within the city; will you wipe out the place and not forgive it for the sake of the fifty innocent who are in it? Far be it from You to do such a thing, to bring death upon the innocent as well as the guilty, so that the innocent and the guilty fare alike. Far be it from You! Shall not the Judge of all the earth deal justly? (Genesis 18:23–26)

For the first of many times in the Bible, the student improves upon the teaching of the master. If God were perfect, how could Abraham challenge His plans and prevail? God learns from His student Abraham precisely because He is not perfect. Put another way, it is not a necessary fact that God is good. Goodness is not inherent in the very idea of God. God's goodness is contingent; it could be otherwise. God has the capacity to learn, both from mistakes, as in the case of the flood, and from relationships, as in the case of Abraham.

As a model of a higher good, on the other hand, God is an accessible role model whom we can emulate and criticize. The Hebrew God, like His human creations, is a moral agent. As the prophet Isaiah put it, God is "initiator of light and creator of darkness, maker of peace and creator of evil" (Isaiah 45:7). This is a fallibilist theology, not in the sense that God's existence is falsifiable, but in the sense that God is fallible.[19] It is part of His or Her very nature to be able to learn from error.

The *Talmud* tells of a debate between Rabbi Eliezer ben Hurkanus and the sages under the leadership of Rabbi Joshua ben Levi. The legal matter in question was whether a particular sort of stove could become impure and hence unusable. If this were possible, it would cause a great hardship to many poor people who would not be able to afford replacing it. Eliezer said that the stove could become impure, and Joshua, in the name of the majority, denied this.

On that day Rabbi Eliezer brought all the answers in the world [to support his position] but they were not accepted. He said to them, "If the law accords with my opinion, let this carob tree prove it!" The carob tree uprooted itself and moved 50 yards. . . . The [other] rabbis said, "One does not bring proof from a carob tree." He continued, saying, "If the law accords with my opinion, let this stream of water prove it!" The stream thereupon flowed backwards. They said to him, "One does not bring proof from a stream of water." He continued saying, "If the law accords with my opinion, let the walls of this academy prove it!" The walls of the academy thereupon began to fall inward. Rabbi Joshua reproved them, "By what right do you intervene in the debates of scholars." The walls did not fall [all the way] in deference to Rabbi Joshua, but did not stand upright [again] in deference to Rabbi Eliezer. To this day they stand at an angle. He then said to them, "If the law accords with my opinion, let it be proved by heaven." A voice from heaven [immediately] called out, "Why do you disagree with Eliezer, when the law accords with him in every instance?" Rabbi Joshua then stood up and said, "*It is not in heaven*" (Deuteronomy 30:12). [The talmudic editor then asks] "What is the significance of '*It is not in heaven*'?" Rabbi Jeremiah said, "Since the Torah was given at Mt. Sinai we pay no attention to voices from heaven [in deciding the law] since You [i.e. God, the source of heavenly voices] have already written in the Torah at Mt. Sinai, '*Follow the majority* [of the court in determining legal matters]'" (Exodus 23:2). [Later] Rabbi Nathan met Elijah [the prophet] and said to him, "What did the Holy One, blessed be He, do when this happened?" Elijah replied, "He smiled and said, 'My children have defeated me! My children have defeated me!'"[20]

According to this view, even God—the ultimate parent and teacher—can be proven wrong on the basis of critical reasoning in service of a vision of the good life. In the absence of such a vision, in the face of poverty and hardship, the application of reason alone can lead to undesirable consequences. Rabbi Eliezer was eventually denied admission to scholarly discussions of this kind because of his unbending commitment to dry logic and his unwillingness to temper rational justice with loving-kindness.[21]

The search for spirituality, then, involves a quest after a higher good that is grounded in intelligence and freedom rather than authority and servitude and that embraces doubt and inquiry in place of dogma and definitiveness. This ethical ideal demands humility instead of arrogance. It entails hope, creativity, and the ever-present possibility of a better way. This is a higher, not highest, good, because it is fallible rather than absolute or ultimate. It is discovered within the context of learning communities committed to transcendent moral teachings; it is found, in other words, in education.

Spiritual Virtues

In addition to being holistic, we have also said that the concept of goodness is pragmatic. It expresses itself in concrete virtues or examples of excellence that are to be practiced. What are some of the ideal characteristics of people who discover their authentic identities in transcendent visions of morality, meaning, and purpose? How should these virtues look in the "tents" and "dwellings" of learning communities? There are at least four sorts of virtues that follow from the ethical holism defended above: integrity, humility, literacy, and fulfillment.[22]

Integrity

Integrity implies that a person's inner life is in accord with her external behavior. A person of integrity behaves, in both public and private, the way she believes she ought to behave. She believes in her heart that her way is a path to the good life. Being a person of integrity, in other words, requires faithfulness to a vision of the higher good that defines how one ought to live. Mother Teresa once commented that "we are not here to be successful; we are here to be faithful."[23] To be a person of integrity, one must also be a person of faith.

This needs to be a robust, wholehearted, and passionate faith, in which one not only devotes one's self to a higher good but cares deeply about it. The faithful person who exhibits integrity identifies with this faith and finds the ideals of her life in it. She not only believes that it is good, she also experiences a burning desire to incorporate it into every fiber of her being. She identifies with this good and seeks to conform her will to it, to become one with it. A person of integrity desires unification with a higher good.

Finally, a person of integrity not only accepts the ideals that her vision of goodness offers, and she not only cares about emulating them, she actually does so. However, the person of integrity does not practice goodness as a means to some extrinsic end. Her higher good is not an instrumental value. Such a person lives up to her ideals because they constitute the very purpose of her life. Goodness is not a means to an end; it is the end. To have integrity, one must not only be a person of faith, who loves the faith she espouses; one must also be pious in living up to one's ideals.[24]

Humility

This, however, is only part of the story. As depicted, the faithfulness needed for integrity is that of a true believer, a fanatic who might use her commitment to justify any evil and who has the unrealistic expectation that her beliefs are unquestionable and her behavior impeccable. Goodness requires that the passion of the faithful be tempered by the realization that they might be wrong. In short, it requires *humility*.

Too often faith is accompanied by arrogance. Often such arrogance is born of the expectation that we must be perfect. "It ought to be with a sense of relief," writes Harold S. Kushner, "that we come to the conclusion that we are not and never will be perfect.

We are not settling for mediocrity. We are understanding our humanity, realizing that as human beings the situations we face are so complex that no one could possibly be expected to get them right all of the time."[25]

Arrogant faith commonly leads to cruelty and disrespect for others. When we expect perfection of ourselves, opposing views represent the threat of failure rather than the possibility of enrichment. This cannot direct us toward a more elevated moral existence. Attacking one another—physically, emotionally, or intellectually—for our diverse faiths cannot possibly lead to human flourishing according to any genuine vision of goodness.

Thomas Merton calls this sort of arrogance the "disease which is spiritual pride":

> I am thinking of the peculiar unreality that gets into the hearts of the saints and eats their sanctity away before it is mature. There is something of this worm in the hearts of all religious men. As soon as they have done something which they know to be good in the eyes of God, they tend to take its reality to themselves and to make it their own. They tend to destroy their own virtues by claiming them for themselves and clothing their own private illusions of themselves with values that belong to God. Who can escape the secret desire to breathe a different atmosphere from the rest of men? Who can do good things without seeking to taste in them some sweet distinction from the common run of sinners in this world?
>
> This sickness is most dangerous when it succeeds in looking like humility. When a proud man thinks he is humble his case is hopeless.[26]

In the biblical view, all people are created in God's image. Hence, the Hebrew Bible calls us not only to love our neighbors, but also to treat the stranger with kindness, to remember what it was like to be powerless and enslaved. Arrogant faith too often ignores the love we are obliged to show not only to our neighbors, whose communities we share, but also to the stranger, whose communities are different than our own. The sages asked why only one person was created in the first chapter of Genesis. They answered, "so that no one should say, my ancestors are greater than yours," since we all have one ancestor.[27] To follow the rabbinic metaphor, it is because we all have one creator, one ancestor, and share individual responsibility to care for a world that was created for each of us, that we are obliged to adopt our faith humbly. This sort of humble faith entails the recognition that another of God's children, who is as intelligent and free as I, may have discovered a path to goodness that, in my fallibility, I simply fail to comprehend.

Humility requires that we temper passion for the good with respect for others and tolerance of their beliefs and practices. If it is possible that my faith is indeed mistaken and that some other alternative could turn out to be better, then the potential alternatives are worthy of respect. From this it does not follow that every alternative is right, but rather that there is more than one way to understand goodness. This is why the sages said, "there are seventy faces to the *Torah*,"[28] to emphasize the multiplicity of acceptable interpretations of the good life, even within the context of a single tradition.

Literacy

We have seen that concepts of goodness make sense in the context of communities that practice them. We have called these contexts learning communities. For a person to be devoted to a vision of the good, she must engage the teachings of her community. In addition to integrity and humility, in other words, the good life requires *literacy*. This means that one must be fluent in the languages and modes of communication a learning community requires. If the source of the good is artistic, then the spiritual person needs to be familiar with the modes of representation of the artistic medium in question. She needs to converse by means of painting or sculpture or dance; she needs to make classical music or play jazz. If the good is found in scholarly pursuits then the proper languages and tools of inquiry must be learned. If the good is rooted in a national or ethnic group then the languages and customs of that group must be acquired. If the good is to be grounded in a religion, then the spiritual person must understand and be fluent in the languages, liturgies, and rituals of that religion. [29]

Not only are languages and other means of communicating values required; to be literate in the teachings of a learning community a person must be familiar with the narratives, stories, great works, paradigmatic experiments, or exemplary lives, of the context in question. She must know and live the paradigmatic stories of this context. If the context is artistic, then the great works of art, the path-breaking musical compositions, the original choreographic works must be learned. If the good is to be found in the life of a scientist, then paradigmatic experiments and the lives of great scientists must be studied. If it is a religious life that is to be emulated, then the stories of great religious figures need to be told. If we used the term "language" to metaphorically describe the modes of communication to be mastered, then we might say that the spiritual person must be familiar with the literature of the tradition in which her conception of the good is to be rooted.[30]

Finally, not only does the spiritual person need to be literate in the languages and literatures of the tradition to which she is devoted, she needs also to understand how that tradition is to be interpreted. She needs to grasp its rules of inquiry; how decisions are made within the tradition; how texts, stories, experiments, great paintings, astounding compositions, exemplary lives are studied. She must comprehend, in short, the hermeneutics of the tradition in question.[31]

Fulfillment

What does all of this integrity, humility, and literacy lead to? What is the point of it all? The idea that there is a standard of goodness to which I must measure up according to my own faith presupposes the possibility that I might not. Whenever I strive with integrity and humility toward an ethical vision in which I am literate, it is possible that I might sin, miss the mark, stray from the good path. It is a contingent fact that I sometimes measure up; it could always be otherwise. In this respect, it is a miracle that I measure up, if I ever do, and hence, a source of awe and wonder and satisfaction. But the fact that I do live up to my ideals despite the risk of failure is not only a source of awe and wonder, it is an opportunity for joy and celebration as well.

Living up to an ideal was not the product of some external force, some hand other than my own; rather it was a result of a decision *I made*, a discipline I imposed upon myself, a behavior I learned to perform. There may have been other hands in the mix—parents, friends, teachers, lovers, even God. But all the help in the world could not force me to do good if I choose otherwise. In the final analysis, I was the one who measured up. What I do and think matters. I make a difference. I can make an impact on the world. When I stray from the path I believe to be right, even when the price is high and very little appears to be in my control, all is not lost. I can learn; I can return; I can repent; I can change. This is a source of profound fulfillment indeed.

Spiritual fulfillment offers an even more profound joy than this. On the one hand, the fact that what I do matters carries with it an enormous amount of responsibility. The errors in my life are mine and mine alone. This can be a source of great fear; for it is not only possible that at some point I will err, it is likely, indeed, nearly inevitable that I will do so, and I won't be able to blame it on another. But I need not fear my tendency to err. I can accept myself as a person who sometimes gets it wrong, because I know that I can also try afterwards to get it right. The consequence of the possibility of returning, repentance, change, and learning, is the acceptance of myself as I am, with all of my flaws and weakness. Not only do I matter; I matter just the way I am. This is the source of our deepest joy and greatest reason for celebration.

Critical Thinking

Until this point we have discussed the conditions required for goodness to be an ethical concept and the way in which a holistic conception of the good leads us to "dwell apart," immersed in learning communities with value schemes that encompass life as a whole. We have also addressed some of the virtues that need to be manifest in our "tents" and "dwellings" as a consequence of this ethical holism. We must now address the issue of how a holistic conception of the good can teach a comprehensive way of life without leading us to "conspire against" other peoples. How is it possible to foster holistic conceptions of the good that teach us to "dwell apart" without becoming chauvinistic and xenophobic?

Goodness is a synthetic concept that teaches respect for all moral visions that conform to the conditions of ethical discourse. We are all potential moral agents—free, intelligent, and fallible. To achieve this potential requires embracing both a parochial, holistic vision embodied in a particular tradition and an expansive vision committed to the moral capability of all people. This broader vision is shared with other communities and embodied in democratic society. At the heart of such a society beats the concept of critical thinking.

Rationality as a Moral Ideal

The theorists and practitioners of the informal logic movement believe that critical thinking is an essential ingredient of a democratic society. According to Harvey Siegel, a seminal thinker in this movement, being a critical thinker means, "being appropriately moved by reasons."[32] He calls this the "reasons conception" of critical thinking. It is comprised of two components: (1) "The reasons assessment component" entails the ability to correctly evaluate reasoning according to "subject-neutral" criteria used in all frameworks (such as logical reasoning) and "subject-specific" criteria used in individual fields of inquiry and activity (such as historical, literary, and art criticism).[33] (2) "The critical spirit" involves not only the ability to properly assess reasons, but also the desire and inclination to do so, and to believe and act accordingly.[34]

Siegel argues that critical thinking is a central ideal of what we have called learning communities. If democratic society is a community of learning communities committed to transmitting and preserving the conditions of ethical discourse, then on Siegel's account, critical thinking is not only *a* core value, but perhaps *the* core value, of such a society. "Being appropriately moved by reason," in other words, constitutes a standard of excellence—a virtue—to be emulated by those who embrace the view of goodness these communities espouse. To be a critical thinker is a moral ideal.

Siegel considers two possible objections to this position, one based on ideology and the other on indoctrination:

The Ideology Objection
According to the ideology objection, critical rationality is just another ideology. Ideological frameworks determine what counts as a "reason." Hence, there are no subject-neutral "reasons" we can refer to in choosing an ideological framework. Instead, ideology determines the sort of reasons we prefer. If reasons have no value except within an ideology, there is no "good reason" for choosing one ideology over another. Therefore, critical thinking can claim no rational priority over other ideologies.

Siegel calls this view ideological determinism and responds by arguing that if there is no reason to prefer critical thinking, there is also no reason to prefer ideological determinism to any other view. If, on the other hand, there is *some reason* to prefer ideological determinism, then the argument against reason fails and the determinist doctrine turns out to be false. This is because the very idea that ideologies are *not adopted* on the basis of ideology-neutral reasons appears itself to *have been adopted* on the basis of a reason.[35]

The problem with this response is that it is only effective if one already accepts the force of reasons. The ideologist does not. He has no interest in the rationality of any ideology whatever, including critical thinking, since he already admits that all ideologies are chosen irrationally. On his account, there needs to be no reason for accepting ideological determinism.[36]

Siegel's response to the ideology objection holds only if he can offer some justification of rationality that will be accepted by the ideologist. Siegel argues that the very request for a justification proves the value of rationality since such a request calls for a reason. This, however, will not do, since it is Siegel who is in fact calling for a reason to justify rationality and not the ideologist.

A student complains when asked to provide reasons for her opinions. "Your interest in rationality is based on ideology," she tells her instructor. "You are trying to impose your value commitment to critical thinking on me. I don't accept your values, because my culture and ideology are different from yours, and you have no right to require me to adopt your values in this coercive way. Why should I accept your values when I am perfectly satisfied with my own?"

"The very fact that you have just now asked why," responds the instructor, "suggests that your values may not be as different from mine as you have supposed. To ask why is to ask for a reason supporting my commitment to rational argument. This shows that you are already committed to the value of reasons. I assume this means that, if I produced a sufficiently convincing argument, you would adopt my view because you believe that reasons have the power to convince. Since you have already assumed the persuasive power of reasons, no further reasons are necessary. I am not imposing values on you at all, but rather trying to teach you skills the force of which you already presupposed when you asked them of me."

"My question demonstrates nothing of the kind," responds the student. "You have misinterpreted my intentions according to your own rational bias. I asked you why I should adopt your view merely as a rhetorical device to show that there is no reason in the world that could convince me to adopt your view, since I abhor the very idea of rational argument. It stems from your ideology, not mine."

"I see," says the instructor nervously. "It appears that you already have excellent reasoning skills."

"Who cares?" responds the student.

The objection of the ideologist appears to prevail over the defense of rationality. Critical thinking is not justifiable by its own standards. Does this mean that critical thinking cannot be a moral ideal of learning communities and open society? Only if critical rationality is the basis for all justifications, including that of rationality itself. I argue instead that critical intelligence should not be viewed as the ultimate court in which all attitudes are to be judged but rather as an assumption necessary for moral conversation to make sense. Before turning to this alternative, however, it will be useful to consider Siegel's response to a second objection.

The Indoctrination Objection

A second objection to critical thinking as a moral ideal is based on indoctrination—the inculcation of beliefs without reference to reasons or evidence.[37] If reasons are not neutral but subject to ideology, there would be no difference between rational and irrational inculcation of belief, and hence no distinction between education and indoctrination. The very process of criticism would be learned uncritically, by means of indoctrination. One consequence of this would be that there would be no basis on which to criticize ideas with which one disagreed, or to ask questions when one was in doubt. Indeed, the very democratic society that protects the freedom to question old ideas and conceive new ones would be in jeopardy.

Siegel responds to this objection by distinguishing between the inculcation of ideas that can later be shown to be rational and those that cannot. The former he refers to as ideas that are redeemable by reason, since the ideas are initially inculcated without the benefit of rationality and "redeemed" later when the young person can understand them critically. Siegel argues that only the inculcation of nonredeemable ideas constitutes indoctrination. Inculcating ideas that are redeemable by reason does not constitute indoctrination because the child can employ the proper reasoning once she is old enough to grasp the sort of reasoning that is required.[38]

This response is also problematic. Consider, for example, the value of rationality itself. Is rationality redeemable by reasons once inculcated? No, since justification of rationality depends upon the very sort of reasoning that has been indoctrinated. The value of critical thinking, it seems, must be adopted uncritically. If rationality itself is not redeemable by reasons, the entire project of conceiving critical thinking as a moral ideal of free society falters.[39]

A friend once asked a mathematician where she learned to think so logically.

"My mother was very logical," the mathematician responded. "She gave me reasons for everything."

"Did she ever offer you reasons to justify why her reasoning should be followed?" asked the friend.

"I never thought about that," the mathematician responded. "I guess she didn't."

"You mean that you followed all of those reasons that your mother fed you without a justification as to why you should do so? Why did you do that?"

"I don't know. I suppose it was because she was my mother."

"This doesn't sound logical to me at all," said the friend. "In fact, it sounds like you were indoctrinated by your mother to accept the power of reasons just like orthodox believers are sometimes indoctrinated to embrace the power of God."

"Perhaps," responded the mathematician. "But now that I am mature and well educated, I can see that my mother was right all along.

"How could you think otherwise? You've already been indoctrinated to think as you do."

"I guess I don't know," said the mathematician somewhat flustered.

"Does that mean that your penchant for logical reasoning was in fact acquired illogically?" asked the friend.

"Perhaps it does," responded the mathematician.

The fact that Siegel does not succeed in derailing the ideology and indoctrination objections does not mean that ideological indoctrination is either inevitable or desirable. But how can critical thinking be defended against these objections, and how can the difference between education and indoctrination be upheld, in light of these difficulties? An answer lies in recalling that critical thinking is part of the very concept of goodness because intelligence is one of the assumptions required for ethical discourse to be meaningful rather than the basis on which ethics is justified.

Intelligence as a Condition of Goodness

As a result, in part, of the failure by the likes of Siegel to demonstrate the self-justifying nature of rationality, it has become popular to seek core spiritual commitments in non-rational ideologies that embrace extreme inwardness, solidarity, or transcendence. Commitment to criticism is belittled in favor of a spirituality of the heart, or the group, or the divine rather than the mind. It is hard, it is said, to muster a passion for something as dry and heartless as rationality. This sort of intellectualism leaves many people uninspired and uninterested.

Yet it is precisely the sort of critical intelligence that Siegel describes that makes possible the very *morality* of the ethical vision with which these critics wish to be inspired. The problem with Siegel's commitment to criticism is not his insistence on the need to be passionate about reason but his assumption that this passion is warranted because rationality is self-justifying rather than because it is a condition of moral agency and ethical discourse. It is ultimately the moral life that calls for commitment and demands devotion. Rationality is required in so far as it serves the moral life. In other words, the commitment to criticism follows from the quest for goodness; *ethics is prior to epistemology.*

Siegel's justification of the "reasons conception" of critical thinking suggests as much, since it appeals to the very assumptions necessary for ethical conversation to be meaningful and for democracy to thrive. He offers four reasons for his view: (1) critical thinking facilitates respect for persons treated as ends rather than means; (2) it fosters independence, self-sufficiency, and empowerment; (3) it enables initiation into the rational traditions of inquiry; and (4) it generates skills essential for democratic citizenship. These are closely tied to the assumptions that make ethical discourse possible.[40]

"Respect for persons" follows from the recognition that people have the capacity to be moral agents. Respect for their ideas follows from the realization that we are fallible, that our views might be wrong and another's right. "Independence, self-sufficiency and empowerment" flow from the concept of free will, which assumes that, within limits, we can take control of our lives. "Initiation into rational traditions" is required to become part of a learning community, which enables the differentiation between positive and negative values. Indeed, many of the very standards that can be used as a basis for criticism are to be found within the rational traditions of inquiry.

Siegel's justification of critical thinking, in short, is simply a review of what we have called the assumptions of ethical discourse, dressed in slightly different garb. And the possibility of moral deliberation that these assumptions guarantee is the first of the four characteristics of the good life that the search for spirituality seeks to attain. It would appear that even Siegel must admit that critical thinking is not an end in itself, but an essential means to discover and sustain a good life. The critical spirit is not antithetical to spirituality, then, but one of the very conditions we must accept if the concept is to make any sense. The search for spirituality entails a quest for a higher, more elevated, more worthwhile, more moral life, and there can be no genuine moral life that is unintelligent!

Spiritual Inspiration

To say that the critical spirit lacks the power to inspire is to misconceive the nature of inspiration. To be inspired is not to have merely acquired a positive emotional disposition toward some

attitude or action, it is to have acquired such an emotional disposition grounded in a conception of what lends value to the attitude
or action in question. This requires an ethical vision that is rooted
outside of self and community; and for such a vision to be ethical, it must be intelligent!

The claim that an intelligent approach to spirituality is unin-
spiring, then, literally makes no sense. Only an intelligent approach
to spirituality has the capacity to inspire. All other claims to inspiration are mere illusions that confuse either the ephemeral emo-
tionalism of the moment or the charismatic influence of an individual or group with the genuine emotional power of reason in
the service of the good. Feelings of attraction to ideas or people
have the capacity to inspire a purposeful life only in the context of
a community committed to a higher good. To inspire allegiance,
however, feelings of this kind must make sense within that context and it must be possible to communicate what makes them
worthy of being embraced. They must, in short, be intelligent
feelings—emotions that make sense under the circumstances.
Feelings that are purely personal cannot be shared or communicated because they lack the needed context. They lead not toward
empowerment but emptiness. Amidst such meaninglessness, there
is no way to make sense of that which is supposed to be inspiring.

One important task of parenting is to teach children what sorts
of emotions are appropriate for which circumstances so that they
will understand how to interpret what they are feeling. A friend's
daughter once demonstrated extreme sadness at the death of an
acquaintance whom she hardly knew. She cried in school and received much attention from her friends. Although she empathized
with her daughter's sadness, my friend pointed out that the intensity of her daughter's feelings did not correspond to the impact
of this particular tragic event on her life. Perhaps the intensity of
her reaction was an expression of emotions connected with some
other events about which she was unable to communicate. If so,
it would be important to discover what those events were and to
understand whether the intensity of emotion was appropriate to

them. This sort of disciplining of emotion according to context, along with the associated inquiry and understanding, is an example of "intelligent feelings."

Thomas Moore put the point as follows:

> Without an education, the heart presents itself as a cauldron of raw emotions, suspicious desires, and disconnected images. Dreams appear stupefying, longings inappropriate, and relationships confounding. Without an animating, educated heart, the intellect appears superior, and we give too much attention and value to it. Our institutions and ideas then lack the humanizing breath of the soul. Education of the proper kind brings into view the order and sense in matters of the heart that otherwise seem illusive, and position the heart to play a significant role in affairs of the mind.[41]

Of course, all feelings cannot and should not be disciplined in this way. Spontaneous feelings of elation, sadness, or fear are sometimes best left alone. But those emotions that are intended to motivate us to a more elevated form of life certainly should be cultivated and controlled. Symbols, events, or speeches can generate emotional reactions that can motivate us to change our lives. If such motivation is to lead us to embrace doctrines or ideas that strengthen our moral potential, such feelings require interpretation within a context that is dedicated to enhancing our authentic selves, to becoming the best that we can be. Such a context requires a vision of a higher good that entails intelligence. It is only within such a context that the concept of inspiration as motivation to embrace something of value makes sense.

Within this context, it is easy to see how the association of personal charisma with spiritual inspiration is dangerous. It can lead to confusion between the attractiveness of an individual or group and the worth of the ideas and behaviors being promoted. The spiritual power of leaders and educators must ultimately derive from the genuine worth of the causes they promote and not the ephemeral attractiveness of good looks, or a silver tongue, or an attractive personality. This is not to say that these qualities cannot and should not be used in the service of goodness but only with great caution. And they should not be confused with goodness itself.

The potential of human beings to understand concepts, draw conclusions, attribute meanings, and form intentions—our capacity for criticism—can itself be a source of inspiration. Because of this ability we can decide how to behave, we can learn from our mistakes, and we can change course. This is the key to spiritual integrity, humility, and literacy. It is the source of moral discovery and personal as well as collective fulfillment. The capacity to criticize is thus the foundation of freedom and intrinsic moral worth. To be uninspired by rationality, or intelligence, or criticism is to be unmoved by the potential of the human spirit for good and evil; it is to deny the very likeness to which the Bible bears witness between humans and the divine.

It follows that the search for spirituality cannot be irrational or uncritical. Acquiring a transcendent vision of the good within a learning community entails acquiring critical thinking skills that are shared by other traditions and that can be used to judge between them once those skills have been learned. This is what makes communication among communities that embrace goodness possible, and what is missing in communication between communities that do not embrace ethical discourse. It is the possibility of criticism inherent in the very nature of goodness and the participation of my community in a community of communities that embraces the values of criticism, moral agency, ethical discourse, and democratic society that is our best protection against chauvinism and xenophobia. And the commitments of this society are part of the very concept of a good life.

It does not follow, however, that faith in a higher good flows from rational argumentation alone. Rather it is nurtured in caring communities that bear witness to the possibility of human goodness. Belonging, in other words, is logically prior to believing; the most compelling evidence for theological ideas is found in communal practices. The sages held, for example, that when nonbelievers treat others with kindness they are considered as if they were believers since they practice respect for the divine spark and moral potential within each person. Nel Noddings is correct in saying that the best preparation for the moral life is in the feeling that one has been properly cared for. It is out of the security of feeling cared for that one can come to believe in the potential goodness of the human spirit, and hence in the possibility of a higher good.[42]

A Loving Rationality

The central prayer of Jewish liturgy is a quote from Deuteronomy (6:4–5), "Hear, O Israel! The Lord is our God, the Lord alone." Following this, the text reads, "You must love the Lord your God with all your heart and with all your soul and with all your might." The sages were sensitive to the emotional complexities of being commanded to love, so they introduced this passage in the liturgy by reciting, "With a great and abiding love have you loved us, O Lord our God."[43] God has expressed love and caring by giving the *Torah*, a vision of the good life, a way to become the best that we can be. Because we feel secure in God's love for us as expressed through the gift of *Torah*, we can return that love by living the good life that God set out to teach us.

This is a model for parents as well. We teach our children how to be good, according to our best understanding of what that means, first through our love and caring. This is expressed in our willingness to teach them the way we believe to be best. By doing so, we teach them how to choose a moral life, and through that life, how to be intelligent, rational, and critical. They return that love by using the very rational tools that are built into the concept of goodness we have taught them, sometimes even to prove us wrong. The origins of reason, therefore, are to be found in love!

The second of the Ten Commandments appears to offer a curious contradiction to this view. It says:

You shall not make for yourself a sculptured image, any likeness of what is in the heavens above, or on the earth below. . . .
You shall not bow down to them or serve them. For I the Lord
your God am an impassioned God who visits the iniquities of
the fathers upon the children, upon the third and fourth generations of those who reject [hate] Me, but showing kindness
to the thousandth generation of those who love Me and keep
My commandments. (Exodus 20:4, Deuteronomy 5:8)

On the face of it, this seems to suggest that children are held accountable for the sins of their parents. This poses a problem to
the idea of individual freedom, since free will suggests that each
person should be held accountable only for his or her own transgressions.[44]

There is, however, another way to read this passage that beautifully illustrates the point I have been making. Children who have
been raised on hatred, who have not been cared for, who have
lived with abuse and anger, will carry the scars of this abuse for
three and four generations. It is very hard to shake the psychological consequences of being raised with hatred or without care.
It is well known that the children of substance-abusers are more
likely to abuse substances and that the children of child-abusers
are more likely to abuse their children. It is no accident that Marx's
theory of a-morality, social pessimism, and revolution was born in
circumstances that preferred the unchecked consequence of brutal
market forces to a society that takes care of those in need. Under
such circumstances, it is hard to see the possibility of goodness.On
the other hand, the child who is cared for and raised in love will
carry the power of that love for a thousand generations. The power
of love for goodness and optimism far outstrips the potential of
hatred for emptiness and pessimism. I am acquainted with more
than one young child who was abused by a parent yet who, when
removed from the hateful environment and placed in the care of
loving adoptive parents, recovered from the abuse to become a
sensitive and productive human being.

This sort of turnaround can also appear in adulthood. In her recent novel, *The Wonder Worker,* Susan Howatch revisits Venetia Hoffenberg, who had been introduced as the unmarried Venetia Flaxton in *Scandalous Risks.* In the earlier novel, she became involved with the married dean of an Anglican cathedral. He used her to fulfill his own need to be adored by a younger woman, but he was unable to consummate the relationship in a way that met her desires.[45] In *The Wonder Worker,* the mistreatment of that episode leads Venetia to divorce, alcoholism, and despair. Yet, due to the unconditional love and attention of an older Anglican priest, whom she meets after her divorce, she is able to heal the pain of her old wounds in order to pursue a new life.[46] Venetia's recovery illustrates the power of goodness to heal a wounded soul, constrained by her past from leading a fulfilling life.

This power is demonstrated in the capacity of our children and students to improve upon what we have taught them, not in their ability to imitate our own thinking. Indeed, it was the unwillingness of Venetia's parents to allow disagreement in family conversations that led her to seek validation from "her dean" as she called him. By failing to acknowledge their daughter's right to her own views, these parents failed to confirm her sense of self-worth and hindered her development as an independent and self-confident person.

Critical reasoning is inherent in the very concept of goodness and hence in the very possibility of searching for spirituality. We can choose between conceptions of the good on the basis of reasons, therefore, but to embrace the possibility of goodness itself requires optimism that comes from having been cared for, from being loved. And the person who is able to rise above her circumstances and discover the possibility of goodness and rationality amidst a life of pain and suffering should be recognized as a moral hero.

Spirituality, like rationality, is born not of criticism but of love, the love of God for humankind, of parents for children, of teachers for students, of neighbors for neighbors, of neighbors for strangers.[47] It does not follow, however, that spirituality, or the good life, or ethical ideals, or critical thinking are irrational, for the very transcendent vision of goodness into which one is initiated in love necessarily entails an intelligent dimension required by the conditions of ethical discourse. It is not love and reason, affect and cognition, the emotions and the intellect, the mind and the heart that are at odds, but loving rationality on the one hand versus uncaring determinism on the other. The enemy of spirituality is not reason but apathy born of the feeling that whatever I do, it will make no difference.

The path from moral crisis to spiritual fulfillment calls for faithful and humble devotion to a higher good that inspires the pursuit of holistic ethical ideals. Following this path requires literacy in the languages, literatures, and interpretations of communities that teach an ethic of relation and that provide a context for becoming the best that we can be. Communities of this kind embrace emancipated societies that enable free moral agents to choose intelligent lives and to criticize the policies and practices of those in power. Such lives nurture integrated rather than fragmented personalities whose inner, collective, and outer selves are in harmony instead of conflict. The question is: How can such intelligent lives and integrated personalities best be fostered?

CHAPTER SEVEN

Educating
Spirituality

*You must love the Lord your God with all your heart and with all
your soul and with all your might. Take to heart these words with
which I charge you this day. Impress them upon your children. Recite
them when you stay at home, when you are away, when you lie down
and when you get up. . . inscribe them on the doorposts of your house
and on your gates.*

—Deuteronomy 6:5–9

Rabbi Akiba once was asked: "Which is more important, the study
or practice of *Torah*?" He responded that "study is more important,
because it leads to practice."[1] Akiba's response can be understood
in at least three ways. According to the first interpretation, the
point of study is to acquire rational understanding, to be able to
derive one precept from another, to think clearly about the re-
quirements of scripture. Proper practice, in this view, is a logical
consequence of genuine study, a necessary outcome of acquiring
justified beliefs. The aim of education is to cultivate critical thinking so that justified behavior will follow rational belief. In this
view, being educated involves becoming a more *rational* person.

A second view is committed to practical knowledge rather than
rational understanding. Proper practice and behavior are believed
to flow naturally from that knowledge. Education, in this view, is

not about cultivating critical rationality but about achieving predetermined ends that are not part of the educative process. Since
the question of what practice to follow is predetermined, learning what to think and do requires no independent judgment.
Proper beliefs and behaviors can be learned mechanically by means
of training. This is an instrumental approach according to which
being educated means becoming more skilled.

On the third interpretation, the study of *Torah* is a form of spiritual practice, and the practice of its precepts is a form of study.
Study celebrates divine love and enriches the practice of God's
commandments. Practicing them deepens our grasp of their meaning in our lives. This understanding is reinvested in sacred study
that yields new insight and, in turn, enables practice to become
more joyous. The way of *Torah* is acquired through its study, practice, and celebration. This is a *teleological* rather than an instrumental approach to education. Since it leads to practicing the very
vision of goodness being studied, it is an end in itself. Being educated, in this view, means becoming a good person.

From the discussion in the previous chapter we can see that
education cannot be mainly about becoming more rational. Dogmatic rationalism ultimately undermines the promise of intelligence, freedom, and fallibility inherent in the very critical spirit
rationality purports to embrace. Moreover, nondogmatic critical
rationality is neither an end in itself nor a self-justifying educational ideal; it is a prerequisite for the possibility of goodness, a
condition that must be admitted if there are to be any ideals at all.
Critical rationality is not the end of education, therefore, but a
means necessary to acquire an ethical vision. Becoming educated
is not about becoming rational for its own sake, but about becoming intelligent in order to be good.

I argue in this chapter that the instrumental view offers no better answer than the rational perspective to the question of what
it means to become an educated person. Although means-ends
reasoning is an essential value of some accounts of goodness, it is
an entirely different matter to view education itself primarily as a
means to an end. Education can be filled with techniques, tech-

nologies, instruments, and means of all kinds. However, to understand the primary value of education in these instrumental terms alone is to miss the point. Education is not about acquiring just any knowledge, but that which is worthwhile; and to judge the worth of something requires a vision of the good.[2]

This brings us to the teleological interpretation of Akiba's response, that becoming educated is about realizing one's moral potential by affirming purpose in one's life. Education is not valuable as a means to an end outside of itself according to this view. On the contrary, without education, the very idea of value has no meaning. Failing to recognize the intrinsic worth of education misses not only the point of what it means to be educated, but of what it means to be a moral and a spiritual being as well. Unfortunately, it is precisely this mistake that advocates of radical subjective, collective, and objective spirituality often make in considering what it means to educate.

Instrumental Education

A common critique of educational institutions is that, by becoming instruments of achievement or oppression, they have lost their moral focus. Yet proponents of this critique often proceed to embrace the very instrumentalism they previously rejected. Education can be an instrument to transform individuals and solve social problems, they argue, so long as my own ideology prevails. But this argument will not do.

First, it is doubtful whether educational institutions can live up to the expectations of this view. By conceiving of education as a means and individual or social transformation as the end, it expects too much of educational institutions and too little of the surrounding society. Students only spend a limited amount of time in educational institutions. Most of their lives are lived with families and friends in communities and social settings outside of these institutions. If educational programs try on their own to promote values without the support of the extra-educational environment, then it is highly unlikely that these values will have a significant impact on the lives of students. Forces much more powerful than educators and children usually bring about individual transformation and social change. This is not to say that educational institutions have no role to play in promoting desirable social ends. But the success of such efforts is more dependent on the extra-institutional forces than on the institutions themselves.[3]

Second, the more we view the relation between educational means and ends in terms of prediction and control, the less we allow education to serve moral ideals that require the exercise of judgment and the possibility of choice. Instrumentalism deprives education of its moral character because its mechanistic viewpoint suppresses the intelligent understanding required of teaching. Consequently, training becomes the preferred mode of instruction even when teaching is in order. The result is a tendency toward indoctrination, which is a-moral.[4]

Third, instrumentalism leaves education without a coherent end in view. Not surprisingly, the educational visions often associated with this attitude are closely allied with the "places" in which they "locate" goodness: (1) Those who understand spirituality as completely inward tend to conceive of education as "deconstruction." (2) Those who view spirituality in terms of radical solidarity often see education as "reconstruction." (3) Those who "locate" the spiritual life in dogmatic objectivism usually understand education in terms of "reproduction." In each case, the educational ends they propose tend to be either incoherent or mechanistic. This leads to conflicts with the conditions of ethical discourse that undermine the possibility of these ends being worthwhile altogether. The result is that the ends of education become impossible to comprehend.

Deconstruction

Those who "locate" goodness wholly inside of us often claim that education involves nurturing attitudes and experiences that lie within the child rather than imposing collective or transcendent values on the child from without. According to this view, the task of education is to enable a student to "deconstruct" or expose to criticism the underlying assumptions that are imposed by external forces such as family and community, religion and tradition, and school and society. This is intended to liberate the inherent good that lies within and protect the learner from the imposition of misleading and misguided rules, formulas, and standards. Sylvia Ashton Warner summed up the point well when she wrote: "What a dangerous activity teaching is, all of this plastering on foreign stuff. Why plaster at all when there is so much already inside?"[5]

Like the radically inward conception of spirituality with which it is associated, this attitude has a long pedigree. Plato depicted the great teacher Protagoras as espousing the view that "man is the measure of all things," and that any given thing "is to me such as it appears to me, and is to you such as it appears to you." This implies that "my perception is true for me; for its object is at any moment my reality, and I am . . . a judge of what is for me, that it is, and of what is not, that it is not."[6] In this view, education involves clarifying the subjective truth that lies within.

The eighteenth-century romantic philosopher Jean-Jacques Rousseau took a similar position by idealizing the "noble savage"—the natural person uncorrupted by civilization. If education represents initiation into civilized culture such as that of eighteenth-century France, in Rousseau's view the child is better left uneducated to allow its natural goodness to emerge untainted.[7] The twentieth-century psychoanalyst Sigmund Freud held that a person becomes neurotic—mentally unstable—when parental values represented in civilized culture too aggressively repress human drives for pleasure and survival.[8] It follows, argued advocates of the child-centered movement in the early decades of this century, that education should enable those repressed inner drives to be expressed and that the needs of the child rather than those of society ought to dictate the content of the curriculum. John Dewey called this "the curriculum of the child"[9] or "education from within"[10] and saw it as an extreme version of progressive education.

Many of these ideas became popular again in the so-called "humanistic education" of the later part of this century. Theodore Roszak wrote, for example, that "we all bring into school a wholly unexplored, radically unpredictable identity. To educate is to unfold that identity—to unfold it with the utmost delicacy, recognizing that it is the most precious resource of our species, the true wealth of the human nation."[11]

Most recently, these notions have resurfaced in "postmodern" education. According to Stanley Aronowitz and Henry Giroux, postmodern criticism contends that traditional choices of subject matter and methods of instruction in the humanities and the natural, social, and historical sciences—"the canon"—presuppose an exclusionary social hierarchy. "Post-modern education deconstructs the canon in crucial ways."[12]

> [T]he traditional curriculum must meet the test of relevance to a student-centered learning regime where "relevance" is not coded as the rejection of tradition but is a criterion for determining inclusion. . . . The canons are no longer taught as self-evident repositories of enlightenment. Rather, the teacher is obliged to encourage students to interrogate the values underlying a work of literature, or a traditional history.[13]

The end of this sort of education is for students to "appropriate the canon of legitimate thought without reference to prior pledge of relevance. . . . Freedom consists in the capacity of people and groups to transform knowledge in accordance with their own plans."[14]

The idea that education entails nurturing the good that lies within is extraordinarily important, but it does not follow that pedagogy should focus on subjectivity alone. If goodness is *only* "located" within, then the only acceptable criterion for evaluating the worth of subject matter to be learned is found within learners themselves. However, it follows from the idea that assumptions are subject to criticism that the values used to critique them emanate from *outside* the self. The very idea of education makes no sense without values independent of self. What would a teacher be able to teach, and why should the student want to learn, when everything needed to live well is already found within? Plato put it this way:

> If what every man believes as a result of perception is indeed true for him; if just as no one is a better judge of what another experiences, so no one is a better judge of what another is entitled to consider whether what another thinks is true or false, and . . . every man is to have what is right for himself alone and they are all right and true—where is the wisdom . . . of setting up to teach others and be handsomely paid for it, and where is our comparative ignorance . . . when each of us is the measure of his own wisdom . . . for to set about overhauling and testing one another's notions and opinions when those of each and every one are right, is a tedious and monstrous display of folly.[15]

It follows that there is little for the student to comprehend or understand on this account and that the possibility of teaching and genuine learning is greatly restricted. The moral choices available to the student are severely limited by this centering on the self. Additionally, the moral content required for teaching is so undermined by extreme subjectivism that any effort to touch upon matters that require intelligent judgment—respect for others, the significance of democratic society, the power of divine love—will necessarily tend toward indoctrination. What remains is a morally vacuous training to meet the perceived instrumental needs of the student.

Reconstruction

Those who "locate" goodness entirely within the collective tend to conceive education in terms of the transformation of society according to a particular ideological vision. The task of education on this account is more the *reconstruction* of social life than the *deconstruction* of externally imposed values. It aims to defend the interests of the oppressed and the alienated rather than to protect the good that lies within. Reconstructionism uses education as a tool to awaken the oppressed and the alienated from "false consciousness" in order to empower them to reclaim their lost heritage, discover their collective will, reaffirm their particular identity, and create a more tolerant, multicultural-cultural society.[16]

Often, education as reconstruction is rooted in neo-Marxist theory. Karl Marx argued that knowledge and goodness are tools in the hands of those in power. Knowledge and moral ideals are always determined by an ideology that follows the dictates of class-consciousness. The underclasses, in Marx's view, are alienated from the fruits of their labors because what they produce is owned by the capitalists.[17] If knowledge is the product of educational institutions, and if it reflects class-consciousness, then a curriculum that ignores a group's consciousness alienates its members from the products of their educational labors. If we want to address the problems of the alienated underclasses in society, it is argued, we must begin by reflecting their consciousness in the schools.

One contemporary version of this approach is called "critical pedagogy." It grew out of a neo-Marxist tradition known as "critical theory" that was founded in Frankfurt, Germany, during the nineteen-thirties. Jürgen Habermas, who was mentioned in Chapter 4 as an example of collective spirituality, is one of the leading critical theorists writing today. According to Peter McLaren, "Critical theorists begin with the premise that men and women are essentially unfree and inhabit a world rife with contradictions and asymmetries of power and privilege."[18] In this view, "knowledge is a social construction deeply rooted in a nexus of power relations."

> Critical pedagogy asks how and why knowledge gets constructed the way it does, and how and why some constructions of reality are legitimated and celebrated by the dominant culture while others clearly are not. . . . The crucial factor here is that some forms of knowledge have more power and legitimacy than others.[19]

The concept of culture—the practices, ideologies, and values groups use to make sense of the world—helps us to understand who has power and "how it is reproduced and maintained in the social relations that link schooling and the wider social order."[20] The concept of ideology refers to "the production and representation of ideas, values, and beliefs and the manner in which they are expressed and lived out by both individuals and groups."[21] Power relations among cultures sometimes produce within individuals distorted conceptions of their place in the sociocultural order. This often happens when the ideology of the "dominant" culture subordinates less powerful cultures through the process of hegemony—the maintenance of domination through consensual social practices in government, education, religion, and the media. The task of critical pedagogy is to "empower" the student to become aware of and liberated from the hegemonic forces that dominate her in order to express the values, beliefs, and practices of those who share her own social, historical, and economic experience.[22]

Religious educators in secular society have been known to adopt this way of thinking when they view secular culture as "dominant" and their own particular religious perspectives as "dominated" because members of their faith communities are "alienated" from the traditions of their ancestors or from God. North American Jewish educators, for example, have often seen their task as encouraging youngsters to become "more Jewish" than their parents, by which they mean more observant of religious traditions, or more committed to Jewish causes, or more passionate about Zionism and the state of Israel. In the terms of critical pedagogy, the task is to encourage youngsters to reject the "false consciousness" of their parents who have embraced a "dominant" secular or Christian culture that has alienated them from their history and heritage. While this may not be the rhetoric that Jewish educators commonly use, the logic of Jewish educational practice often conforms to this sort of attitude.

Reconstructionist accounts of education remind us of the intersubjective, cultural character of knowledge and of the need for students to identify with the cultural origins of the subject matter they study for it to have meaning for them. Reconstructionism, however, appears to take an additional step in suggesting that class, culture, race, or gender-consciousness determine, rather than merely influence, belief and behavior. Hence, we are not accountable for the consequences of what we do. This undermines one of the central conditions that make moral discourse possible. What sense is there to moral claims if one cannot choose to adopt and enact them? Suppose my beliefs and behaviors are determined by an ideology that follows the dictates of history, social status, or economic class. What, then, of my freedom to choose what to believe and how to behave? The very moral outrage at oppression and domination, which is the important contribution of critical pedagogy, becomes incomprehensible when these deterministic assumptions are adopted. To make moral judgments we must assume the free will of the agents involved; and this is precisely what critical pedagogy appears to deny.

This difficulty is compounded by the radically relativistic account of truth and goodness that are inherent in this view. If each class or culture has its own knowledge and values, then the very idea that there can be standards on which we decide which knowledge and values to embrace is undermined. Indeed, it is difficult to understand what it might mean to adopt such standards. If the claim that truth and values are *always* relative to culture is true, then the claim is false. Such a claim is not relative to a *particular* culture, but absolute. It is said to apply to *all* claims in *all* cultures. If truth is *always* relative, it can *never* be so. The very idea of relativism is that *nothing* is true in *every* circumstance, not even relativism itself. Hence, education as reconstruction undermines not only the condition of free will, but those of intelligence and fallibility as well. The possibility of understanding standards is denied, since the very existence of standards is undermined.

It is no wonder that reconstructionists often see no difference between education and indoctrination. The very idea of a moral agent whose will and intelligence are to be disciplined through education is rejected, since there is no moral agent to begin with.

Without intelligence and choice, we live in an amoral world in which might makes right and the only source of justification is power. In such a world, there are only victims and victimizers, controllers and controlled, oppressors and oppressed, powerful and powerless. In such a world, spirituality, goodness, and education—all of which enhance moral agency—are impossible; there is only indoctrination, the very point of which is to incapacitate the moral agent within.[23]

The source of these difficulties is that reconstructionism exaggerates an important observation. Surely ideology influences belief and behavior, but it is neither the determining nor the sole influence over them. Many factors influence decisions we make about what to believe and how to behave. Some are ideological. Others stem from different social influences such as peer pressure, economic circumstances, social status, religious background, and, of course, critical reason. None of this precludes the possibility that I can decide what to believe and how to behave or that, if I want my beliefs and behaviors to be good, I can seek to embrace them intelligently.

Reproduction

Those who "locate" goodness in a rigid view of that which transcends self, community, and nature often view education as the reproduction in the new generation of that which was found in the old. In the 1920s, for example, Franklin Bobbitt launched an educational movement known as the science of curriculum making. The task of education, according to this position, is to prepare the young for adult life. The goal of the curriculum is to reproduce the current adult society.[24] This sort of reproductive view is common today among neo- and ultra-conservative groups.

John Dewey referred to this orientation as "traditional education."[25] Critical pedagogues call it "social reproduction," by which they mean the ways in which schools and other educational institutions reproduce inequitable social relations, structures, and attitudes across the generations.[26] Using the ancient Greek concept of *mimesis,* which refers to the reproduction of reality through an imitative process, Philip Jackson calls this the *mimetic* tradition of education. In this "subject-centered" tradition, he writes, "knowledge is 'presented' to the learner, rather than 'discovered' by him or her [and] can be 'passed' from one person to another or from a text to a person."[27]

> A crucial property of mimetic knowledge is its reproducibility. It is this property that allows us to say it is "transmitted" from teacher . . . or . . . text to student. . . . It does not entail handing over a bundle of some sort as in an actual "exchange" or "giving." Rather, it is more like the transmission of a spoken message from one person to another . . . . [B]oth parties wind up possessing what was formerly possessed by only one of them. What has been transmitted has actually been "mirrored" or "reproduced" without its ever having been relinquished in the process. . . . It can (also) be judged right or wrong, accurate or inaccurate, correct or incorrect on the basis of comparison with the teacher's own knowledge or with some other model as found in a textbook or other instructional materials.[28]

The reproductive account of education reminds us that teaching and genuine learning, which always involve the exercise of intelligence, often require much training and rote learning. The difficulty with this view is that it never seems to move beyond training and rote learning to teaching and understanding. If socialization entails reproducing social and cultural patterns of belief and behavior, and education involves grasping a community's moral ideals, then the problem with this view is that it never moves beyond socialization to education.

To train and socialize intelligent beliefs and behaviors rather than teaching and educating them denies students the opportunity to think for themselves and to choose whether and when to adopt them. When training and socialization become the be-all and end-all of education, then it lapses into a form of indoctrination. It is impossible to comprehend what could be worthwhile about intelligent beliefs that are acquired through socialization and training alone, since restricting the instructional repertoire in this way undermines the conditions required to make sense of the very concept of worth.

Education is not primarily a means to ends outside of itself. It is less a matter of deconstruction, reconstruction, or reproduction than of initiation, renewal, and renaissance. It is dedicated primarily to the celebration of goodness and only secondarily to critical and instrumental reason. It is, in short, more a spiritual than a rational or instrumental value. To understand what this entails, we need first to look at what it would mean to educate intelligent spirituality. We can then turn to the concept of liberal education more generally. We will see that the education of intelligent spirituality is what we ought to mean by the concept of a liberal education.

Spiritual Education

If spirituality entails discovering our best selves in communities committed to a higher good, then educating spirituality involves initiating new members into such communities and renewing the commitment of continuing members to their ethical visions. This is accomplished through the study, practice, and celebration of goodness. Education, in this view, initiates into ethical communities with common conceptions of the good rather than epistemological communities that share forms of knowledge.[29] It is about becoming a good person who acquires knowledge as her ethics demands. This is not a means to an end; it is an end in itself, a source of meaning in life, a purpose of existence. This is why the sages said that one good deed leads to another.[30] The study, practice, and celebration of the good life is self-justifying and self-reinforcing. Goodness begets goodness.

This is not to say that there are not advantageous by-products of education such as better jobs or improved economies. However, if we view these by-products as the primary ends of education, we confuse means and ends by transforming jobs, economies, rationalities, or knowledge into the purposes of existence when they ought to be viewed as resources for good living. A conception of worth should govern thinking about what knowledge is most worth knowing and what job worth having.

A student of mine once informed me that I needed to award her a certain grade because she would loose her merit scholarship without it. I replied that the scholarship was intended to reward academic achievement as assessed by faculty and recorded in grades. The point of assessment is to evaluate what a student has learned, not to insure financial aid. And the purpose of learning is to enhance one's moral insight, not increase one's material worth; to become better at *living well* or *practicing a valued craft,* not at *earning a living.* Professionals who graduate from educational institutions require not merely *practical skill* but also *purposes for which to practice.*

This does not mean that education is completely without goals. After all, it does serve a higher good. However, this is a teleological rather than an instrumental attitude. Unlike instrumental ends that are often chosen on the basis of enlightened self-interest, teleological ends are discovered in the context of communities committed to a higher good.[31] The study of goodness does not entail pursuits that are external to its vision. Rather, it is part of the very pursuit of that vision, since coming to understand the good is required to enact it intelligently. To say that study leads to practice means that achieving a genuine understanding of goodness entails fueling a desire to actualize it.

We are so accustomed to speaking of education and related concepts, such as teaching and learning, in instrumental terms that the very notion of an inherently valuable education conflicts with our instinctive linguistic associations. To speak of education teleologically, therefore, requires talking about concepts such as study, practice, and celebration in unfamiliar ways.

Study

What sort of study enables initiation into and renewal of transcendent visions of the good? An answer lies in the subject matter to be studied, the manner in which that material is engaged, the reasons for doing so, and the outcomes to be expected.

The Subject Matter
The subject matter of spiritual education is the language, literature, and hermeneutics of an approach to the good life. To be initiated into a community's concept of goodness entails becoming *literate* in that concept. It means learning to speak its languages, perform its rituals, sing its songs, and dance its dances. It means listening to its stories, laws, rules, standards, and customs and learning to recount and reenact them at the appropriate times and in the accepted manners. It also means learning to interpret those stories, rules, and customs and to apply them to new and ever-changing circumstances. To be initiated into a vision of the good life is not only to be trained in the rudiments of that vision. It is also to be taught to understand it, to operate within it, not only to be shaped and molded by it, but also to shape and to mold it. Education as renewal refers not only to the regeneration of what was, but also to the creation of what is new on the basis of what came before.

There is no one body of material that students need to master or no single curriculum framework that educators must employ to accomplish this initiation and renewal process. It requires neither what Paul Hirst and Richard Peters called "forms of knowledge,"[32] what Joseph Schwab called "structures of disciplines,"[33] what Philip Phenix called "realms of meaning,"[34] or what Elliot Eisner called "forms of representation."[35] The spiritual subject matter demands, instead, initiation into the languages, literatures, and hermeneutics of communities that draw on a variety of religious, spiritual, ethical, intellectual, and aesthetic resources to express their conceptions of goodness.[36]

Religious resources are available both in the formal experience of institutional religion and the informal religiosity of everyday life. One involves learning from rituals, texts, traditions, and history; the other entails responding with awe, wonder, and appreciation to the miracles of daily life.[37] Spiritual resources are found in theologies that seek higher goods both within and beyond the confines of space and time.[38] Ethical resources include traditions of virtue that address the joys and sorrows of life. There are also important intellectual dimensions to spirituality. History, philosophy, literature, and natural science, to name but a few, all have enormous potential for spiritual guidance and fulfillment. Finally, conceptions of the good require the capacity to express original ideas and feelings using the creative and performing arts.

The Manner of Instruction

A nondogmatic, transcendent vision of goodness cannot be satisfied with regenerating that which has existed, with mere training and reproduction. Independent deliberation and decision-making are also required. This is accomplished through inquiry and criticism, which demonstrate that there might be a better way, innovation and creativity, that chart what that better way might be, and hope, which motivates us to enact the innovations we conceive based on traditions we received. Just as the subject matter of spiritual education entails the virtue of literacy, its manner calls for the virtue of humility. This necessitates recognizing the fallibility not only of my tradition but also of my comprehension, criticism, and creativity. It also calls for the realization that the alternatives may have more to recommend them than we previously might have thought.

Lee Shulman writes of the "knowledge-base of teaching"—what teachers need to know to practice their craft.[39] What do spiritual pedagogues need to know to transmit the subject matter outlined above? They need subject-neutral critical thinking skills that transcend disciplines and traditions, the subject-specific thinking of their own ethical tradition and of relevant cognitive traditions, familiarity with at least one empirical discipline that teaches the fallibility of its results, and appreciation for aesthetic forms of representation that celebrate creativity and hope. They also need what Shulman calls "pedagogic content knowledge"—intuitions learned from experience about enabling others to inquire as well as the inquiry skills themselves.

Elliot Eisner points out that, in addition to the published curriculum they convey explicitly, teachers transmit values and ideas
implicitly in the educational environments they create and the
topics they exclude.[40] What is the implicit teaching of spiritual
pedagogy and what gets left out? Optimism is implied, while pessimism is left out. Moral vision is engaged, amoral emptiness
ignored. Freedom is supposed, determinism denied. Intelligence is
assumed, ignorance battled; fallibility suggested, perfectionism rejected; hope promoted, despair discouraged; creativity encouraged,
conformity constricted. Confidence in humankind with all of our
limitations is embraced while reliance on the dogmatic is disre-
garded. Faith in a higher good is championed and the expectation
of nothingness is suppressed.

What of the hidden curriculum? Are tacit messages intentionally or unconsciously submerged by spiritual pedagogy? This assumes a hermeneutic of suspicion according to which dominant
cultures camouflage important messages that, if explicit, would be
rejected.[41] The very idea of manipulating a student to adopt a behavior or belief that he might otherwise reject, whether accidentally
or purposefully, is antithetical to spiritual education. This denies
the freedom of the learner, undermines her capacity to acquire understanding, and thwarts her ability to question or disagree. Such
an approach robs the learner of moral agency and runs contrary
to the possibility of ethical discourse. Spiritual pedagogy rejects the
psychology of victimhood inherent in the hermeneutic of suspicion. Victory over victimhood is achieved by rejecting powerlessness—by recognizing that, although I control only a small portion
of life, if I take responsibility for that which is within my grasp, I
can make a difference in the world.

The Rationale
What is the rationale for this spiritual curriculum and pedagogy?
The answer is, to strengthen the moral agent within each person.
But why strengthen the moral agent within? What is the value of
moral agency? The answer is, that without moral agency the very
idea of value is meaningless. If education entails initiation into an

ethical vision dependent on moral agency, then in the absence of education nothing can be considered worthwhile. One could, of course, choose to reject the possibilities of freedom, intelligence, and fallibility as have the extreme subjectivists, the advocates of radical solidarity, and the dogmatic objectivists. But, transmission of those modes of spirituality tends to favor indoctrination over education. This precludes spirituality as the affirmation of ethical vision and returns us to the moral crisis of modernism.

Why reinforce moral agency? The answer is, that without it there is no goodness, no education, no moral discourse, indeed, no civilized life altogether. Moral agency is important because without it the very idea of importance is meaningless. It is significant because it constitutes the basic condition of significance. Goodness is not studied to achieve some extrinsic end; it is the end. Its value is intrinsic. It is study for its own sake. The subject matter of spiritual education is grounded in the virtue of literacy and its manner in the virtue of humility. Similarly, the rationale for this curriculum finds its home in the virtue of integrity, in the passionate commitment to live in harmony with one's faith in a higher good.

Desired Outcomes

What outcome is to be expected from such a curriculum? An answer lies in the virtue of fulfillment. The person who has been educated spiritually understands that she matters, that what she thinks is significant, and that what she does can make a difference. Such a person is not afraid of the world, or scared of intellectual challenge, or frightened by new ideas. She is open to the possibility of a better tomorrow, confident, hopeful, and optimistic. By the same token she is deeply committed to a vision of the good, either the one in which she has been educated, or another that she has chosen with the tools that she acquired through the educational process. Put simply, such a person is empowered.[42]

How can we identify good examples of this orientation to empowerment through pedagogy? This question calls for a value judgment about what to count as *good* spiritual pedagogy. As aesthetic creations in their own right, instances of spiritual pedagogy should be judged as other intrinsically valuable cultural artifacts, not on the basis of the products they produce but in terms of the excellence of the process and product combined, on the grounds of the quality of the whole. Elliot Eisner refers to the background required to make such judgments as *connoisseurship,* that is, the expert knowledge of one who has been initiated into a community of ethical, cognitive, and aesthetic discourse and who is able to communicate that expertise through a variety of forms of representation. The communication of judgments made by the connoisseur he calls *educational criticism.*[43] This is a form of qualitative inquiry that has connections to art and literary criticism.

In contrast to quantitative educational assessment that measures quality in terms of student achievement or changes in student behavior, qualitative evaluation seeks a thick description of a whole pedagogic event as it transpires in its natural setting. In order to assess quality, it articulates the cultural norms that guide teachers and students in deciding to behave as they do, describes how a pedagogic event is experienced by the participants from an insider's point of view, and presents a vivid description of the event with special attention to a particular focus or perspective.

Data are collected through observation of the events while in progress, interviewing of participants, and examination of documents such as program advertisements, written curricula, course syllabi, examinations, and other participant products. Descriptions are composed of those aspects of the events about which judgments need to be made. Should a teacher be retained? How can instruction be improved? Is one curriculum preferable to another? Should this student be promoted? What sorts of experiences should be funded? Educational criticism then asks, is this effort good enough to meet the ethical, cognitive, or aesthetic standards of the tradition in which this pedagogic effort resides? Following Dewey, Eisner sees the task of criticism as the reeducation of perception in order to identify new solutions to old problems and new problems to be solved.[44]

This does not preclude the use of quantitative measures in assessing the quality of a pedagogic event, but it requires that they be used as one among a number of indicators of excellence, rather than as the sole criterion against which we judge the value of an educational experience. It is entirely appropriate, for example, to ask about the level of proficiency with which students have learned to master certain mathematical concepts, reading skills, or writing competencies. But the questions of which concepts, skills, and competencies are most worth mastering and of what level of mastery is most desirable are only answerable within the framework of a vision of excellence. Ultimately, quantitative assessment in education is always subject to qualitative judgments, to the standards of excellence being applied.

Practice

Spirituality is not only a theoretical but also a practical endeavor. It is not merely about knowing or thinking but also about living. To speak of spiritual education in the theoretical realm of study alone would be like studying music theory but never listening to or making music, exploring aesthetics without ever engaging a work of art. It would be similar to considering poetics but never reading or writing a poem, or inquiring into the history and philosophy of science without ever witnessing or executing a scientific experiment. Educating spirituality requires practice, not mere study.

What kind of practice is this? It is the practice of living the good life that a community's transcendent vision prescribes. Spiritual education requires not only that we learn about the good, and not only that we engage in the study of goodness for its own sake, but also that we actually do good deeds, lead a good life, enact what we learn, implement what we have studied. Indeed, according to this view, we cannot fully comprehend any vision of the good unless we experience it in action.

We learn to emulate moral ideals not only by studying books but also by example. Every teacher, college professor, school principal, clergy-person, youth leader, parent, grandparent, and neighbor teaches by example. If we are not prepared to ask of ourselves what we ask of our students, children, and grandchildren, then there is little reason for them to practice what we preach. We teach as much by who we are and what we do as by what we say. This is the import of the biblical injunction to follow divine teachings at home and away, in the morning and at night. Goodness is taught by thoughtful example not only at school, or summer camp, or in the church or synagogue or mosque but in every aspect of life.

Insiders and Outsiders

The requirement of practice in spiritual education leads to an important distinction relating to study as well. The point of practicing goodness in everyday life is different from the goal of studying about those practices in the academy. Part of the academic ethos has been to separate the object of study, to place it over against oneself in order to analyze, examine, and dissect it. Although postmodern and hermeneutic critics have challenged this analytic and objective ethos, few scholars suggest that high schools, colleges, and universities should become places in which students are initiated into cultures and traditions other than those sanctioned by the academy itself.

Anthropologists distinguish between the insider's and outsider's perspective.[45] The goal of spiritual education is not to examine a vision of the good with dispassion, from an outsider's point of view, as if it belongs to someone else. The sort of study that leads to the practice of *Torah* advocated by Akiba requires engagement from *within*. Languages, literatures, and hermeneutics are approached as if they belong to me, to my family, my people, and my God. Identification with a community is a prerequisite rather than an outcome of such an education.[46]

This is one of the paradoxes of spiritual education. In order to invite someone to identify with a vision of goodness we must already assume that they do. A willingness to take on this insider perspective is part of what makes initiation possible; by acting *as if* I am an insider, I can learn to become one.[47] Its purpose is to enable the initiate to identify with the good, to join communities that embrace it, to construct his moral ideals around it, find the purpose of his life within it, devote himself to this good as the transcendent source of life's meaning. The point of spiritual education is not to objectify the good but to "subjectify" it, to enable the student to commit himself to it, become one with it, so that its ways become his. The task in other words, is to become an insider, to live inside a particular vision of the good life.

Herein lies the fallacy of much thinking about religious instruction that views its task as transmitting knowledge rather than goodness. To study *about* the Eucharist—the Christian ceremony in which wine is transformed into the blood of Jesus and bread into his flesh—but never to experience it as a believing Christian cannot be the end of Christian education. The Christian vision of goodness involves embracing this practice as one's own, not merely knowing about it. This can not be accomplished without experiencing the Eucharist and practicing it on a regular basis.

Similarly to study *about* Jewish dietary practice or Sabbath observance or synagogue liturgy without ever experiencing them in the context of regular religious practice is insufficient for Jewish education, if one believes that embracing Judaism involves accepting these practices as one's own. It is not enough to know about the Eucharist or how to chant the synagogue service. It is not even enough to have experienced these practices once or twice. To be educated in these visions of the good life requires that these practices be incorporated into daily life, that they become part and parcel of a person's way of being.[48]

It follows that to educate spirituality parents and children, teachers and students, camp counselors and campers, must engage virtues sincerely, as genuine insiders, because they have come humbly to believe that these virtues represent the best way to be, at least for now. We may "try them on for size," but at some point we have to decide whether or not "they fit."[49]

Passion and Intelligence
This having been said, we should not minimize the importance of the outsider's point of view. It is the ability to view the world not

only from our own points of view, but also from the perspective of others, that makes possible the sort of humility and tolerance necessary for genuine spirituality. Academic study does not initiate us into our particular communities, but it does invite membership into the community of communities that embraces the assumptions of moral agency and ethical discourse which are essential to democracy. This sort of study provides the tools of critical inquiry necessary for spiritual pedagogy that are sometimes absent within historical faith traditions.

Becoming spirituality educated, then, involves learning about a tradition both as an insider and an outsider. Initiation into and renewal of a vision of goodness entail acquiring the perspective of two communities, that of the community of primary identity and that of the community of communities we have called open society that shares a common commitment to the conditions of ethical discourse. Spiritual pedagogy acknowledges no dichotomy between passion and intelligence. Just as there can be no moral intelligence without passionate commitment, there can be no genuine spiritual passion that is not rooted in intelligent deliberation.[50]

Celebration

What is the consequence of practicing goodness in this thoughtful way? One answer is joy and celebration! We genuinely believe that the life we exemplify is the best for us (at least for now) and we are sincerely committed to the idea that this way of life is an honest reflection of a higher good. The fact that we can actually incorporate this good into our daily lives, therefore, is a source of great joy and a reason for extraordinary celebration. Spiritual education entails not merely the study and practice of moral ideals, it also involves celebrating the good in daily life.

Celebrating Ethical Ideals
Spiritual communities celebrate ethical ideals in a variety of ways and places: religious and civic holidays, life-cycle events and rites of passage, daily prayer and sacred study. For Christians, Christmas

celebrates the birth of a redemptive ideal and Easter the value of sacrifice as a means of atonement. Jews celebrate redemption at Passover and the role of sacrifice in atonement on *Yom Kippur*— the Day of Atonement. Modern nations often enshrine civic visions of redemption in holidays of national liberation and secular sacrificial ideals in commemorations of those who lost their lives in battle.

The celebration of ethical ideals on these occasions often involves ceremony, ritual, and tradition. These are enacted in public arenas such as places of government, worship, or learning. They are also enacted in private arenas such as home and hearth, family and friendship. People share gifts, or words, or rituals that become important moments and memories in their lives. The institution of marriage, for example, celebrates important ideals. Often families, friends, and couples develop traditions through which they share and pass on to children the meaning those ideals hold for them. In schools, the celebration of moral ideals is an ongoing process that can be seen in school assemblies, in classroom decorations, even relations among staff or between teachers and students. These ideals can be felt in the very atmosphere of the school and are referred to by educational scholars as an implicit dimension of learning in school.[51]

Ethical ideals are also celebrated in daily life through prayer, study, and the sanctification of the mundane. The traditional Jew, for example, recites approximately one hundred blessings each day. There are blessings for washing hands, for arising in the morning, for getting dressed, for nearly every normal act of everyday life. These blessings always associate the act with an idea, a meaning. They are not only forms of worship but also formulas for education, for learning to see goodness in the most mundane moments of life. Through this process, Jews not only learn about the good, they enact it as well, bringing it into every moment and aspect of their existence. The recitation of blessings sanctifies the normal routine of daily life. They become one with their vision of a higher good. Max Kadushin called this normal mysticism.[52]

To say that every moment can be sanctified is to recognize that goodness lies around every corner, that whatever trial or tribulation life may hold, it is none the less inherently good, that life is to be celebrated, not merely lived. How do spiritual communities celebrate goodness? We do so by attending to the inherent goodness in every moment of existence, seeking to enact the vision of a higher good at every turn, and transforming the instrumental and the mundane into the sanctified and the holy.[53]

This sort of pedagogy elevates learning to a higher plain. By enabling learners to understand a positive account of goodness through spiritual practice, it not only prepares the ground for moral agency, it celebrates the higher good to which it is devoted. This celebratory attitude is not restricted to a particular religious point of view; there is potential joy in every act of teaching and in every instance of genuine learning. To experience this joy we need to notice the wonders of teaching and the miracle of learning, to recognize that every teaching act has the capacity to reinforce the ethical conditions goodness requires. We also need to attend to the meaning and purpose with which our lives are infused when we learn to express our devotion to a higher good.

The Joy of Teaching and Learning

Too often the images and terminology we associate with education are expressed in the language of enslavement and drudgery. We speak of study as labor or work—home*work*, seat*work*, class*work*. We train rather than educate teachers to assign this work. The reward for this study is conceived not in the joy of learning or in the value of the material but in the currency of grades, advancement, and acceptance into prestigious institutions that will facilitate high-paying jobs with power and authority. I recently had occasion to advise some young parents who were concerned about getting their child into the "right" preschool so that she could enter the "proper" private elementary school in order to go to the "best" high school so that she would get into Harvard. Harvard, I pointed out, does not read their applicants' preschool transcripts. I was saddened on another occasion when a friend objected to my use of the image of the teacher as a metaphor for God, because the popular association with teaching is mechanical, authoritative, and negative.

In contrast, some colleagues and I once conducted a study of teacher motivation to see why people aspire to, or remain in, the teaching profession when the conditions of employment are often not as advantageous as in some other careers. The answer from teachers of a variety of disciplines and age groups who had been born and educated all over the world was surprisingly uniform. "It is because of how I feel when I see it in their eyes," they said, "when they have understood what I am trying to teach them, and their mind has been opened. When their eyes are opened like that, and I had something to do with opening them . . . there is no feeling in the world quite like it." This does not describe an experience of enslavement, mechanism, or drudgery. It depicts rather an experience that is uplifting, energizing, enlightening—literally, eye-opening![54]

One of the most inspiring pieces of writing in the philosophy of education appears in the final chapter of Thomas Green's *The Activities of Teaching.* The knowledge that we transmit in schools, Green points out, is mostly contingent. The fact that Columbus arrived in North America in 1492 or that Lincoln delivered the Gettysburg Address is not necessary. It is a mere custom that in proper English spelling 'i' precedes 'e', except after 'c', or when sounding like 'ay' as in 'neighbor' and 'weigh.' And it is an accident of nature that water freezes at 32 degrees Fahrenheit. Under different conditions all of these "facts" could have turned out otherwise. Moreover, Green continues, student learning is not a necessary consequence of even the very best teaching. That students learn anything at all also could be otherwise. It is a miracle, therefore, when students do learn; learning, in short, is a source of great awe and wonder.[55]

That teaching is uplifting and eye-opening and learning miraculous and wondrous are not oppressive ideas. On the contrary, they are occasions for exuberance, joy, and celebration. Why is it that the institutions most closely associated with education are so often depicted in terms so very contrary to these? The answer lies in the instrumentalization of education that flattens its moral ideals, diminishes its uplifting, inspiring, and energizing qualities, and replaces them with mechanisms, techniques, and methods. By confusing means with ends, this process transforms the joyous into the laborious, the eye-opening into mind-closing, the liberating into the enslaving, the wondrous into the mundane, the holy into the profane. There is a need to recapture the joy of teaching and learning.

Rabbi Isaac Luria, the great sixteenth-century mystic of Safed, believed that the world was created in a cosmic catastrophe. The divine essence from which God attempted to create the world was so powerful that it burst the vessels through which it was being transformed from heavenly to earthly matter. The divine sparks from these vessels were scattered throughout the world and set-tled within each person where they lie dormant to this day. To re-deem the world, we must light those divine sparks within each of us so that God's creative efforts can be completed as originally in-tended. Teaching and learning are holy acts in which the divine sparks that lie dormant within us are kindled so that our minds and hearts can be engulfed in a blaze of devotion to worthwhile endeavors. The moments in which the fires of learning are lit through teaching are a blessing, for through them our troubled world can be repaired. When practiced in this spirit, teaching and learning become celebrations of goodness.[56]

This is not to deny that there is a darker side to existence and that there is evil in the world. The very fact of moral agency means not only that we have the capacity for enormous good, but also for extraordinary evil. The conclusion of the rabbinic dictum cited above that "one good deed leads to another," is that "one trans-gression," one evil act, also "leads to another."[57] Just as goodness begets goodness, evil begets evil. A primary task of education is to deflect that potential evil within each of us by teaching us to renew goodness in our lives each day, each hour, each moment.

An approach to spirituality that embraces intelligence responds to the moral crisis of modernism. This entails discovering our best selves in communities that teach us to care for one another by emulating a higher good. This view "locates" spirituality not only in communities of primary identity but also in communities of communities that embrace the assumptions of democracy and ethical discourse. Educating this sort of spirituality is not a matter of cultivating critical rationality as an end in itself; nor is it a means to extrinsic ends such as deconstruction, reconstruction, or reproduction. It involves instead initiation into and renewal of communal visions of a higher good through studying, practicing, and celebrating them for their own sakes. What is the relation between this particularistic concept of education and the more general notion of "liberal education"?

Liberal Education

If liberal education entails the preparation of the democratic public, then it involves the reinforcement of the conditions of moral agency and ethical discourse: critical intelligence, freedom, and fallibility. But this is just what we have seen to be the essence of spiritual education. Educating spirituality is not in conflict with liberal society as is sometimes supposed. On the contrary, spiritual education as conceived here just is liberal education, if by this term we mean the sort of education necessary to prepare leaders and citizens for the responsibilities of power in open, liberal democracies. This involves initiation of new members into learning communities committed to a higher good and renewal of that commitment on the part of continuing members. It also involves initiation into and renewal of commitment to a community of communities that share a common faith in freedom as opposed to determinism, intelligence as opposed to ideology; fallibilism as opposed to subjectivism, relativism, or dogmatism.

Preparing Democratic Leaders

Liberal education is often associated with the preparation of leaders for democratic societies. This includes political and organizational leadership as well as practitioners of the so-called learned professions such as law, medicine, teaching, and divinity. The problem with Plato's conception of leadership, discussed in Chapter 2, is that he focused on its coercive rather than its educational power. In Plato's view the philosopher-ruler has the right to exercise coercive power because he understands the truth about justice. Isaiah Berlin has called this the "positive" conception of freedom because it authorizes leaders to enforce an attitude or behavior that will free the subject from error.[58] On these grounds many non-Christians and non-Moslems have been put to their deaths throughout the ages, as have many non-Fascists and non-Communists during this century.

But if our moral commitments must be more tentative and more humble, then the guardian can no longer be certain that the individual whose soul he claims to be saving or liberating is not actually dying on the altar of a personal folly. Berlin suggests, therefore, that we adopt a "negative" conception of freedom. According to this view, the leader will be authorized to prevent an individual or group from imposing its will on another and to protect the rights of every individual or group to pursue a chosen vision of happiness provided it does not infringe on anyone else's.[59]

This expects far too little of our leaders and ourselves. To understand leadership in terms of coercive power alone is to forfeit its moral authority, which lies not in forcing others to conform to particular views but in teaching them to do so. Leaders teach not only or even primarily through discourse, although dialogue, discussion, analysis, and explanation are undoubtedly important media. Leaders teach first by example, by who they are, by sincere commitment to a transcendent moral vision. In a democratic society leaders should be model educators! This is why we are often disappointed when leaders fall short of our moral expectations for them, because in doing so they betray the very vision we hope to learn from them.

Democratic leaders are the guardians neither of positive nor of negative freedom but of the very possibility of freedom itself, that is, of moral agency and ethical discourse. They are not only educators but potential defenders of intelligent spirituality as well. *In an open society, all genuine leadership involves spiritual leadership.* Berlin is correct that coercive power is only justified when the possibility of freedom is threatened, but leadership has other positive educative roles such as persuading others to adhere to a vision of goodness and to treat one another with kindness.[60]

Preparing Democratic Citizens

In a democratic society not only are leaders spiritual educators but citizens also become leaders when they accept the responsibilities of self-control and self-governance and when they teach by example. *Every democratic citizen is a potential spiritual educator.* This is the import of the biblical idea that the Israelites are to be "a kingdom of priests and a holy nation" (Exodus 19:6). In a society in which moral agency is fostered, every citizen shares the burdens of service to the holy. This is why the concepts of education and democracy are so deeply intertwined, because education is the process of cultivating moral agency and ethical discourse, while democracy can be viewed as that society designed to protect them.

There are, at least, three models of initiation into this view of democratic citizenship. According to the first, state schools are the main source of education. They must therefore promote primary identification with a vision of the good. By allowing the state to support schools that embrace particular ethnic groups or ethical traditions, this approach runs contrary to the radical pluralism often found in state schools. These might be thought of as spiritual magnet schools. Instead of—or in addition to—special attention to particular academic, social, or artistic interests, such schools would address particular spiritual, ethical, or cultural concerns.

In countries, such as the United States, where there is complete separation of church and state, these schools might promote ethnic, racial, cultural, or gender identification. Bilingual education would find support in this view, as would special attention to hyphenated identities—Latin, African, or Asian American. In countries such as the United Kingdom and Canada, where there is state support of religious education, opportunities for particular religious instruction in the state school is in order.

What this approach rules out, however, is an education that avoids addressing life's most basic issues, either in order not to offend the affinities of one particular group or to appease the desires of another. This sort of avoidance, which is so prevalent in today's state schools, leads to education by reference to the lowest common ethical denominator. Here, the Enlightenment failure to offer an adequate vision of the good is evident. It is not enough to protect the rights of individuals to pursue their own versions of happiness. Liberal society requires individuals who actively embrace alternative visions of the good life; and the task of liberal education is to promote them. Provided they also embrace the conditions of ethical discourse, these schools ought to initiate youngsters into the community of ethical communities through embracing, rather than sidestepping, particular traditions.[61]

According to a second model for educating democratic citizens, the state school should not be in the business of promoting primary identity. This task should be reserved for religious and ethnic subcultures that are organized independently of the public or state sphere. In this model, state schools can only provide a portion of that which is required for a genuine liberal education. This must be supplemented by initiation into some particular community or tradition outside of state-sponsored institutions. In the United States, this has often been the province of the church Sunday school or the Synagogue Hebrew school. For this approach to make a difference, however, much greater cooperation is needed between the state and religious institutions in developing the identities of the student than has been prevalent heretofore. Amy Gutman put the point this way:

> A democratic state of education recognizes that educational authority must be shared among parents, citizens, and professional educators even though such sharing does not guarantee

that power will be wedded to knowledge, that parents can successfully pass their prejudices on to their children, or that education will be neutral among competing conceptions of the good life. . . . A democratic state of education is . . . committed to allocating educational authority in such a way to provide its members with an education adequate to participating in democratic politics, to choosing among (a limited range of) good lives, and to sharing in the several sub-communities, such as families, that impart identity to the lives of its citizens.[62]

A third alternative provides liberal education in independent schools such as Catholic parochial or Jewish day schools that address the whole child in a single educational setting. Schools such as these serve the ends of liberal education only if they aim to initiate the child not only into a particular community of primary identity but also into the democratic community as a whole.

Sectarian Education in Liberal Society

Herein lies the rationale for sectarian education in a liberal society. For much of this century, the American Jewish community placed its faith in state-sponsored public schools to prepare their youth to engage in business, politics, and the professions while relying on supplemental synagogue schools to serve its particular religious and ethnic needs. In contrast, the Catholic community operated a separate school system to provide for the education of its youth. Ironically, today the trends are reversed. The all-day Jewish school system in the United States is on the rise, while the Catholic schools are having difficulty preserving their unique educational missions as purveyors of Catholic tradition and faith.

Until recently, the concern over separate day schools voiced within the Jewish community was that it separated—ghettoized— young Jews from their fellow citizens, which prohibited their proper integration into American society. Similarly, the challenge to the identity of Catholic education in the United States today is in part based on its commitment to preserve and transmit a distinct set of spiritual values in a world of rampant relativism that accepts the equal moral legitimacy of all views without critique.

However, the earlier concern of American Jews and the more recent challenge to Catholic parochial education is not well founded. The idea that there is a completely neutral common culture that can be forged in a melting pot is a myth that has been broken by the crisis of Enlightenment. There can be no common democratic community other than through particular learning communities. About this, the multicultural critique is undoubtedly correct. The notion of neutrality was a not-so-veiled attempt to impose a single cultural model on us all. At first, this was an Anglo-Protestant model. It later became secularized. It has often been unsympathetic to particular religious, ethnic, cultural, or racial affiliations and traditions, especially those that are non-Protestant, non-Anglo, non-European, non-male, and non-white. This neutral society has clearly failed to foster a spiritually compelling conception of the good life in many of its constituents.

This having been said, the very commitment to transmit a moral vision calls upon each community to embrace a transcendent vision of goodness consistent with moral agency and ethical discourse.[63] The state has a genuine interest not only in the schools it sponsors to promote the common good but in every school, public or private, secular or religious. However, the state would be well advised not to establish any particular comprehensive vision of the good, such as a particular religious tradition, but instead to support the common faith that every tradition must embrace if it is to prepare its adherents for participation in the common public domain.

Spiritual Renaissance

Without the support of the communities in which they educate, however, schools cannot deliver spiritual and liberal education. For example, consider again the continuity movement of North American Jewry mentioned previously: it follows from this analysis that one problem with this movement lies in its adherence to an instrumental view of education in which identity and continuity become the external ends that educational institutions are to produce. The irony is that, so long as leaders view education as a means to external ends, they will imperil their ability to accomplish those ends, since the very commitment to the ends they seek to promote only makes sense within the framework of the traditions that education celebrates. But what is the alternative?

I propose a movement of spiritual renaissance and renewal in which adults and children—leaders, educators, parents, and students—take upon themselves the collective and individual commitment to become initiated into and to renew Jewish life through intensive study, practice, and celebration of *Torah*. This involves changes in adult individual and collective behavior prior to asking such changes of children. It requires the development of new Jewish theologies that respond to a postmodern age in which the question of how to be Jewish that occupied previous generations is transformed into today's question of why be Jewish, indeed, why be anything at all in post-Enlightenment, emancipated culture.

Often within North American Jewry, it is assumed that this sort of intensive schooling is only possible in a separate, all-day, sectarian school system. I am inclined to agree. But the crux of the matter is not whether this school system functions independently from the state or, as was the case in many large metropolitan Jewish communities prior to the Second World War, in partnership with and as an intensive supplement to public schools. The central question here is not which sort of schooling is best but in what kind of community will that schooling reside. Will the adults, the families and homes they nurture, the neighborhoods and environments they cultivate, the synagogues they found, and the social institutions they foster, model the values and ideals of the schools and other organizations charged with the responsibility of teaching their children? Will education be seen as the province of children alone, or part of the ongoing renewal of commitment to a life of *Torah*?

American Jews have been enamored with the success of Jewish educational summer camps because they create precisely the sort of communal immersion experience of which I am speaking. However, these summer camps are artificial environments that do not always reflect the values of the adult societies they serve. Jewish renaissance requires not merely that we send our children to summer camp but that we also transform the character of our communities to reflect the values those camps promote so that they will no longer be artificial. Our very lives and those of our communities must become the intensive spiritual hothouses that summer camps represent. I call this *organic community*[64] because there is a natural flow of complementary and mutually reinforcing ideas and ideals, study and practice, from the home to the neighborhood, the school to the synagogue, the youth group and summer camp to the cultural center and the social-welfare organization. Communal norms can only be transmitted when the study, practice, and celebration of goodness is valued as highly by parents, grandparents, aunts, uncles, and neighbors as it is expected to be valued by their children.[65]

This is not only a model for Jewish renewal but for other communities as well. Protestant churches, Catholic parishes, and Moslem mosques—even state schools—are capable of spearheading intensive communal experiences with passion and humility, piety and tolerance. This will require a transformation of the role into which many of these institutions have allowed themselves to be cast. It is possible to accomplish such a transformation by teaching that it is not a compromise to espouse passionate commitment to moral agency and ethical discourse, and to the god or good that flow from such a commitment.[66]

Can this sort of synthesis between spiritual commitment and liberal society work? There is something quite odd about asking whether such pedagogy "works." The very question presupposes the sort of instrumental view of education that we have seen to be problematic. The question to be asked of such a pedagogy is not whether it works, but whether the ends that it celebrates are desirable.

Organic Communities

Sociologists distinguish between communities that grow out of the natural circumstances of the extended family and those created for instrumental purposes such as the division of labor and economic growth. Ferdinand Tonnies used the German term *Gemeinschaft* to denote the former and *Gesellschaft* to capture the latter. *Gemeinschaft* is a romantic concept that depicts premodern, rural folk communities in which there is a commonality of commitment rooted in tribal and familial ties. *Gesellschaft*, on the other hand, is a rational idea that describes modern, urban, stratified, and industrialized societies in which people of different families, cultures, faiths, and ethical persuasions share overlapping economic and political interests.[67]

Emile Durkheim pointed out how *Gemeinschaft*-type communities are characterized by "mechanical solidarity." Belief and conduct are uniform across the community, governed by exterior constraint associated with social pressure. *Gesellschaft*-oriented societies, on the other hand, are united by "organic solidarity," generated by mutual self-interest and interdependence. The former are homogeneous, closed communities, the latter heterogeneous, instrumental, open societies.[68] And neither on its own is up to the challenges of education conceived as a spiritual activity associated with a vision of goodness.

Many *Gemeinschaft*-type communities, such as the Pennsylvania Amish or the ultra-orthodox Hassidim, function as dogmatic, closed societies for which Durkheim's "mechanical solidarity" is apt. However, it is possible to conceive of close, caring communities in which mechanical forms of solidarity rooted in training form the basis of deeper understandings of collective norms acquired through the process of teaching. Similarly, in many *Gesellschaft*-oriented societies, people live unfettered by communal memory and tradition. Often, however, they also suffer an absence of meaning and purpose. Connections to others are instrumental, not "organic" as Durkheim put it, and normative commitments tend to be weak because self-interest is the first priority.[69]

Goodness is holistic and pragmatic. It is tied to tradition and community through a comprehensive vision of life exemplified in concrete virtues. In this respect, its transmission requires support from the sort of caring, nurturing community associated with *Gemeinschaft*. However, goodness is also ethical and synthetic. It assumes freedom, intelligence, and fallibility, and it interacts with other traditions that do the same. For ethical visions to flourish they require regular contact with a variety of competing ideals that can stimulate conversation and criticism. This is most likely to happen in open, *Gesellschaft*-type societies.

Spiritual renaissance through education, therefore, requires the constitution of communities that bridge the rift between these romantic and rational conceptions of social organization. Durkheim's notion of "organic solidity," in other words, that reaches beyond mutual self-interest to genuine interdependence, requires *Gemeinschaft*-type communities rooted in memory and meaning which are open to *Gesellschaft*-oriented societies that embrace growth and innovation. Such communities should evidence both caring and intelligence, conveying passionate commitment to ethical vision on the one hand and openness to critique and creativity on the other. Social associations that evidence these characteristics have the capacity to educate. Consider the following examples.

"A Congregation of Learners"

Isa Aron and her colleagues provide an important illustration of how educational institutions and adult communities—in this case, synagogue schools and congregations—can weave spirituality into their curricula.[70] In her earlier work, Aron drew upon John Westerhoff's distinction between "instruction"—training and teaching—and "enculturation"—"loving induction into culture and community."[71] Instruction, she argued, can be successful only when buttressed by a supportive adult community. If the child's identification with that community is marginal, the instructional material it calls her to learn will lack meaning and relevance. The first task of elementary Jewish education, at least in the supplemental system where the support of adult communities is weak, is not instruction but enculturation.[72] As we put the point above, identity and continuity are not the products but the prerequisites of education.

More recently, Aron and her colleagues sought to strengthen adult communities to facilitate enculturation and instructional support by engaging congregations in the educational missions of their supplemental schools. The task is nothing less than to transform the entire synagogue into "a congregation of learners."[73] Jonathan Woocher identifies three ingredients that can help to transform congregations into learning communities. First, he addresses the nurturing, warmth, and security often missing in highly individualized societies. Second, he writes of the structure and content in life often absent in secular culture. Finally, he discusses the importance of enacting master stories that enable people to see themselves as part of larger, more significant wholes. These can be accomplished, Woocher argues, through renewal of commitment to the study of sacred texts that recount and interpret master stories, to caring and loving-kindness, and to the ritual and pageantry of Jewish life. I have called these the study, practice, and celebration of a vision of the good life.[74]

One synagogue that participated in this project was the Leo Baeck Temple in West Los Angeles.[75] Education director Linda Rabinowitch Thal writes:

> We are told that the world stands, and consequently any authentic Jewish community must stand, on the pillars of *Torah* (study), *avodah*—"worship," and *gemilut chasadim* (deeds of loving-kindness). These pillars are also portals, gateways for reentry into Jewish life. We must be prepared to greet congregants at each of these portals because each individual and family may choose a different point of entry. We must also be sure that the community into which we usher those who cross any of these thresholds is so vibrant and contains such a richly woven tapestry of Jewish possibilities that they will be drawn from

their particular antechamber of welcome into the sanctuary of vital Jewish living. This vibrancy depends upon using our own stories, our symbols, our ritual, and our texts. It is the interconnectedness of the pathways that lead from one portal to another, that provides the possibility of personal integration and allows individuals and families to experience Jewish life as a whole garment. . . . If . . . we can make the synagogue into a community that helps us to find sanctity in all parts of our lives, we will have established the kind of place that allows us to live with a sense of wholeness.[76]

Educating Synagogues

Another example of spiritual renewal through organic community can be found in Joseph Reimer's recent book, *Succeeding at Jewish Education: How One Synagogue Made it Work*.[77] Reimer offers an ethnographic study—a "thick" description based on the reflections of a participant observer—of one synagogue that succeeded in incorporating some of the principles sketched out by Jonathan Woocher and Isa Aron for the creation of a "congregation of learners." Reimer calls it "the educating synagogue."

> Much has been written about formal education of children in synagogue schools. Less has been written about the synagogue as a social and religious institution. But almost nothing has been written about the educating synagogue: the ways that the American synagogue presents its Judaic mission to its constituency . . . how the religiously committed synagogue leadership and the majority of members who do not share those commitments are actively engaged in trying to communicate with and understand one another.[78]

Based on his data, descriptions, and analysis Reimer concludes that "educating synagogues" require certain crucial ingredients. One of these is a clear message that I have referred to in these pages as a vision of the good. He calls it a "distinctive Torah":

I believe that collective self-definition is a key to synagogue education. If Temple Akiba, or any of its sister congregations, hopes to educate the next generation to live as Jews in America, they will have to define a Judaism that is both identifiable and meaningful. Congregants—young and old—have to know what Judaism is so that they might embrace it as their own. Has it distinctive features? Do these features make a difference in their lives? Will belonging enhance their lives?

The rabbis and educators at Temple Akiba have risen to the challenge of giving a definition of Judaism. They are not afraid to say, "In this we believe and in this we don't." . . . They will stand up for a more intensive Jewish education than was offered previously even against calls for less. They will use all the means available to them to announce who they are and what they stand for, even when doing so creates conflict . . . When there is a clear message that gives shape to the educational agenda, children and adults sense that message and respond to it. They are challenged.[79]

Informal Education

Research on youth programming constitutes another example of spiritual renaissance through organic community. It has long been recognized that nonformal experiences such as summer camps, youth groups, and educational tours have a significant impact on religious identification. Fifteen programs were studied that targeted eighteen- to twenty-two-year-old participants and had acknowledged histories of success. Program staff, participants, and supporters uniformly understood their success in terms of participants becoming more "involved or affiliated," "connected or committed to," a Jewish group. Six common themes emerged as characteristics of programs that achieved this sort of success among significant portions of their constituents. They included (1) the quality of professional and peer leadership, (2) attention to group process, (3) autonomous peer involvement, (4) a vision of the role

Judaism plays in the lives of participants, (5) a significant commitment of participant time, and (6) a dedicated place in which groups can meet.[80]

> In sum, our study of good Jewish youth programs has suggested that we can contribute to Jewish continuity through strengthening the preparation of personnel, especially contact staff and peer leaders, the continuing education of current staff and lay leaders, the improvement of curricula, and the recruitment . . . of participants.[81]

Taken together with Aron's work on learning congregations and Reimer's examination of educating synagogues, this description of good youth programs suggests the outline of a theory of organic spiritual community grounded in practice and devoted to the study and celebration of a vision of the good life. Organic communities draw on spiritual resources to enculturate and initiate their youth as well as those who seek to join them as adults. They are caring communities that study sacred teachings and master stories, and that celebrate through ritual and pageantry. They have strong leaders, are concerned about process, have a sense of autonomy, require a commitment of time from their constituents; dedicate sacred space in which to congregate, and articulate clearly and unapologetically, a vision of the life they call their members to lead.

The Educational Task
The task of education—liberal and spiritual—is not to reform the community by means of our children. It is to renew the community by reinvigorating and recommitting *ourselves* to become spiritual role models and democratic leaders whose daily lives are filled with the study, practice, and celebration of a higher vision. It is to create organic communities out of fragmented ones in which our children will be able to thrive, uplifted by authentic moral identities rooted in the resources of religion, ethnicity, culture, nationality, race, gender, or sexual preference.

In the final analysis, investment in good spiritual pedagogy is investment in a community's highest and most sacred values and commitments. To place a priority anywhere else is to misconceive the very idea of a priority, which in the end must serve the higher good that spiritual pedagogy promotes. Falling prey to such misconceptions flattens the moral significance of any other investments we prioritize, indeed, of the very idea of setting priorities altogether. In short, if the education of intelligent spirituality is not our first priority, then the standards we might use to assess the value of other priorities lose their meaning. Those standards derive their significance from the conditions of critical intelligence, freedom, and fallibility that are at the heart of the process of spiritual pedagogy.

The prophet Micah said that people are expected to do three things in life: to do justice, to love mercy, and to walk humbly with their God (Micah 6:8). We have seen that love of mercy is the well-spring of the intelligence necessary for moral discourse. Justice is a consequence of free will, of our capacity to make and enact moral decisions. Humility is an outgrowth of recognizing our fallibility. Embracing these attitudes is what enables us to discover a higher good, to follow a life path that nourishes our souls and encourages us to flourish, to become the best that we can be. These are the commitments that stand at the heart of the free society that allows each to walk with his or her own God provided they are gods of goodness and truth rather than of emptiness, apathy, determinism, and despair.

The Psalmist symbolized this vision in the city of Jerusalem, literally the city of peace and wholeness. He feared that his own vision of goodness and social justice would be snuffed out when the Temple dedicated to the worship of his God was destroyed in Jerusalem by the Babylonians in the year 586 BCE. But he did not despair, he turned, instead, to teaching the memory of what Jerusalem meant to his people. "If I forget you, O Jerusalem," he wrote, "may my right hand wither; may my tongue cleave to my mouth, if I fail to remember you, if I fail to put you above my highest joy"

(Psalm 137:5–6). Because of teachings such as this, the memory of Jerusalem and the ethical vision for which it has stood throughout the ages, a vision of universal social justice rooted in passionate commitment to a particular religious faith, has been transmitted across the generations. It is the initiation into this vision embodied in a spiritual community and renewed each day through study, practice, and celebration that belongs, to use the Psalmist's uplifting phrase, above our highest joys.

Notes

Preface

1. For example, Robert J. Nash, *Faith, Hype, and Clarity: Teaching about Religion in American Schools and Colleges* (New York: Teachers College Press, 1999), pp. 11–13.

2. Evelyn Underhill, *Mysticism: The Nature and Development of Spiritual Consciousness* (Rockport, Mass.: One World Publications, 1993). Nash calls this neo-gnosticism, after the second-century mystical movement that saw direct personal experience of God as the key to salvation (*Faith, Hype, and Clarity*, pp. 130–53).

3. Richard Carlson, *Don't Sweat the Small Stuff . . . and It's All Small Stuff: Simple Ways to Keep Little Things from Taking over Your Life* (New York: Hyperion, 1977).

4. For example, Thomas Merton, *New Seeds of Contemplation* (New York: New Directions, 1961), pp. 29–63.

5. Bernard Williams, *Ethics and the Limits of Philosophy* (Cambridge: Harvard University Press, 1985), pp. 6–7.

6. See, Iris Murdoch, *The Sovereignty of the Good* (London: Routledge, 1970), pp. 77–104.

7. Charles Taylor calls this a work of retrieval in *The Ethics of Authenticity* (Cambridge: Harvard University Press, 1991), p. 23.

8. For example, Michael J. Sandel, *Liberalism and the Limits of Justice* (Cambridge: Cambridge University Press, 1998), pp. 133–74, and John

Kekes, *Moral Wisdom and Good Lives* (Ithaca: Cornell University Press, 1995).

9. For example, John Rawls, *A Theory of Justice* (Oxford: Oxford University Press, 1971).

10. In *Ethics and the Limits of Philosophy,* Bernard Williams distinguishes between ethics in the classical sense and a modern use of morality as referring to right action (pp. 6–7). Also Iris Murdoch, *The Sovereignty of the Good,* p. 53.

11. See, John Dewey, "Religion Versus the Religious," in *A Common Faith* (New Haven: Yale University Press, 1976), pp. 1–28.

12. Thomas Green also seeks to include arts and sciences not usually associated with ethics and the sacred, in *Voices: The Educational Formation of Conscience* (Notre Dame: University of Notre Dame Press, 1999), pp. ix–xii.

13. Immanuel Kant, *Critique of Pure Reason,* Norman Kemp Smith, trans. (London: Macmillan, 1970), pp. 22–25.

14. This shift from analysis and the priority of the right, to synthesis and the priority of the good, is central to the communitarian critique of liberal moral philosophy. Liberal political and ethical theorists such as John Locke, Immanuel Kant, and more recently, John Rawls, are concerned with the analysis and justification of individual rights. Communitarians such as Michael Sandel, Charles Taylor, and Alasdair MacIntyre argue that individual rights and the nature of a just society can only be properly understood within the context of a communal vision of the good. See Stephen Mulhall and Adam Swift, *Liberals and Communitarians* (Oxford: Blackwell, 1992).

15. *New York Times Magazine: A Special Issue,* "God Decentralized," December 8, 1997, p. 55.

16. Robert Bellah et al., *Habits of the Heart: Individualism and Commitment in American Life* (New York: Harper and Row, 1985), p. 237.

17. Aristotle, *Nicomachean Ethics,* Book II, chapter 6, in Richard McKeon, ed., *The Basic Works of Aristotle* (New York: Random House, 1941), pp. 957–59; and Moses Maimonides, *Mishneh Torah: Laws Concerning Moral Dispositions and Ethical Conduct,* chapter 1, in Isadore Twersky, ed., *A Maimonides Reader* (New York: Behrman House, 1972), pp. 51–53, and *Eight Chapters,* chapter 4, in ibid., pp. 364–76.

Chapter One: Spiritual Awakening

1. Elie Wiesel, *The Fifth Son* (New York: Summit Books, 1985), pp. 11–14.

2. Adapted from Elie Weisel, *The Gates of the Forest*, Frances Frenaye, trans. (New York: Schocken Books, 1995).

3. See Philip Wexler, *Holy Sparks: Social Theory, Education, and Religion* (London: Macmillan, 1997), pp. 4–11, and Roof Wade, *A Generation of Seekers: The Spiritual Journeys of the Baby Boom Generation* (New York: Harper-Collins, 1993).

4. Paul Tillich, *Theology of Culture* (Oxford: Oxford University Press, 1959), pp. 40–52.

5. See Iris Murdoch, "On 'God' and 'Good'," in *The Sovereignty of the Good* (London: Routledge, 1970), pp. 46–76.

6. For example, Nel Noddings, *Caring: A Feminine Approach to Ethics and Moral Education* (Berkeley: University of California Press, 1984), pp. 40–46.

7. For example, John Dewey, "Faith and Its Object," in *A Common Faith* (New Haven: Yale University Press, 1976), pp. 29–58. Also, Michael Oakeshott, "Religion and the Moral Life," in *Religion, Politics, and the Moral Life*, Timothy Fuller, ed. (New Haven: Yale University Press, 1993), pp. 39–45.

8. See Paul Tillich, "Theology of Education," in *Theology of Culture*, pp. 146–57.

9. Some of these ideas are developed more fully in H. A. Alexander, "Teaching Theology in Conservative Ideology: Historical Judaism and the Concept of Education," *Conservative Judaism* 48, 4 (1996), pp. 35–52, and "On the Possibility of Teaching Theology," *Panorama: International Journal of Comparative Religious Education and Values* 7, 1 (1995), pp. 83–93.

10. Michael Oakeshott calls this view "religion as the completion of morality," in "Religion and the Moral Life," pp. 41–45.

11. See Simon Rawidowicz, *Israel: The Ever-Dying People and Other Essays*, B. C. I. Ravid, ed. (Rutherford: Farleigh Dickinson University Press, 1986), pp. 135–36.

12. H. A. Alexander, "Teaching Religion," *Religious Education* 89, 1 (1994), pp. 4–7.

13. Unless otherwise indicated, all translations of the Hebrew Bible follow, *TANAKH: A New Translation of the Hebrew Scriptures according to the Masoretic Text* (Philadelphia: Jewish Publication Society of America, 1985).

14. Torah in its most limited sense refers to the Five Books of Moses. It also refers to the whole of the Hebrew Bible. But in its broadest sense, the term encompasses the whole Jewish interpretive tradition with which these texts have been read for thousands of years.

15. See, Michael Walzer, *Exodus and Revolution* (New York: Basic Books, 1985), especially pp. 131–49.

16. For example, Harry A. Wolfson, "What Is New in Philo?" in *From Philo to Spinoza: Two Studies in Religious Philosophy* (New York: Behrman House, 1977), pp. 17–38.

17. Ernest Gellner, *Reason and Culture* (Oxford: Blackwell, 1992), p. 2.

18. Benedict Spinoza, *Theologico-Political Treatise,* R. H. M. Elwes, trans. (New York: Dover, 1951), pp. 175–244.

19. David Hume, *Dialogues Concerning Natural Religion* (New York: The Free Press, 1972), Parts III–VIII.

20. Immanuel Kant, *Religion Within the Limits of Reason Alone* (New York: HarperCollins, 1960).

21. Immanuel Kant, *Critique of Practical Reason,* T. K. Abbott, trans. (New York: Prometheus Books, 1977), p. 46, and *Foundations of the Metaphysics of Morals,* Lewis White Beck, trans. (Indianapolis: Bobbs-Merrill, 1976), pp. 22–64.

22. Thus, Bruce A. Ackerman writes that to accept Kantian-style liberalism, "one need take no position upon a host of Big Questions of a highly controversial character," *Social Justice in the Liberal State* (New Haven: Yale University Press, 1980), p. 361. Also Ronald Dworkin, "Liberalism," in S. Hampshire, ed., *Public and Private Morality* (Cambridge and New York: Cambridge University Press, 1978), pp. 113–43.

23. John Locke, *An Essay Concerning the True Original Extent and End of Civil Government,* in Ernest Barker, ed., *Social Contract* (Oxford: Oxford University Press, 1975), pp. 45–76.

24. David E. Purpel, *The Moral and Spiritual Crisis in Education: A Curriculum for Justice and Compassion in Education* (Granby, Mass.: Bergin and Garvey, 1989), pp. 28–64.

25. Robert Fulghum, *All I Really Needed To Know I Learned in Kindergarten: Uncommon Thoughts on Common Things* (New York: Ivy Books, 1988), pp. 3–6.

26. Robert Bellah and his colleagues write that contemporary religious individualists often see themselves as "spiritual" rather than "religious," as in "I'm not religious but I'm very spiritual," *Habits of the Heart: Individualism and Commitment in American Life* (New York: Harper and Row, 1985), p. 246.

27. Martin Heidegger, *Being and Time,* J. Macquarrie and E. Robinson, trans. (New York: Harper and Row, 1962), pp. 152–53.

28. Hans-Georg Gadamer, *Truth and Method* (New York: Seabury Press, 1975), pp. 235–74.

29. Karl-Otto Apel, "The A Priori of Communication and the Foundation of the Humanities," in Fred R. Dallmayr and Thomas A. McCarthy, eds., *Understanding and Social Inquiry* (Notre Dame: University of Notre Dame Press, 1977), pp. 292–315.

30. Alasdair MacIntyre, *After Virtue: A Study in Moral Theory* (Notre Dame: University of Notre Dame Press, 1984), pp. 244–63.

31. Some critics of modern thought argue that the shift from the priority of the right to that of the good is not a sufficiently dramatic departure from Lockean and Kantian metaphysics and epistemology to capture the radical deviation from liberalism represented by the recent spiritual awakening. Understanding spirituality, this line of thinking suggests, requires an entirely new, nonempirical metaphysics and epistemology. See, for example, Douglas Sloan, *Insight-Imagination: The Emancipation of Thought and the Modern World* (Westport, Conn.: Greenwood, 1993), pp. 3–51. But this appears to embrace the problematic assumption that our conceptions of what ought to be are dependent in some important sense on our views about how we can come to know about what is the case. Surely metaphysical and epistemological concerns must be part of any serious consideration of spirituality. I argue with the communitarians, however, that these concerns can only be sensibly articulated in the broader context of a conception of the good.

32. Robert Nozick, *Philosophical Explanations* (Cambridge: Harvard University Press, 1981), p. 8.

Chapter Two: Spirituality and the Good Life

1. The Hebrew for Egypt, *Mitzraim*, can be vocalized as narrow straits, *meitzarim*. See Richard N. Levy, ed. *On Wings of Freedom: The Hillel Haggadah for the Night of Passover* (Hoboken: B'nai Brith Hillel Foundations and KTAV, 1989), pp. 16, 23–24.

2. Immanuel Kant, *Critique of Practical Reason*, T. K. Abbott, trans. (New York: Prometheus Books, 1996), pp. 108–10, and *Foundations of the Metaphysics of Morals*, Lewis White Beck, trans. (New York: Bobbs-Merrill, 1976), pp. 22–64.

3. John Stuart Mill, *Utilitarianism*, chap. 2, in *Utilitarianism, On Liberty, Essay on Bentham* (New York: Meridian, 1962), pp. 256–62.

4. John Locke, *An Essay Concerning the True Original Extent and End of Civil Government*, in Ernest Barker, ed., *Social Contract* (Oxford: Oxford University Press, 1975), pp. 76–100.

5. See, for example, Hermann Cohen, *The Religion of Reason Out of the Sources of Judaism* (New York: Fredrick Unger, 1972), pp. 35–49, 236–68.

6. William James, "The Will To Believe," in *Essays on Faith and Morals* (New York: Meridian, 1970), pp. 32–62.

7. See, for example, Ronald J. Faley, *Bonding with God: A Reflective Study of Biblical Covenant* (New York: Paulist Press, 1997), and Eugene B. Borowitz, *Renewing the Covenant: A Theology for the Postmodern Jew* (Philadelphia: The Jewish Publication Society, 1991).

8. G. E. Moore, *Principia Ethica*, Thomas Baldwin, ed. (Cambridge and New York: Cambridge University Press, 1994).

9. Friedrich Schleiermacher, "The Nature of Religion," in *On Religion: Speeches to Its Cultured Despisers*, John Oman, trans. (New York: Harper Torchbooks, 1958), pp. 26–118.

10. Søren Kierkegaard, *Fear and Trembling* (Princeton: Princeton University Press, 1954), pp. 30–64, especially p. 53.

11. John Dewey, *Democracy and Education* (New York: The Free Press, 1997), pp. 180–93, and *Experience and Education* (New York: Macmillan, 1997).

12. Richard S. Peters, "Education as Initiation," in R. D. Archambault, ed., *Philosophical Analysis and Education* (New York: Humanities Press, 1972), pp. 87–111.

13. Paul H. Hirst, "Liberal Education and the Nature of Knowledge," in Richard Peters, ed. *Philosophy of Education* (Oxford: Oxford University Press, 1973), pp. 87–111.

14. Benjamin Bloom et al., *A Taxonomy of Educational Objectives*, Handbook 1: *Cognitive Domain* (New York: Longmans, 1956), pp. 25–43.

15. See, H. A. Alexander, "Rationality and Redemption: Ideology, Indoctrination, and Learning Communities," in *Philosophy of Education Yearbook 1996* (Champaign: The Philosophy of Education Society, 1997), pp. 65–73.

16. Alasdair MacIntyre, *Whose Justice, Which Rationality?* (Notre Dame: University of Notre Dame Press, 1989), pp. 1–11.

17. Christopher Lasch, *The Culture of Narcissism: American Life in an Age of Diminishing Expectations* (New York: W. W. Norton, 1991), pp. 71–103.

18. See Harvey Siegel, *Educating Reason: Rationality, Critical Thinking, and Education* (New York and London: Routledge, 1988), pp. 32–47.

19. Charles Taylor, *The Ethics of Authenticity* (Cambridge: Harvard University Press, 1991), pp. 4–8, 109–21.

20. John A. T. Robinson, writing about *Honest To God* in the *Sunday Mirror*, April 7, 1963, quoted in Susan Howatch, *Scandalous Risks* (New York: Fawcett Crest, 1990), pp. 3, 29, 105, 123.

21. John A. T. Robinson, *Honest To God*, quoted in ibid., p. 157.

22. *A Time to Act: Report of The National Commission on Jewish Education* (Cleveland: The Commission on Jewish Education in North America, 1990). H. A. Alexander and Joel Grishaver, *If We Don't Act Now: Report of The Commission on the Jewish Future of Los Angeles* (Los Angeles: Jewish Federation Council, 1991).

23. David Schoem, *Ethnic Survival in America: An Ethnography of a Jewish Afternoon School* (Atlanta: Scholars Press, 1989).

24. H. A. Alexander, Elon Sunshine, and Michelle Dorph, "Education and Jewish Continuity," *Avar V'Atid: A Journal of Jewish Education, Culture, and Discourse* 4, 1 (1997), pp. 101–8.

25. Sidney Simon, Leyland Howe, and Howard Kirschenbaum, *Values Clarification: A Handbook for Teachers and Students* (Dodd Mead, 1984).

26. Emile Durkheim, *Moral Education: A Study in the Theory and Application of the Sociology of Education* (New York: The Free Press, 1986).

27. Lawrence Kohlberg and Elliot Turiel, "Moral Development and Moral Education," in G. Lesser, ed., *Psychology and Educational Practice*

(Chicago: Scott Foresman, 1971), pp. 439–54. Also Robert E. Carter, *Dimensions of Moral Education* (Toronto: University of Toronto Press, 1984), pp. 43–105.

28. Lawrence Kohlberg, *The Philosophy of Moral Development: Moral Stages and the Idea of Justice* (New York: HarperCollins, 1981). Also, Donald R. C. Reed, *Following Kohlberg: Liberalism and the Practice of Democratic Community* (Notre Dame: University of Notre Dame Press, 1977), pp. 163–220.

29. Plato, *The Republic*, H. D. P. Lee, trans. (New York: Penguin Books, 1972), Part I, pp. 51–99.

30. Karl R. Popper, *The Open Society and Its Enemies*, Volume 1: *The Spell of Plato* (London: Routledge and Kegan Paul, 1963), pp. 120–37.

31. Of course, Abraham and Moses challenged God to live up to His own principles, whereas Descartes challenged first principles; and these do not call for precisely the same sorts of questions. But, challenging God potentially undermines first principles as powerfully to the biblical mind as did Cartesian skepticism to the medieval. For, if God is the source of moral authority and can be shown to be wrong according to his own standards, then how can we be certain that God's moral pronouncements in other cases are reliable?

32. Charles Taylor, "What Is Human Agency?" in *Human Agency and Language* (Cambridge: Cambridge University Press, 1988), pp. 15–44; also "The Self in Moral Space," *Sources of the Self: The Making of Modern Identity* (Cambridge: Harvard University Press, 1989), pp. 25–52.

33. See Charles Lamore, "The Right and the Good," in *The Morals of Modernity* (Cambridge: Cambridge University Press, 1996), pp. 19–40.

34. See John McPeck, *Critical Thinking and Education* (New York: St. Martin's Press, 1981), and Harvey Siegel, *Educating Reason*, pp. 5–31.

35. See Michael J. Sandel, *Liberalism and the Limits of Justice* (Cambridge: Cambridge University Press, 1988), pp. 7–11.

36. Harold S. Kushner, *How Good Do We Have To Be? A New Understanding of Guilt and Forgiveness* (Boston: Little, Brown, 1996), pp. 54–55.

37. Moses Maimonides, "Laws Concerning Repentance," in Isadore Twersky, ed., *A Maimonides Reader* (New York: Behrman House, 1989), pp. 77–78.

38. Charles Taylor, *Sources of the Self*, pp. 25–52.

Chapter Three: Subjective Spirituality

1. Jules Harlow, ed., *Mahzor for Rosh Hashanah and Yom Kippur: A Prayer Book for the Days of Awe* (New York: The Rabbinical Assembly, 1973), pp. 240–41.

2. See, Philip Birnbaum, trans., *High Holiday Prayer Book* (New York, The Hebrew Publishing Company, 1989), pp. 361–62.

3. Plato, *The Republic,* H. D. P. Lee, trans. (New York: Penguin Books, 1972), Part V, Book IV, pp. 183–200.

4. Plato, *Phaedrus and the Seventh and Eighth Letters,* Walter Hamilton, trans. (New York: Penguin Books, 1973), pp. 55–66.

5. See, Moshe Idel and Bernard McGinn, *Mystical Union in Judaism, Christianity, and Islam: An Ecumenical Dialogue* (New York: Continuum, 1996).

6. Anne E. Carr, Preface, in Lawrence S. Cunningham, ed., *Thomas Merton, Spiritual Master: The Essential Writings* (New York: Paulist Press, 1992), p. 6.

7. Thomas Merton, *New Seeds of Contemplation* (New York: New Directions, 1972), pp. 34–35.

8. Merton, *New Seeds of Contemplation,* pp. 35–36.

9. Ibid., p. 1.

10. Ibid., p. 3.

11. Ibid., pp. 4–5.

12. Ibid., p. 26.

13. Ibid., p. 64.

14. David Biale, *Gershom Scholem: Kabbalah and Counter-History* (Cambridge: Harvard University Press, 1982), pp. 1–8.

15. Perle Besserman, *Kabbalah and Jewish Mysticism: An Essential Introduction to the Philosophy and Practice of the Mystical Traditions of Judaism* (Boston: Shambhala, 1997), pp. 140–42.

16. See Aviezer Ravitzky, *Messianism, Zionism, and Jewish Religious Radicalism* (Chicago: University of Chicago Press, 1996).

17. For example, David Ariel, *The Mystic Quest: An Introduction to Jewish Mysticism* (New York, Schocken Books, 1988); Aryeh Kaplan, *Meditation and Kabbalah* (York Beach, Maine: Samuel Weiser, 1986); Daniel Matt, *The Essential Kabbalah: The Heart of Jewish Mysticism* (San Francisco: Harper San Francisco, 1995).

18. Perle Besserman, *Kabbalah and Jewish Mysticism*, pp. 4–5.

19. This notion of hidden divine light bears some similarity to George Fox's and Robert Barclay's Quaker idea of the "hidden light." See H. Van Etten, *George Fox and the Quakers*, E. Kelvin Osborn, trans. (1959), and L. Eeg-Olofsson, *Conception of the Inner Light in Robert Barclay's Theology* (1954).

20. Gershom Scholem, *Major Trends in Jewish Mysticism* (New York: Schocken Books, 1973), pp. 244–86, and *Shabbatai Sevi: The Mystical Messiah* (Princeton: Princeton University Press, 1975), pp. 22–93.

21. See, for example, Arthur Green, *Tormented Master: The Life and Spiritual Quest of Rabbi Nahman of Bratslav* (Woodstock, Vt.: Jewish Lights Press, 1992).

22. For a contemplative interpretation of Hasidism, see Rachel Elior, "HaBaD: The Contemplative Ascent to God," in Arthur Green, *Jewish Spirituality: From the Sixteenth Century Revival to the Present* (New York: Crossroads, 1987), pp. 157–205.

23. Lawrence Kushner, *God Was in This Place and I Did Not Know It: Finding Self, Spirituality, and Ultimate Meaning* (Woodstock, Vt.: Jewish Lights Press, 1994), pp. 177–80.

24. Martin Buber, *Hasidism and Modern Man* (New York: Harper and Row, 1958), pp. 21–43.

25. Martin Buber, *I and Thou*, Walter Kaufman, trans. (New York: Charles Scribner's Sons, 1970), p. 59. Years later, this aspect of Buber's thought was very influential on feminists such as Nel Noddings. See her *Caring: A Feminine Approach to Ethics and Moral Education* (Berkeley, University of California Press, 1984), pp. 73–74.

26. Nel Noddings, *Caring*, p. 30.

27. See, for example, Georg Wilhelm Friedrich Hegel, *Phenomenology of Spirit* (Oxford: Oxford University Press, 1979), Friedrich Schleiermacher, *On Religion: Speeches To Its Cultured Despisers*, John Omar, trans. (New York: Harper Torchbooks, 1958), Jean-Jacques Rousseau, *Confessions* (New York: Knopf, 1992), William Wordsworth, *Selected Poems*, John O. Hayden, ed. (New York: Viking Press, 1994).

28. Charles Taylor, *Sources of the Self: The Making of Modern Identity* (Cambridge: Harvard University Press, 1989), pp. 361–62. There is a new

pantheism afoot today in the form of earth and other forms of nature worship. These bear some similarity to Rousseau's naturalism. Although space does not permit discussing every example of the new spiritualism, some of the concerns voiced below in connection with radical subjectivism that are an outgrowth of this sort of naturalism, might well be applied to this pantheistic revival as well.

29. Michel Foucault, *The History of Sexuality,* Vol. 2: *The Use of Pleasure,* Robert Hurley, trans. (New York: Random House, 1990), p. 29.

30. Michel Foucault, *The History of Sexuality,* Vol. 3: *The Care of the Self,* Robert Hurley, trans. (New York: Random House, 1986), pp. 37–68.

31. Michel Foucault, *The Essential Foucault 1954–1984,* Vol. 1: *Ethics, Subjectivity, and Truth,* Paul Rabinow, ed., Robert Hurley and others, trans. (New York: The New Press, 1997), p. 294.

32. Quoted in C. Erricker, J. Erricker, C. Ota, D. Sullivan, and M. Fletcher, *The Education of the Whole Child* (London: Cassell, 1997), p. 10.

33. Richard Rorty, *Contingency, Irony, and Solidarity* (Cambridge: Cambridge University Press, 1989), pp. 23–43.

34. David A. Cooper, *The Heart of Stillness: The Elements of Spiritual Practice* (New York: Bell Tower, 1992), p. 215.

35. Ramana Maharishi, *The Spiritual Teaching of Ramana Maharishi* (Boulder and London: Shambhala, 1972), p. 92, quoted in ibid., p. 215.

36. Thomas Merton, *New Seeds of Contemplation,* p. 2.

37. See, for example, Elliot W. Eisner, *The Enlightened Eye: Qualitative Inquiry and the Enhancement of Educational Practice* (New York: Merrill, 1997), pp. 1–8.

38. Elliot W. Eisner, *Cognition and Curriculum Reconsidered* (New York: Teachers College Press, 1994), pp. 20–38.

39. Alfred Schutz, *On Phenomenology and Social Relations,* Helmut R. Wagner, ed. (Chicago: University of Chicago Press, 1970), pp. 53–95, and George Rickey, *Constructivism: Origins and Evolution* (New York: George Braziller, 1995).

40. Nel Noddings, *Caring,* p. 201.

41. Ibid., pp. 46–58. Also, Carol Gilligan, *In a Different Voice: Psychological Theory and Women's Development* (Cambridge: Harvard University Press, 1993), pp. 128–50.

42. See, for example, Jacques Derrida, *Of Grammatology* (Baltimore: Johns Hopkins University Press, 1977), and Michel Foucault, "The Cultivation of the Self," in *The History of Sexuality*, Vol. 1: *The Care of the Self*, pp. 27–68.

43. Thomas Merton, *New Seeds of Contemplation*, pp. 41–42.

44. Richard Rorty, "The Contingency of Selfhood," in *Contingency, Irony, and Solidarity*, pp. 23–43.

45. H. A. Alexander, "Is Phenomenology the Basis of Qualitative Inquiry?" *Proceedings of the Philosophy of Education Society 1987* (Champaign: The Philosophy of Education Society, 1988), pp. 379–89.

46. See, Charles Taylor, *The Ethics of Authenticity* (Cambridge: Harvard University Press, 1991), pp. 31–42. Franz Rosenzweig makes a similar claim in evaluating Buber's subjective spirituality, see "The Builders," in *On Jewish Learning* (New York: Schocken, 1955), pp. 72–94.

47. Christopher Lasch, *The Culture of Narcissism: American Life in an Age of Diminishing Expectations* (New York: W. W. Norton, 1991), pp. 27–70.

48. Perle Besserman, *Kabbalah and Jewish Mysticism*, pp. 124–38.

49. Thomas Merton, *New Seeds of Contemplation*, p. 52.

50. Ibid., p. 56.

51. According to philosopher Ludwig Wittgenstein, we can understand one another only because concepts such as "caring" are used in accordance with public criteria. See Ludwig Wittgenstein, *Philosophical Investigations*, third edition (Englewood-Cliffs: Prentice-Hall, 1973), sec. 202, p. 81e, and Saul Kripke, *Wittgenstein on Rules and Private Language* (Cambridge: Harvard University Press, 1982).

52. *Babylonian Talmud, Hagiga*, p. 14b.

Chapter Four: Collective Spirituality

1. E.g., Reinhold Niebuhr, *Politics and Faith: A Commentary on Religious, Social, and Political Thought in a Technological Age* (New York: George Braziller, 1968).

2. Bernard Lewis, *The Arabs in History* (New York and Oxford: Oxford University Press, 1993).

3. See Arnold M. Eisen, "Secularization, 'Spirit,' and the Strategies of Modern Jewish Faith," in Arthur Green, ed., *Jewish Spirituality: From the*

Sixteenth-Century Revival to the Present (New York: Crossroads, 1987), pp. 283–316.

4. Plato, *The Republic*, H. D. P. Lee, trans. (New York: Penguin Books, 1972), Part VII, Book VI, pp. 265–78.

5. Aristotle, *Nicomachean Ethics*, in Richard McKeon ed., *The Basic Works of Aristotle* (New York, Random House, 1941), Book I, Chapters 4–13, pp. 936–52.

6. Alasdair MacIntyre, *Whose Justice? Which Rationality?* (Notre Dame: University of Notre Dame Press, 1988), pp. 98–99.

7. Moses Maimonides, *Guide to the Perplexed*, M. Friedlander, trans. (New York: Dover, 1956), pp. 221–50.

8. Thomas Aquinas, "On the Way in Which Divine Truth Is Made Known," *Summa Contra Gentiles*, in A. Pegis, trans., *On the Truth of the Catholic Faith* (New York: Doubleday, 1955), pp. 63–75.

9. Jean Jacques Rousseau, *Social Contract*, Maurice Cranston, trans. (New York: Penguin Classics, 1983), Book II, pp. 69–100.

10. Adam Smith, *An Inquiry into the Nature and Causes of the Wealth of Nations* (New York: Knopf, 1994), Vol. II, pp. 180–81.

11. Karl Marx, *The German Ideology*, in David McLellan, ed. *Karl Marx: Selected Writings* (Oxford: Oxford University Press, 1977), pp. 158–91.

12. Gustavo Gutierrez, *A Theology of Liberation* (Maryknoll, N.Y.: Orbis Books, 1988). Also Neil Ormerod, *Introducing Contemporary Theologies* (Maryknoll, N.Y.: Orbis Books, 1997), pp. 144–54.

13. Leonardo Boff and Clodovis Boff, *Introducing Liberation Theology* (Maryknoll, N.Y.: Orbis Books, 1996), p. 1.

14. Leonardo Boff, *Eccesiogenesis* (Maryknoll, N.Y.: Orbis Books, 1986). Also Neil Ormerod, *Introducing Contemporary Theologies*, pp. 154–63.

15. For Example, Eliezer Schwied, *The Zionism After Zionism* [*Hatzionut Sheaharei Hatzionut*] (Jerusalem: The World Zionist Organization, 1996).

16. Berl Katznelson, "Revolution and Tradition," in Arthur Hertzberg, *The Zionist Idea* (New York, Atheneum, 1969), pp. 392.

17. See Steven J. Zipperstein, *Elusive Prophet: Ahad Ha'Am and the Origins of Zionism* (Berkeley: University of California Press, 1993).

18. For example, Theodor Herzl, "The Jewish State," in Arthur Hertzberg, *The Zionist Idea*, pp. 204–25, and Max Nordau, "Zionism," in ibid., pp. 242–46.

19. The neo-Marxist critiques of post-Zionist thought outlined below can help redress some of the practical and ethical errors of the founders, but for reasons to be articulated as we proceed, the relativism inherent in this position makes it an unlikely candidate to envision higher ideals for the future of Israeli society.

20. Mordecai Kaplan, *Judaism as a Civilization: Toward a Reconstruction of American Jewish Life* (Philadelphia: Jewish Publication Society, 1994), pp. 127–508.

21. See Bernard Reisman, *The Chavurah: A Contemporary Jewish Experience* (New York: Union of American Hebrew Congregations: 1977).

22. Both Heschel's and Soloveitchik's thought includes doses of subjectivism and objectivism. Heschel has sometimes been compared with Merton, yet he also placed great emphasis on ritual. Soloveitchik, who also exhibits strong existentialist tendencies, was a leading authority of Jewish law. I discuss them under the heading of collectivism here not to deny subjective or objective dimensions to their work, which in no way contradict collectivism, but to illustrate how solidarity can be tied to transcendence.

23. Abraham Joshua Heschel, *God in Search of Man* (New York: Harper and Row, 1955), p. 31.

24. Ibid., pp. 355–56.

25. Ibid., p. 120.

26. Ibid., p. 121.

27. Joseph Soloveitchik, *The Lonely Man of Faith* (New York: Doubleday, 1992), p. 20 .

28. Ibid., p.22.

29. Jonathan Cohen, "Strauss, Soloveitchik, and the Genesis Narrative," *The Journal of Jewish Thought* 5 (1995), p. 128; Joseph Soloveitchik, *The Lonely Man of Faith*, p. 64.

30. Jonathan Cohen, "Strauss, Soloveitchik, and the Genesis Narrative," pp. 130–31.

31. Joseph Soloveitchik, "My Lover's Voice Calls," in *The Lonely Man of Faith*.

32. Wilfred Sellars, *Science and Metaphysics* (London: Routledge and Kegan Paul, 1968), p. 222.

33. Richard Rorty, *Contingency, Irony, and Solidarity* (Cambridge: Cambridge University Press, 1989), p. 192.

34. Jürgen Habermas, *The Philosophical Discourse of Modernity*, Fredrick Lawrence, trans. (Cambridge: MIT Press, 1987), and J. M. Bernstein, *Recovering the Ethical Life: Jürgen Habermas and the Future of Critical Theory* (London: Routledge, 1995), pp. 88–135.

35. For example, Mitchell Cohen, *Zion and State: Nation, Class, and the Shaping of Modern Israel* (Oxford: Oxford University Press, 1987).

36. See H. A. Alexander, "Cognitive Relativism in Evaluation," *Evaluation Review* 10, 3 (1986), pp. 259–80.

37. Abraham Joshua Heschel, *God in Search of Man* (New York: Harper and Row, 1955), pp. 114–24.

38. This chapter addresses only the relativist assumptions that proponents of multiculturalism too often embrace. For a thorough and fair analysis of the historical, conceptual, and educational issues surrounding multicultural education, see James A. Banks, *Multiethnic Education: Theory and Practice*, second edition (Boston: Allyn and Bacon, 1988).

39. This is sometimes called "semantic holism"; for example, H. A. Alexander, "Liberal Education and Open Society: Absolutism and Relativism in Curriculum Theory," *Curriculum Inquiry* 19, 1 (1989), p. 21.

40. This is sometimes called "incommensurability," ibid., p. 22.

41. This is sometimes called "theory laden perception," ibid., pp. 23–27.

42. Willard V. O. Quine, "Ontological Relativity," in *Ontological Relativity and Other Essays* (New York: Columbia University Press, 1977), pp. 32–67.

43. Peter Berger, Brigette Berger, and Hansfried Kellner, *The Homeless Mind: Modernization and Consciousness* (New York: Vintage Books, 1974), pp. 184–85.

44. D. Z. Phillips, *Faith and Philosophical Enquiry* (London: Routledge and Kegan Paul, 1970) p. 237.

45. See Roger Trigg, *Reason and Commitment* (Cambridge and New York: Cambridge University Press, 1973), pp. 1–27.

46. Ludwig Wittgenstein, *Philosophical Investigations* (New York: Macmillan, 1953), sections 1–7, pp. 2e–5e.

47. It is possible that Heschel did not embrace this sort of relativism intentionally but inherited it when he adopted philosophical language in

which it is implicit. The deeper insight behind the relativistic language is that *coming to know God* through religious experience is not at all the same as *coming to know of God's existence* through rational argumentation. The latter is not a religious activity, the former is. See Michael Peterson, William Hasker, Bruce Reichenbach, and David Basinger, *Reason and Religious Belief* (Oxford: Oxford University Press, 1991), pp. 13–31.

48. Boethius, *The Consolation of Philosophy* (New York: Viking Press, 1987).

49. See Alasdair MacIntyre, "The Rationality of Traditions," In *Whose Justice? Which Rationality?* pp. 349–69.

50. Karl Popper, "Facts, Standards, and Truth: A Further Critique of Relativism," in *The Open Society and Its Enemies,* Vol. II: *The High Tide of Prophecy: Hegel, Marx, and the Aftermath* (London: Routledge and Kegan Paul, 1963), pp. 369–96.

Chapter Five: Objective Spirituality

1. Simon Blackburn discusses a somewhat similar concept in *Essays in Quasi-Realism* (Oxford: Oxford University Press, 1993), especially pp. 3–11.

2. Paul Tillich, *Biblical Religion and the Search for Ultimate Reality* (Chicago: University of Chicago Press, 1955), pp. 81–83.

3. Plato, *The Republic,* H. D. P. Lee, trans. (New York: Penguin Books, 1972), Part VII, Book VII, pp. 278–86.

4. Ibid., Part VIII, Book VII, pp. 300–304.

5. This is not to say that Buber and Soloveitchik, and to some degree Heschel, are not also Jewish existentialists, but only that I referred to their thought earlier to illustrate relational and collective aspects of spirituality. I will touch on Rosenzweig below to make a point about the Jewish emphasis on ritual.

6. Shalom Spiegel, *Amos vs. Amaziah,* Essays in Judaism, No. 3 (New York: The Jewish Theological Seminary of America, 1957).

7. One might ask whether Moses' response to the rebels was not overly harsh. Perhaps he should have intervened on their behalf as well. See, Michael Walzer, *Exodus and Revolution* (New York: Basic Books, 1985), pp. xi, 55–60.

8. Paul Tillich, *Dynamics of Faith* (New York: HarperCollins, 1986), p. 1.

9. Ibid. p. 4.

10. Ibid., pp. 9–10.

11. Ibid., p. 11.

12. Ibid., p. 10–11.

13. Ibid., p. 16. Also, Tillich, *The Courage to Be* (New Haven: Yale University Press, 1978), pp. 186–90.

14. Tillich, *Dynamics of Faith,* p. 17.

15. Ibid., p. 20.

16. Ibid., p. 28–29.

17. Franz Rosenzweig, *On Jewish Learning* (New York: Schocken, 1965), pp. 72–92.

18. Ibid., p. 75.

19. Ibid., p. 76.

20. Parker J. Palmer, *The Courage to Teach: Exploring the Inner Landscape of a Teacher's Life* (San Francisco: Jossey-Bass, 1998), p. 32.

21. Franz Rosenzweig, *On Jewish Learning,* p. 120.

22. Ibid.

23. Ibid., p. 122.

24. Ibid., p. 120.

25. Shimon Hurwitz, *Being Jewish* (Jerusalem: Feldheim, 1978), p. 15.

26. Mayer Schiller, *The Road Back* (Jerusalem: Feldheim, 1978), pp. 211–12.

27. Janet Aviad, *Return to Judaism: Religious Renewal in Israel* (Chicago: University of Chicago Press, 1983), pp. 157–61. See also Samuel Heilman, *Defenders of the Faith: Inside Ultra-Orthodoxy* (New York: Schocken, 1992), and M. Herbert Danzger, *Returning to Tradition: The Contemporary Revival of Orthodox Judaism* (New Haven: Yale University Press, 1989).

28. Abraham Joshua Heschel, *God in Search of Man* (New York: Harper and Row, 1955), pp. 320–21.

29. Hayim Soloveitchik, "Rupture and Reconstruction: The Transformation of Contemporary Orthodoxy," *Tradition* 28, 4 (1994), pp. 64–130.

30. See Robert J. Nash, *Faith, Hype, and Clarity: Teaching About Religion in American Schools and Colleges* (New York: Teachers College Press, 1999), pp. 22–25.

31. Robert Maynard Hutchins, *The Great Conversation* (Chicago: Encyclopaedia Britannica, 1952), and *The Learning Society* (New York: Fredrick A. Praeger, 1968).

32. Mortimer J. Adler, *Reforming Education: The Opening of the American Mind* (New York: Macmillan, 1988), pp. xix–xxxiii, 318–50.

33. For a critique of this view, see H. A. Alexander, "Liberal Education and Open Society: Absolutism and Relativism in Curriculum Theory," *Curriculum Inquiry* 19:1 (1989), pp. 11–32.

34. Alan Bloom, *The Closing of the American Mind: How Higher Education has Failed Democracy and Impoverished the Souls of Today's Students* (New York: Simon and Schuster, 1987), p. 25.

35. Ibid., p. 26, emphasis added.

36. Ibid., p. 344.

37. Ibid., p. 381.

38. Douglas Sloan, *Insight-Imagination: The Emancipation of Thought and the Modern World* (Westport, Conn.: Greenwood Publishers, 1993), pp. 3–10.

39. M. Scott Peck, *The Road Less Traveled: A New Psychology of Love, Traditional Values, and Spiritual Growth* (New York: Simon and Schuster, 1978), p. 226.

40. Ibid., p. 223.

41. Ibid., p. 232.

42. Paul Tillich, *The Courage to Be*, pp. 40–56.

43. Ibid., pp. 151–90.

44. For an interesting analysis of the religious and intellectual failings of fundamentalism, see Robert J. Nash, *Faith, Hype, and Clarity*, pp. 40–57.

45. There are textual arguments against religious dogmatism that are beyond the purview of this volume. One would be hard pressed, for example, to defend a literalist account of revelation based on Exodus 19–20. There was so much noise, fire, and smoke that the people were afraid to even listen to God's voice. They asked Moses to approach God on their behalf. Divine revelation is mediated, therefore, with all the hermeneutic complexities this implies. See, for example, David Couzens Hoy, *The Critical Circle: Literature, History, and Philosophical Hermeneutics* (Berkeley: University of California Press, 1982). Moreover, a coercive conception of divinity undermines God's moral authority and ignores repeated biblical polemics against the abuse of power (e.g., Deuteronomy 17: 15–20,

1 Samuel 8). Deuteronomic references to reward and punishment should be understood as natural consequences of life choices, built into the very moral fabric of the human condition.

46. See Abraham Joshua Heschel, "Religion in a Free Society," in *The Insecurity of Freedom* (New York: Schocken Books, 1972), pp. 3–23.

47. Susan Howatch, *Absolute Truths* (New York: Fawcett Crest, 1994).

48. See Michael Polanyi, *Science, Faith, and Society* (Chicago: University of Chicago Press, 1964), pp. 63–84.

49. See Ignacio L. Gotz, "On Spirituality and Teaching," *Philosophy of Education Yearbook 1997* (Champaign: The Philosophy of Education Society, 1998) and Reinhold Niebuhr, *The Nature and Destiny of Man,* vol. 1 (New York: Scribner's, 1964), pp. 194–95.

50. Robert Nozick, *Philosophical Explanations* (Cambridge: Harvard University Press, 1981), p. 5.

51. August Comte, "A General View of Positivism," in Getrud Lenzer, ed., *August Comte and Positivism: The Essential Writings* (New York: Transaction Publishers, 1998), pp. 309–89.

52. A. J. Ayer, *Logical Positivism* (New York: The Free Press, 1966).

53. Perhaps this is why some very orthodox believers are comfortable becoming scientists. They adopt a mechanistic view of both religion and science that allows each to remain compartmentalized and unaffected by the other.

54. See H. A. Alexander, "Science and Spirituality: Tradition and Interpretation in Liberal Education," *Curriculum Inquiry* 22, 4 (1992), pp. 383–400.

Chapter Six: Intelligent Spirituality

1. Charles Taylor, *The Ethics of Authenticity* (Cambridge: Harvard University Press, 1991), p. 58.

2. Lionel Trilling, *Sincerity and Authenticity* (Cambridge: Harvard University Press, 1982), pp. 3–5.

3. Charles Taylor, *The Ethics of Authenticity,* p. 40.

4. Ibid., pp. 28–29.

5. Ibid. p. 41. See also H. A. Alexander, "Jewish Education and the Search for Authenticity: A Study of Jewish Identity," in David Zisenwein

and David Schers, eds., *Making a Difference: Jewish Identity and Jewish Education*, Studies in Jewish Education, Identity, and Community (Tel Aviv: Tel Aviv University School of Education, 1997), pp. 37–66.

6. See Thomas F. Green, "Teaching, Acting, and Behaving," *Harvard Educational Review* 34, 4 (1964), and *The Activities of Teaching* (Troy, N.Y.: Educator's International Press, 1998). Also H. A. Alexander, "What Is the Power of Jewish Education? Lipset's Analysis in Philosophical Perspective," in Seymour Martin Lipset, *The Power of Jewish Education* (Los Angeles: Wilstein Institute of Jewish Policy Studies, 1994).

7. See H. A. Alexander, "Teaching Theology in Conservative Ideology: Historical Judaism and the Concept of Education," *Conservative Judaism* 48, 4 (1996), pp. 35–52; "On the Possibility of Teaching Theology," *Panorama: The International Journal of Comparative Religious Education and Values* 7, 1 (1995), pp. 83–93; and "Teaching Religion," *Religious Education* 89, 1 (1994), pp. 4–7.

8. Lee S. Shulman, *Communities of Learners and Communities of Teachers*, Monographs from the Mandel Institute, no. 3 (Jerusalem: The Mandel Institute, 1997), pp. 22–23.

9. Robert Bellah et al., *Habits of the Heart: Individualism and Commitment in American Life* (New York: Harper and Row, 1985), p. 153; also see p. 333.

10. See Nel Noddings, *Caring: A Feminine Approach to Ethics and Moral Education* (Berkeley: University of California Press, 1984), pp. 79–103.

11. Philip Phenix, "Transcendence and the Curriculum," *Teachers College Record* 73, 2 (1971). Also, Abraham H. Maslow, *Religions, Values, and Peak Experiences* (New York: Penguin Books, 1983), pp. 19–35.

12. John Dewey, *The Quest for Certainty* (New York: Minton and Balch, 1929), pp. 26–48.

13. See Paul Tillich, *The Dynamics of Faith* (New York: HarperCollins, 1986), p. 20.

14. Sarah Lawrence Lightfoot, *The Good High School: Portraits of Character and Culture* (New York: Basic Books, 1983), pp 23–26.

15. Immanuel Kant, *Critique of Pure Reason*, Norman Kemp Smith, trans. (New York: Macmillan, 1970), pp. 532–49.

16. See Franz Rosenzweig, "The Jewish Writings of Hermann Cohn," *Naharaim* (Jerusalem: Mosad Bialik, 1960), pp. 109–53.

17. Rudolf Otto, *The Idea of the Holy* (Oxford and New York: Oxford University Press, 1958).

18. For example, Plato, *The Republic,* H. D. P. Lee, trans. (New York: Penguin Books, 1972), Part VII, Book VI. pp. 264–74, and *Phaedrus and the Seventh and Eighth Letters,* Walter Hamilton, trans. (New York: Penguin Books, 1973), pp. 50–66.

19. See Antony Flew and Alasdair MacIntyre, eds., *New Essays in Philosophical Theology* (New York: Macmillan, 1973), pp. 96–130.

20. *Babylonian Talmud, Bava Metzia,* p. 59b–60a.

21. The *Talmud* records that God was not altogether sanguine about the consequences of these deliberations. Rabban Gamliel, the Patriarch who banned Rabbi Eliezer for refusing to accept the will of the majority, eventually met his own demise for taking that action. God may be willing to accept criticism, but is unforgiving about the uncompromising exercise of power. See, Milton Steinberg, *As a Driven Leaf* (New York: Behrman House, 1996).

22. These are probably necessary but not sufficient conditions for someone to be considered a good person.

23. Quoted in Harold S. Kushner, *How Good Do We Have to Be? A New Understanding of Guilt and Forgiveness* (Boston: Little, Brown, 1996), p. 170.

24. See Martin S. Cohen, *In Search of Wholeness: The Pursuit of Spiritual Integrity in a Delusional World* (London, Ont.: Moonstone Press, 1996).

25. Ibid. p. 54.

26. Thomas Merton, *New Seeds of Contemplation* (New York: New Directions, 1972), pp. 48–49.

27. *Mishnah Sanhedrin,* 4:5.

28. *Numbers Raba,* 15:3.

29. See Charles Taylor, *Sources of the Self: The Making of Modern Identity* (Cambridge: Harvard University Press, 1989), pp. 32–40, and John Dewey, *Democracy and Education* (New York: The Free Press, 1997), pp. 14–18.

30. See Michael Rosenak, *Roads to the Palace* (Oxford: Berghan Books, 1995), pp. 19–20; Michael Oakeshott, "The Study of 'Politics' in a University," *Rationalism in Politics and Other Essays* (London: Methuen, 1962), pp. 303–13; and R. S. Peters, "Reason and Habit: the Paradox of Moral Education," in *Moral Development and Moral Education* (London: George Allen and Unwin, 1981), pp. 45–60.

31. See H. A. Alexander, "Literacy, Education, and the Good Life," in David Zisenwein and David Schers, eds., *Present and Future: Jewish Culture, Identity, and Language,* Studies in Jewish Culture, Identity, and Community (Tel Aviv: University of Tel Aviv School of Education, 1999), pp. 35–62.

32. Harvey Siegel, *Educating Reason: Rationality, Critical Thinking, and Education* (New York: Routledge, 1988), p. 32.

33. Ibid., 34–38.

34. Ibid., 38–42.

35. Ibid., pp. 71–72.

36. H. A. Alexander, "Rationality and Redemption: Ideology, Indoctrination, and Learning Communities," *Philosophy of Education Yearbook 1997* (Champaign: The Philosophy of Education, 1997), pp. 65–73, and Harvey Siegel, "Can Reasons for Rationality Be Redeemed?" in ibid., pp. 74–76.

37. See Thomas F. Green, "Indoctrination and Beliefs," in I. A. Snook, ed., *Concepts of Indoctrination* (London: Routledge and Kegan Paul, 1972), pp. 44–45.

38. Harvey Siegel, *Educating Reason,* pp. 81–85.

39. H. A. Alexander, "Rationality and Redemption," p. 69.

40. Harvey Siegel, *Educating Reason,* pp. 55–61.

41. Thomas Moore, *The Education of the Heart* (New York: Harper-Collins, 1996), p. 5. Also, Ronald de Souse, *The Rationality of Emotion* (Cambridge: MIT Press, 1995), pp. 171–203, and Daniel Goldman, *Emotional Intelligence* (New York: Bantam Books, 1995).

42. Nel Noddings, *Caring,* pp. 64, 67, 193–97.

43. Philip Birnbaum, trans., *Daily Prayer Book* (New York: Hebrew Publishing Co., 1997), p.74.

44. Deuteronomy 24:16 appears to contradict the view that the children should be punished for the sins of the parents: "Parents shall not be put to death for children, nor children for parents: a person shall be put to death only for his own crime." See also Ezekiel 18.

45. Susan Howatch, *Scandalous Risks* (New York: Fawcett Crest, 1990).

46. Susan Howatch, *The Wonder Worker* (New York: Alfred A. Knopf, 1997).

47. C. J. B. Macmillan, "Love and Logic in 1984," *Philosophy of Education 1984* (Normal, Ill.: The Philosophy of Education Society, 1985), pp. 3–16, and Barbara Arnstine, "Rational and Caring Teachers: How Dis-

positional Aims Shape Teacher Preparation," *Philosophy of Education 1990* (Normal, Ill.: The Philosophy of Education Society, 1991).

Chapter Seven: Educating Spirituality

1. *Babylonian Talmud, Kidushin,* p. 40b.

2. Richard S. Peters, "Education as Initiation," in R. D. Archambault, ed., *Philosophical Analysis and Education* (New York: Humanities Press, 1972), pp. 87–111.

3. David E. Purpel, *The Moral and Spiritual Crisis in Education: A Curriculum for Justice and Compassion in Education* (Granby, Mass.: Bergin and Garvey Publishers, 1989), pp. 1–13, and David Tyack and Larry Cuban, *Tinkering Toward Utopia: A Century of School Reform* (Cambridge: Harvard University Press, 1995), pp. 1–10.

4. See H. A. Alexander, Elon Sunshine, and Michelle Sullum Dorph, "Education and Jewish Continuity," *Avar V'Atid: A Journal of Jewish Education, Culture, and Discourse* 4, 1 (1997), pp 101–8.

5. Sylvia Ashton-Warner, *Teacher* (London: Virago, 1980), quoted in C. Erricker et al., *The Education of the Whole Child* (London: Cassell, 1997), p. 5.

6. F. M. Cornford, *Plato's Theory of Knowledge* (London: Routledge and Kegan Paul, 1959), p. 152a.

7. Jean-Jacques Rousseau, *Emile,* P. D. Jimack, ed., Babara Foxley, trans. (Everyman's Library, 1974), pp. 5–10.

8. Sigmund Freud, *Civilization and Its Discontents,* James Strachey, trans. (New York: W. W. Norton, 1989).

9. John Dewey, "The Child and the Curriculum," in *The School and Society and The Child and the Curriculum* (Chicago: University of Chicago Press, 1991), pp. 3–31.

10. John Dewey, *Experience and Education* (New York: Macmillan, 1997), pp. 17–23.

11. Theodore Roszak, *Person/Planet* (London: Granada, 1981), quoted in C. Erricker et al., *The Education of the Whole Child,* p. 13.

12. Stanley Aronowitz and Henry A. Giroux, *Postmodern Education: Politics, Culture, and Social Criticism* (Minneapolis: University of Minnesota Press, 1991), p. 17.

13. Ibid., p. 15.

14. Ibid., p. 22.

15. F. M. Cornfeld, *Plato's Theory of Knowledge*, pp. 161–62.

16. William Pinar refers to this orientation as "reconceptualist," because it reconceives earlier curriculum theories, *Curriculum Theorizing* (Berkeley: McCutchan, 1983). I prefer "reconstructionist," because it emphasizes continuity from George Counts's *Dare the School Build a New Social Order?* (Chicago: University of Chicago Press, 1934) to Michael Apple's *Ideology and Curriculum* (London: Routledge and Kegan Paul, 1979).

17. Karl Marx, *Economic and Philosophical Manuscripts,* in David McLellen, ed., *Karl Marx: Selected Writings* (Oxford: Oxford University Press, 1977), pp. 75–77; Marx, *Grundrisse,* in ibid., pp. 362–65, and *Capital,* in ibid., pp. 515–17.

18. Peter McLaren, *Life in Schools: An Introduction to Critical Pedagogy in the Foundations of Education* (New York: Longman, 1989), p. 166.

19. Ibid., p. 169.

20. Ibid., p. 171.

21. Ibid., p. 176.

22. Ibid., pp. 180–91.

23. This is ironic since Max Horkheimer launched critical theory—from which critical pedagogy derives its assumptions—with his own critique of instrumentalism; see his *Critique of Instrumental Reason* (New York: Continuum, 1996), especially pp. 136–58. However, so long as ideology is relative to social class, and culture determines behavior, it is hard to see how to escape these instrumentalist consequences.

24. Herbert M. Kliebard, *The Struggle for the American Curriculum 1893–1958,* second edition (New York: Routledge, 1995), pp. 89–122.

25. John Dewey, *Experience and Education,* p. 17.

26. See Peter McLaren, *Life in Schools,* pp. 186–90.

27. Philip W. Jackson, *The Practice of Teaching* (New York: Teachers College Press, 1986), p. 117.

28. Ibid., p. 118.

29. See Richard Peters, "Education as Initiation."

30. *Mishnah Avot* 4:2.

31. Michael J. Sandel, *Liberalism and the Limits of Justice* (Cambridge: Cambridge University Press, 1998), p. 22.

32. Paul Hirst, "Liberal Education and the Nature of Knowledge," in Richard Peters, ed., *Philosophy of Education* (Oxford and New York: Oxford University Press, 1973), pp. 87–111.

33. Joseph Schwab, "The Structure of the Disciplines," in Ian Westbury and Neil J. Wilkof, *Science, Curriculum, and Liberal Education* (Chicago: Chicago University Press, 1978), pp. 229–72.

34. Philip Phenix, *Realms of Meaning: A Philosophy of Curriculum for General Education* (New York: McGraw-Hill, 1964), pp. 3–14.

35. Elliot W. Eisner, *Cognition and Curriculum Reconsidered* (New York: Teachers College Press, 1994), pp. 39–60.

36. H. A. Alexander, "Literacy, Education, and the Good life," in David Zisenwein and David Schers, eds., *Present and Future: Jewish Culture, Identity, and Language,* Studies in Jewish Culture, Identity, and Community (Tel Aviv: Tel Aviv University School of Education, 1999), pp. 35–62.

37. Michael Rosenak, *Commandments and Concerns: Jewish Religious Education in Secular Society* (Philadelphia: The Jewish Publication Society, 1987), pp. 108–26.

38. Naturalistic ethics are often called secular. I do not find the distinction between religion and secularism especially useful, but I agree with Nel Noddings that intelligent believers and unbelievers have more in common with one another than with unintelligent believers and unbelievers; see her *Educating for Intelligent Belief or Unbelief* (New York: Teachers College Press, 1993), p. xiii.

39. Lee Shulman, "Those Who Understand: Knowledge Growth in Teaching," *Educational Researcher* (February 1986), pp. 4–14.

40. Elliot Eisner, *The Educational Imagination: On the Design and Evaluation of School Programs,* third edition (Upper Saddle River, N.J.: Prentice-Hall, 1994), pp. 87–107.

41. Robert Dreeban, *On What Is Learned in Schools* (Reading, Mass.: Addison Wesley, 1968), Michael Apple, "The Hidden Curriculum and the Nature of Conflict," in *Ideology and Curriculum* (London and Boston: Routledge and Kegan Paul, 1979), pp. 82–104, and, Peter McLaren, *Life in Schools* (New York and London: Longman, 1989), pp. 183–85.

42. The term "empowerment" is used by critical pedagogues who embrace deterministic assumptions to denote the goal of social criticism, e.g., Ira Shor, *Empowering Education: Critical Teaching for Social Change* (Chicago:

University of Chicago Press, 1992). However, empowerment flows from the recognition that I am the master of my own fate, not from the feeling that destiny is controlled by external forces. Of course, critical pedagogues seek to educate for just such a sense of self-mastery. But if my beliefs and behaviors have until now been the product of socially determined ideologies, and if any new view I would adopt is also the product of such social and political forces, how does adopting a new "critical" stance empower *me*? It seems instead that in adopting this new stance, I am merely switching my subservience from one ideological master to another.

43. Elliot W. Eisner, *The Educational Imagination: On the Design and Evaluation of School Programs,* third edition (Upper Saddle River, N.J.: Prentice-Hall), pp. 212–344; also, his *The Enlightened Eye: Qualitative Inquiry and the Enhancement of Educational Practice* (New York: Merrill, 1997), pp. 63–168.

44. Elliot W. Eisner, *The Art of Educational Evaluation: A Personal View* (Philadelphia: Falmer Press, 1985), p. 105, and John Dewey, *Art as Experience* (New York: Perigee Books, 1980), pp. 298–325.

45. See Alfred Schutz, *On Phenomenology and Social Relations,* Helmut R. Wagner, ed. (Chicago: University of Chicago Press, 1970), pp. 85–95.

46. See John Westerhoff, *Will Our Children Have Faith?* (New York: Seabury Press, 1976), and Isa Aron, "The Malaise of Jewish Education," *Tikkun 4* (1989), pp. 32–34.

47. See Raymond Holley, *Religious Education and Religious Understanding: An Introduction to Religious Education* (London: Routledge and Kegan Paul, 1978).

48. Teaching *about* religion is sometimes associated with the "phenomenological approach" to religious education. See Terence J. Lovat, *What Is This Thing Called Religious Education?* (Sydney: Social Science Press: 1989), pp. 51–84.

49. Teaching students to embrace particular traditions is sometimes called "confessional" religious education. For a thorough discussion of the tensions between this sort of religious education and the values of academic life, see Trevor Cooling, *A Christian Vision for State Education* (London: Society for Promoting Christian Knowledge, 1994).

50. H. A. Alexander, "Intelligence and Passion in Teaching," in *Philosophy of Education Yearbook 1997* (Champaign: The Philosophy of Education Society, 1998), pp. 209–13.

51. Elliot W. Eisner, *The Educational Imagination*, pp. 87–107

52. Max Kadushin, *The Rabbinic Mind* (New York: Bloch, 1972), pp. 194–272; also his *Worship and Ethics: A Study in Rabbinic Judaism* (New York: Bloch Publishing, 1963), pp 13–17.

53. Philip Wexler has something like this in mind when he writes of "resacralizing" everyday life (p. 6), social theory (pp. 88–90) and education (pp. 133–52) in *Holy Sparks: Social Theory, Education, and Religion* (London: Macmillan, 1997).

54. H. A. Alexander, Gail Dorph, and Ron Wolfson, "Opening Their Eyes: Being a Teacher in Jewish Schools," *Jewish Education* 56, 4 (1987), pp. 29–33.

55. Thomas F. Green, *The Activities of Teaching* (Troy, N.Y.: Educators International Press, 1998), pp. 193–214.

56. See Gershom Scholem, *Shabbatai Sevi* (Princeton: Princeton University Press, 1973), pp. 1–102.

57. *Mishnah Avot* 4:2.

58. Isaiah Berlin, "Two Concepts of Liberty," in *Four Essays on Liberty* (Oxford and New York: Oxford University Press, 1969), pp. 131–34.

59. Ibid., pp. 122–31.

60. See Charles Taylor, "What's Wrong with Negative Liberty?" in *Philosophy and the Human Sciences* (Cambridge and New York: Cambridge University Press, 1988), pp. 211–29.

61. See Amy Gutman, *Democratic Education* (Princeton: Princeton University Press, 1987), pp. 48–70.

62. Ibid., p. 42.

63. Ibid., pp. 71–94, and John Dewey, *A Common Faith* (New Haven, Yale University Press, 1976), especially pp. 22–57.

64. Joseph Schwab called this "milieu"; see his "The Practical: Arts of Eclectic," and "The Practical: Translation to Curriculum," in Ian Westbury and Neil Wilkof, eds., *Science, Curriculum, and Liberal Education* (Chicago: University of Chicago Press, 1978), pp. 339–40 and pp. 365–68.

65. See Lawrence Cremin, "Toward an Ecology of Education," *Public Education* (New York: Basic Books, 1976), pp. 27–53.

66. See George W. Nobbit and Van O. Dempsey, *The Social Construction of Virtue: The Moral Life of Schools* (New York: SUNY Press, 1996).

67. Ferdinand Tonnies, *Community and Society (Gemeinschaft und Gesellschaft)*, Charles P. Loomis, trans. (New York: Harper and Row, 1957).

68. Emile Durkheim, *The Division of Labor in Society*, W. D. Halls, trans. (New York: Macmillan, 1984).

69. Thomas Green, *Voices*, pp. 50–60.

70. Isa Aron, Sarah Lee, and Seymour Rossel, *A Congregation of Learners: Transforming the Synagogue into a Learning Community* (New York: UAHC Press, 1995).

71. John Westerhoff, *Will Our Children Have Faith?* (New York: Seabury Press, 1976).

72. Isa Aron, "The Malaise of Jewish Education," *Tikkun* 4 (1989), pp. 32–34.

73. Isa Aron, "From Congregational School to Learning Congregation: Are We Ready for a Paradigm Shift?" in *A Congregation of Learners*, pp. 56–77, and "Avocational Teaching: The Genesis and Diffusion of an Idea" *Religious Education* 92, 4 (1997), pp. 430–39, and Sharon Feiman-Nemser "Teach Them Diligently to Your Children: An Experiment in Avocational Teaching," *Religious Education* 92, 4 (1997), pp. 440–58.

74. Jonathan Woocher, "Toward a 'Unified Field Theory' of Jewish Continuity," in Isa Aron et al., *A Congregation of Learners*, pp. 14–55.

75. Linda Rabinowitch Thal, "Reimaging Congregational Education: A Case Study of a Work in Progress," in Isa Aron et al., *A Congregation of Learners*, pp. 185–227.

76. Ibid., pp. 215–17.

77. Joseph Reimer, *Succeeding at Jewish Education: How One Synagogue Made It Work* (Philadelphia: Jewish Publication Society, 1997).

78. Ibid., p. 3

79. Ibid., p. 184.

80. H. A. Alexander and Ian Russ, "Good Jewish Youth Programming," *Agenda for Jewish Education* 3 (1993), pp. 25–30.

81. Ibid., p. 30.

Index

gender: as a basis for collective identity,
78, 180, 201, 211; representation
in multiculturalism, 95
"general will," the social contract as
consensus of for Rousseau, 82
Genesis
1, 89, 112, 153
2, 89–90
3:1–24, 48–49
6:9–8:19, 147
9:21, 147
18:16–33, 115; 18:23–26, 40, 148
Giroux, Henry, 176
God, ix, 10, 12, 103, 109–10, 121 (see
also divinity)
as fallible, 10, 41, 147–50
human sharing of moral agency
with, 48–49
image of the teacher as metaphor
for, 196
for Kant, 146–47
knowledge of for mystics, 116
love for us expressed through the
gift of Torah, 166, 172
in Luria's interpretation of
Kabbalism, 59–60
name change in Exodus 6:2–7, 114
relationship with, 72, 112, 121,
229n47; in Christian
contemplative tradition, 57–58;
by means of rituals, Buber's
attitude toward, 61, 119–20
seen as changing course in
response to humans, 40–41,
115–16; with Abraham at
Sodom and Gomorrah, 40,
222n31; in the incident of the
golden calf, 109–10, 112,
114–15
theology used as term broader
than study of, 5–6
understanding of, place in Jewish
religious experientialism, 88

will of: expression of for dogmatic
objectivists, 112; leaders
presumed to represent among
religious extremists, 131–32
God, existence of: place in Jewish
religious experientialism, 88;
positivist method used to deny,
136; as prime mover for
Aristotle, 14; relativistic
defense of faith in, 95, 102–3
Golden Calf, the, 109–10, 112,
114–15, 138
good, the, xii, xv–xvi, 6, 12, 146,
219n31 (see also higher good);
found in collective identity,
77–78, 80, 94–98; outwardness
as primary path to for
objectivists, 110–12; for Plato
and Aristotle, 56, 113, 127;
relationship to individual
rights, xii–xiii, 216n14; for
subjective spirituality, 56, 62,
63, 67–68, 68–71; vision of (see
ethical vision)
good life, xii, 26, 65–66, 110, 129;
approaches to as subject matter
of spiritual education,
185–86; criteria for concepts
of, 41–50, 140–41, 162;
education as partner in
conceptualizing, 34–35; led
by integrated personalities,
137–38; for Maimonides, xvi;
for Marx, 82; medieval
approaches to, 13–14, 16;
sought in subjective
spirituality, 55, 64; vision of
(see ethical vision)
goodness, x–xi, 6, 13, 105–6, 110–11,
140, 188
celebration and practice of in
learning communities, 183,
184–93

religious education: in after-school
or Sunday schools, 18, 34, 201;
in day schools, 18, 202–3,
207–8, 211; educational
summer camps, 205, 211
jihad (holy war), 132
John of the Cross, 113
joy: in Judaism, celebration of in
eighteenth-century Kabbalism,
60; role in spiritual education,
193, 195–97; spiritual fulfillment as a source of, 155
Judaism, 9–12, 78–79, 87, 147
continuity crisis, 19; education seen
as answer to, 19, 33–35, 36
existentialism, 113, 119–22, 230n5
law, 60, 119–22, 124, 148–50,
228n22
liturgy and ritual, 111, 123, 192,
194, 228n22; Buber's attitude
toward, 61, 119–20; central
prayer, 166; Passover, 25–26,
194; Yom Kippur, 194
medieval religious philosophy,
13–14
orthodoxy and ultraorthodoxy,
59, 78, 79, 83, 98, 122–25,
131–33; religious experi-
entialism and the New
Orthodoxy, 87–91
religious education (*see* religious
education, Jewish)
spiritual renaissance, 79, 202–5,
207–11
transcendental collectivism, 83,
84–87
transcendental subjective
spirituality tradition, 56–57,
59–61 (*see also* Kabbalism)
Zionism (*see* Zionism)
justice, xii, 36, 150, 212; for Aristotle,
80–81; for Plato, 37–38, 80–81,
199; prophetic call for, 84, 85, 96

Kabbalism, 59–61, 72, 121, 130;
importance of ritual, 111, 113;
revival of, 59, 60–61, 84, 87,
116
Kadushin, Max, 194
Kant, Immanuel, xiii, 130, 146–47,
216n14, 218n22, 219n31;
rational morality, 16, 20–21,
27, 29
Kaplan, Mordecai, 87, 95
Katzenelson, Berl, 85–86, 96
kibbutzim, seen as realization of
Zionist ideals, 85
Kierkegaard, Søren, 28
1 Kings: **19:8,** 75; **19:11–15,** 55, 75
knowledge, 17, 22, 29, 182–84, 196
(*see also* epistemology);
Enlightenment replacements
for scriptural faith, 12–13; seen
as a social construction rooted
in power relations, 82, 178–79
"knowledge-base of teaching," 186
Kohlberg, Lawrence, 35–36
Kook, Abraham Isaac, 59
Korah, rebellion against leadership of
Moses and Aaron, 115–16
Koran, 13, 125
Kushner, Harold S., 47, 60–61, 151–52

labor Zionism, 85–87, 96
language, 5, 34, 111, 129; linguistic
community as a basis for
collective identity, 78; as means
for communicating values,
153–54; role in subjective
spirituality, 66–67; seen as
having meaning only in
particular contexts, 97, 102–3;
as subject matter of spiritual
education, 185–86, 191
Lasch, Christopher, 30, 71
law, Jewish, 60, 119–22, 124, 148–50,
228n22